Ulysses Travel Guide

MONTRÉAL

François Rémillard
Pascale Couture
Francis Giguère
Benoit Prieur
Marc Rigole

Ulysses Travel Publications

Series Director
Claude Morneau

*Research and
Composition of Tours*
François Rémillard

Montréal Panorama
Benoit Prieur

*Additional Research and
Composition*
Francis Giguère
Pascale Couture
Alain Legault
Marc Rigole

*English Editors and
Translation*
Jennifer McMorran
Carol Wood

English Translation
Tracy Kendrick

Contributors
Daniel Desjardins
Sarah Gilbert

Graphic Design
Pierre Daveluy

*Photography
Downtown from
Mont Royal*
Tibor Bognar
(Réflexion)

Cartography
André Duchesne

Special thanks to: Hélène Biron, Claude Charlebois, Sylvie Desmarais, Fernande Kavanagh, Nathalie Lachapelle, Lorette Pierson, Gérald Pomerleau, Joel Pomerleau, Christian Roy, Martin Tavernier

Distributors

CANADA :
Ulysses Books & Maps
4176 Saint-Denis
Montréal, Québec
H2W 2M5
☎ (514) 843-9882
Fax : 514-843-9448

GREAT BRITAIN :
Roger Lascelles
47 York Road
Brentford
OH 45202
☎ 847-0935
Fax : 568-3886

U.S.A. :
Seven Hills Book Distributors
49 Central Avenue
Cincinnati, Ohio, 45202
☎ 1-800-545-2005
Fax : (513) 381-0753

GERMANY :
Brettschneider Fernreisebedarf
GmbH
D-8011 Poing bei München
Hauptstr. 5
☎ 08121-71436
Fax : 08121-71419

NETHERLANDS and FLANDERS :
Nilsson & Lamm
Pampuslaan 212-214
Postbus 195
1380 AD Weesp (NL)
☎ 02940-65044
Fax : 02940-15054

SCANDINAVIA :
Scanvik Books Imports
Esplanaden 8B
DK-1263 Copenhagen K
DENMARK
☎ 33 12 77 66
Fax : 33 91 28 82

Other countries, contact Ulysses Books & Maps (Montréal), Fax : (514) 843-9448

Canadian Cataloguing in Publication Data

Rémillard, François

Montréal

(Ulysses travel guides)
Includes index.
Translation of Montréal

ISBN 2-921444-41-0

1. Montréal (Québec) - Guidebooks. I. Rémillard François. II. Title. III. Series.

FC2947.18M5613 1994   917.14'28044   C94-941010-1   F1054.M8313 1994

"In those days the streets of Montreal were a kind of thruth to me and I roamed them. I learned them block by block from their smells and the types I saw, I came to love the shape of the city itself, its bold masses bulging hard against the sky and the purple semi-darkness of the lower town at evening when Mount Royal was still high and clear against bright sunsets."

The Watch that Ends the Night
Hugh MacLennan

TABLE OF CONTENTS

LIST OF MAPS

Help make Ulysses Travel Guides even better!

The information contained in this guide was correct at press time. However, mistakes can slip in, omissions are always possible, places can disappear, etc. We value your comments, corrections and suggestions, as they allow us to keep each guide up to date.

The best contributions will be rewarded with a free book from Ulysses Travel Publications. All you have to do is write us at the following address and indicate which title you would be interested in receiving (see the list at the end).

**Ulysses Travel Publications
4176 - rue Saint-Denis
Montréal, Québec
Canada H2W 2M5**

TABLE OF SYMBOLS

☎	Telephone number
⇄	Fax number
≡	Air conditioning
⊗	Ceiling fan
≈	Pool
ℜ	Restaurant
⊕	Whirlpool
ℝ	Refrigerator
ℂ	Kitchenette
tv	Colour television

ATTRACTION CLASSIFICATION

★	Interesting
★★	Worth a visit
★★★	Not to be missed

RESTAURANT CLASSIFICATION

$	0 - $30
$$	$ 30 - $ 60
$$$	$ 60 and up

Prices are for 2 people before taxes, drinks and tip.

ACCOMMODATION

Prices are for a standard room for two people, before taxes and during high season.

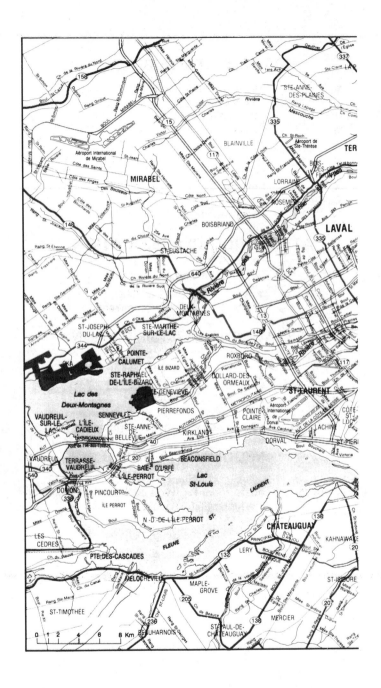

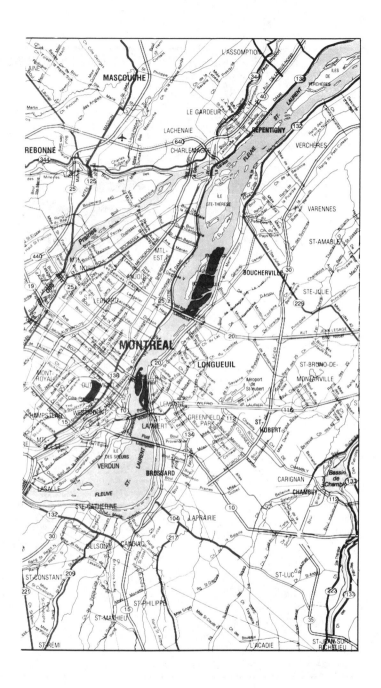

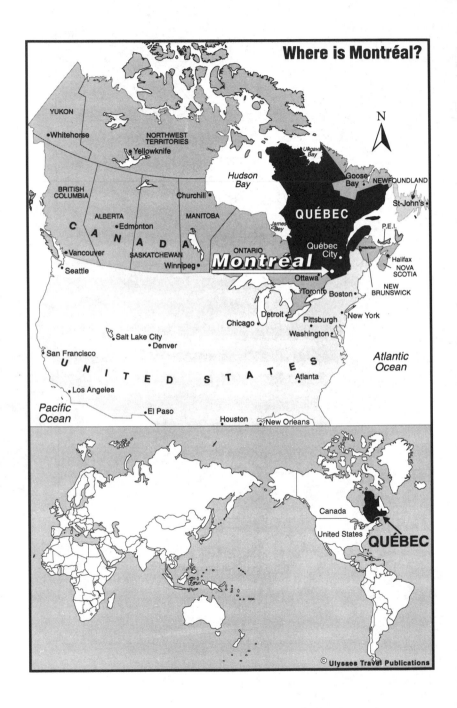

MONTRÉAL: PANORAMA
OF A COMPLEX CITY

Seen as both Latin and northern, cosmopolitan and unmistakably the metropolis of Québec, the largest French-speaking city in the world after Paris, yet also bilingual, Montréal is definitely a city of paradoxes! Visitors to the city appreciate it for many different reasons, for as it succeeds in charming American tourists with its so-called European charm, it also manages to surprise overseas travellers with its haphazard character and nonchalance. Above all, Montréal holds nothing back and visitors find what they are looking for without having to search too far. Montréal is a city that exists in a balance between several different worlds: securely tied to America while looking toward Europe, claimed by two lands, Québec and Canada, and always, it would seem, in the middle of social, economic and demographic changes.

It is difficult to define this city, especially since no postcard cliché truly succeeds in evoking an image of it that is even the slightest bit realistic or honest. If Paris has its great boulevards and squares, New York its skyscrapers and celebrated Statue of Liberty, what best symbolizes Montréal? Its many and beautiful churches? Its Olympic Stadium? Its opulent Victorian residences?

In fact, despite Montréal's rich architectural heritage, it is above all the city's unique, engaging atmosphere that appeals to people. Montréal is a delightful city to visit, an exhilarating place to discover; it is generous, friendly and not at all mundane. And, when it comes time to celebrate jazz, film, humour, singing or Saint-Jean-Baptiste Day, hundreds of thousands of people flood into the streets, turning events into warm public gatherings. There is no doubt that Montréal is a big city that has remained on a human scale. For while its towering glass and concrete silhouette give it the appearance of a North American metropolis, Montréal has trouble hiding the fact that it is primarily a city of little streets, of neighbourhoods, each with its own church, businesses, restaurants, brasseries - in short, each with its own personality, shaped over the years by the arrival of people from all corners of the globe.

Elusive and mysterious, Montréal's magic is nevertheless genuine, and is as mystical for those who experience it on a daily basis, as it is for visitors immersed in it for only a few days.

Montréal and Its History

To understand Montréal's place in the history of this continent, it is first of all necessary to consider the tremendous advantages afforded by its location. Occupying an island in the Fleuve St-Laurent, the main route into northeastern North America, Montréal lies at the point where maritime traffic encounters its first major obstacle: the Rapides de Lachine. From a commercial point of view, this geographical quirk worked to Montréal's advantage for many years, forcing vessels travelling on the river to stop there for transshipment. The city's commercial calling was further reinforced by the proximity of a number of other important waterways, guaranteeing it privileged access to the riches of an immense hinterland. These assets, moreover, have greatly favoured Montréal's growth and evolution throughout its history.

■ The City's Origins

Before the regional balance was disrupted by the arrival of European explorers, what is known today as the island of Montréal was inhabited by Amerindians of the Iroquois nation. These people had probably recognized the location's exceptional qualities, which enabled them to flourish by dominating the St-Laurent valley and playing the role of commercial intermediary for the entire region. In 1535, and then in 1541, Jacques Cartier became the first European to briefly explore the island. He took the opportunity to climb the mountain rising up out of its centre, which he christened Mont Royal (Mont Réal, in old French). In his ship's log, Cartier also mentioned a short visit to a large Amerindian village apparently located on the side of the mountain. Inhabited by approximately 1,500 Iroquoian people, this village consisted of about fifty large dwellings protected by a high wooden palisade. All around, the villagers cultivated corn, squash and beans, thus meeting most of the dietary needs of their sedentary population. Unfortunately, Cartier left only a partial and sometimes contradictory account of this Amerindian community, and thus even today the exact location of the village, as well as the name by which the Amerindians referred to it (Hochelaga or Tutonaguy?), remains unknown. Another enduring mystery that still gives rise to much speculation is the astonishing and rapid disappearance of this village after Cartier's visits. Some 70 years later, in 1603, when Samuel de Champlain travelled through the region, he found no trace of the Iroquoian community Cartier had spoken of. The most popular hypothesis is that the Amerindians of the island of Montréal had, in the meantime, fallen victim to trade rivals and finally been driven from the island.

Be that as it may, Champlain, the founder of New France, quickly took an interest in the location's potential. In 1611, just three years after founding Québec City, he ordered that an area be cleared on the island. He viewed this spot, named Place Royale, as the starting point of a new colony or an outpost for the fur trade. The project had to be postponed, however, since at the time the French, allied with the Algonquins and Hurons, had to cope with attacks by the Confederation of the Five Iroquois Nations. Supported by the merchants of New Amsterdam (which would later become New York), the Confederation was trying to seize complete control of the fur trade. The founding of Montréal was thus delayed for a number of years, and is not attributable to the efforts of Samuel de Champlain, who died in 1635.

■ **Ville-Marie (1642-1665)**

The fur trade was the primary reason for the French colonization of Canada in those years, however it does not appear to have been at the origin of the founding of Montréal. The city, initially christened Ville-Marie, was established by a group of pious French men and women strongly influenced by the currents of religious revival affecting Europe at the time, as well as by the Jesuits' accounts of their time in America. Driven by idealism, they wanted to establish a small colony on the island, in hopes of converting Amerindians and creating a new Christian society. Paul de Chomedey, Sieur de Maisonneuve, was chosen to see this venture through, and was later designated governor of the new colony. Heading an expedition of about fifty people, including Jeanne Mance, de Maisonneuve arrived in America in 1641 and founded Ville-Marie in May of the following year. From the beginning, a great effort was made to hasten the construction of the social and religious institutions that would form the heart of the town. In 1645, work was begun on Hôtel-Dieu, the hospital Jeanne-Mance had dreamed about. A few years later, the first school was opened, under the direction of Marguerite Bourgeoys. The year 1657 was marked by the arrival of the first priests from Paris's Séminaire de Saint-Sulpice, who subsequently, and for many years to come, had a decisive influence on the city's development. Ironically, the primary goal behind the founding of Ville-Marie, the conversion of local Amerindians, had to be quickly abandoned or at least set aside for a certain period of time. In fact, just one year after their arrival, the French had to confront the Iroquois, who feared that the presence of colonists would disrupt the fur trade and put them at a disadvantage. Before long, a permanent state of war set in, threatening the very survival of the colony a number of times. Finally, however, after nearly a quarter of a century of hanging by only a thread, the colony was provided with military protection by King Louis XIV, who had been governing New France himself for two years. From that point on, Ville-Marie, which had already come to be known as Montréal, began to flourish.

Important Dates in Montréal's History

5th century: Nomadic tribes settle in the valley of the Saint-Laurent and on the island known today as Montréal.

1535 : On his second voyage to North America, Jacques Cartier sails up the river to the island of Montréal, where he visits an Amerindian village and climbs the mountain, naming it Mont Royal.

1642 : Under the command of Paul de Chomedey, Sieur de Maisonneuve, a French colony, originally named Ville-Marie, is founded on the island. This small community survived with great difficulty for nearly a quarter of a century, and very quickly abandoned its initial plans to convert the Amerindians to Christianity.

1672 : The main roads of Montréal, a city whose survival is now assured, are delineated for the first time.

1701 : The French and Amerindians sign a treaty, ushering in a period of peace and thus fostering the development of a fur trade centred around Montréal.

1760 : Like Québec City the previous year, Montréal falls into the hands of British troops. The fate of the city and its inhabitants is drastically altered as a result.

1775-1776 : While the American Revolution rages in the United States, an American army occupies Montréal for several months.

1831 : Montréal surpasses Québec City in terms of population, thereby becoming the main urban centre in Canada.

1837 : Riots break out in Montréal, with the Fils de la Liberté (Sons of Liberty), a movement made up of young French Canadians, opposing the Doric Club, composed of loyal British subjects.

1867 : Canadian Confederation expands the domestic market, which, in the following years is very beneficial to Montréal's development and industrialization.

1874 : Creation of Parc du Mont-Royal, laid out by Frederick Law Olmsted, who designed New York's Central Park.

1911 : Due to recent immigration, 10% of Montréal's population is of neither British nor French extraction.

1951 : Montréal's population surpasses 1,000,000, not including the rapidly expanding suburbs.

1966 : Inauguration of the Métro.

1967 : The City of Montréal organizes the successful World Fair.

1970 : In October, a crisis breaks out when the Front de Libération du Québec (FLQ) *kidnaps British diplomat James Cross and minister Pierre Laporte. The Canadian government reacts by enforcing martial law, and the Canadian army takes up position in Montréal.*

1976 : The summer Olympic Games are held in Montréal.

1992 : Montréal vibrantly celebrates the 350ʰ anniversary of its founding.

■ The Fur Trade (1665-1760)

Although the church hierarchy still maintained its authority, and the mystical vocation of the town endured in people's minds, the protection afforded by the royal administration enabled Montréal to prosper as a military and commercial centre from 1665 on. The arrival of French troops and relative "pacification" of the Iroquois which ensued, especially from 1701 on with the signing of the Montréal peace treaty, finally made it possible to capitalize on the town's advantages as far as the fur trade was concerned. Since Montréal was the town located furthest upriver on the St-Laurent, it soon surpassed Québec City as the hub of this lucrative commerce. In addition, more and more young Montrealers nicknamed *coureurs des bois* were leaving the city and venturing deep into the hinterland to negotiate directly with Native fur suppliers. Legalized in 1681, this practice gradually became more organized and hierarchical and the *coureurs des bois* became for the most part paid employess of important Montréal merchants. Montréal, located at the gateway to the continent, also served as the starting point for France's intensive exploration of North America. French expeditions, notably those led by Jolliet, Marquette, La Salle and La Vérendrye, kept pushing the borders of New France further and further. It was by means of these expeditions that Pierre Le Moyne d'Iberville founded Louisiana in 1699. In those years, France claimed the

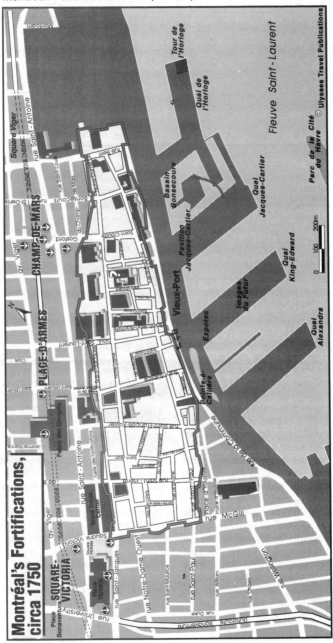

major part of what is now known as North America, an immense territory that enabled France to contain the expansion of the much more densely populated English colonies in the south, between the Atlantic and the Appalachians.

Supported by the royal administration, Montréal continued to grow slowly throughout this period. In 1672, a map was created, delimiting for the first time a number of the city's streets, the most important being Rue Notre-Dame and Rue Saint-Paul. Then, between 1717 and 1741, the wooden palisade surrounding the city was replaced by a stone wall over 5m high to reinforce the city's defences. All in all somewhat slow, the growth of the population nevertheless led to the establishment of areas outside the enclosure from the 1730's on. A clear social distinction gradually developed between the residents of these areas and those of the city centre, where, after a number of devastating fires, only stone buildings were permitted. The core of the city, protected by walls, was occupied mainly by members of the local aristocracy, wealthy merchants and social and religious institutions, while the outlying areas were inhabited primarily by artisans and peasants. With its numerous multi-story stone houses, the centre of Montréal already had the appearance and atmosphere of a peaceful little French city by the middle of the 18th century.

The Seven Years' War, which raged through Europe between 1756 and 1763, was to have enormous repercussions in America, which quickly became a battlefield. The cities of Québec, in 1759, and Montréal, the following year, fell into the hands of British troops. And when the war ended in Europe, France officially ceded control of almost all its North American possessions to England under the Treaty of Paris, thereby signing New France's death sentence. The fate of Montréal and its francophone population, numbering 5,733 inhabitants, was significantly altered as a result.

■ The Transitional Years (1763-1850)

The first decades after the conquest (1760) were characterized by an atmosphere of uncertainty for the city's community. First of all, despite the return of a civilian government in 1764, French-speaking citizens continued to be edged out until 1774, excluded from the Public Administration and higher realms of decision-making. In addition, although Montréal would maintain a dominant role in the lucrative fur trade for a number of decades to come, control of this commerce quickly fell into the hands of the conquerors, particularly a small group of merchants of Scottish extraction. Then, in 1775-1776, the city was invaded once again, this time by American troops, who only stayed for a few months. It was, therefore, at the end of the American Revolution that Montréal and other parts of Canada were faced with the first large waves of English-speaking immigrants, made up of Loyalists (American colonists wishing to maintain their allegiance to the British Crown). Later, from 1815 on, these individuals were followed by large numbers of newcomers from the British Isles, especially Ireland, which at the time was severely stricken by famine. At the same time, the French Canadian population was growing at a remarkable pace, due to a very high birth rate. This rapid increase in the Canadian population had a positive effect on Montréal's economy as the city and country grew more and more dependent upon one another. The rapidly expanding rural areas, particularly in the part of the territory that would later become Ontario, formed a lucrative market for all sorts of products manufactured in Montréal. The country's agricultural production, particularly wheat, which inevitably passed through the port of Montréal before being shipped to Great Britain, ensured the growth of the city's port activities. And then in the 1820's, an old dream was realized with the inauguration of a canal making it possible to bypass the Rapides de Lachine. In fact, Montréal's economy was already so diversified by that time, that it was barely affected when the Hudson's Bay Company took over the Northwest Compagny, which had represented the city's interests in the fur trade. For many years the mainspring of Montréal's economy, the fur trade had become only one activity among many.

During the 1830's, Montréal earned the title of the most populated city in the country, surpassing Québec City. A massive influx of English-speaking colonists disrupted the balance between French and English, and for 35 years, starting in 1831, there was an anglophone majority in Montréal. Furthermore, the different ethnic groups had already started to group together in a pattern that would endure for many years to come: the francophones mainly in the east end of the city, the Irish in the southwest and the Anglo-Scottish in the west. These various ethnic groups did not, however, share the territory without problems. When the *Patriote* Rebellions broke out in 1837-1838, Montréal became the scene of violent confrontations between the members of the Doric Club, composed of loyal British subjects, and the *Fils de la Liberté* (Sons of Liberty), made up of young francophones. It was actually after an inter-ethnic riot, leading to a fire that destroyed the parliament building, that Montréal lost its six-year-old title of capital of united Canada in 1849.

Finally, although Montréal's urban landscape did not undergo any major changes during the first years of the English Regime, British-style buildings gradually began to appear in the 1840's. It was also at this time that the city's wealthiest merchants, mainly of Anglo-Scottish descent, little by little abandoned the Saint-Antoine neighbourhood and settled at the foot of Mont Royal. From that point on, less than a century after the conquest (1760), the British presence was an undeniable part of the city's make-up. It was also at this time that a crucial phase of Montréal's development began.

■ **Industrialization and Economic Power (1850-1914)**

Montréal experienced the most important period of growth in its history from the second half of the 19th century until World War I, thanks to the rapid industrialization starting in the 1840's that continued in several consecutive waves. From then on, it ranked as Canada's undisputed metropolis, and became the country's true centre of development.

The broadening of Canada's internal market - first with the creation of United Canada in 1840 and then, most importantly, the advent of Canadian Confederation in 1867 - reinforced Montréal's industrial sector, whose products were more and more often replacing imports. The main forces that would long lie at the heart of the city's economy were the shoe, clothing, textile and food industries, as well as certain heavy industries, particularly rolling stock and iron and steel products. The geographical concentration of these activities near the port installations and railroad tracks significantly altered the city's appearance. The area around the Canal de Lachine, the cradle of Canada's industrial revolution, followed by the Sainte-Marie and Hochelaga neighbourhoods, filled up with factories and then inexpensive housing intended for workers. The industrialization of Montréal was intensified by the city's advantageous position as a transportation and communications hub for the entire Canadian territory, a position it worked to strengthen throughout this period. For example, starting in the 1850's, a channel was dug in the river between Montréal and Québec City, thus enabling larger ships to go upriver to the metropolis, and at the same time eliminating most of the advantages enjoyed by Québec City's port installations. The rail network which was beginning to extend over the Canadian territory also benefitted Montréal by making the city the centre of its activities. Montréal's industries enjoyed privileged access to the markets of southern Québec and Ontario via the Grand Trunk network, and the west of the country via that of Canadian Pacific, which reached Vancouver in 1866. As far as both domestic and international trade were concerned, Montréal occupied a dominant position in the country during this period.

The city's rapid growth was equally exceptional from a demographic point of view; between 1852 and 1911, the population went from 58,000 to 468,000 (528,000 including the suburbs). This remarkable increase was due to the huge pull of the booming city. The massive waves of immigration from the British Isles, which had begun in the early 19th century, continued for several more years before slowing down appreciably during the 1860's. This deceleration was then amply compensated for by an exodus of peasants from the Québec countryside, attracted to Montréal by the work offered in the factories. The arrival of this mainly francophone population also led to a new reversal of the balance between French and English in Montréal. The population became in 1866, and remains to this day, majority francophone. An entirely new phenomenon began to take shape toward the end of the 19th century, when Montréal started welcoming immigrants from places other than France and the British Isles. Initially, those who came in the greatest numbers were Eastern European Jews fleeing persecution in their own countries. At first, they grouped together mainly along Boulevard Saint-Laurent. A considerable number of Italians also settled in Montréal, mostly, for their part, in the northern section of the city. Thanks to these waves of immigration, Montréal already had a decidedly multiethnic character by 1911, with more than 10% of its population of neither British nor French extraction.

The urbanization resulting from this population growth caused the city to spread out more and more, a phenomenon promoted by the creation of a streetcar network in 1892. The city thus expanded beyond its old limits on a number of occasions, annexing up to 31 new territories between 1883 and 1918. At the same time, efforts were being made to lay out areas where Montrealers could spend leisure time, such as Parc du Mont-Royal

(1874). As far as residential construction was concerned, British inspired styles were most prevalent, notably in working-class neighbourhoods, where row houses with flat roofs and brick fronts would predominate from then on. Furthermore, in order to offer low-cost housing to working-class families, these buildings were more frequently two or three stories high and designed to accommodate at least that many families. More and more affluent Montrealers were settling on the sides of Mont Royal, a neighbourhood that would soon be known as the Golden Square Mile, due to the great wealth of its residents. The industrial revolution had, for that matter, increased the socio-economic divisions within Montréal society. This phenomenon separated the main ethnic groups involved in an almost dichotomous fashion, since the upper middle class was just about entirely made up of Anglo-Protestants, while the majority of unspecialized workers consisted mainly of French and Irish Catholics.

■ **From the First World War to the Second**

From 1914 to 1945, a number of international-scale events hindered the city's growth and evolution. First of all, with the start of World War I in 1914, Montréal's economy stagnated for a certain period of time due to a drop in investments. It regained strength very quickly, though, thanks to the exportation of agricultural products and military equipment to Great Britain. These years, however, were marked above all in Montréal by a political battle waged between anglophones and francophones on the subject of the war effort, a topic which divided the two groups. Francophones viewed the British Empire with mixed feelings and

therefore protested for a long time against any Canadian participation in the British war effort. They were therefore fiercely opposed to the mandatory conscription of Canadian citizens. The anglophones, many of whom still had very strong ties with Great Britain, were in favour of Canada's full involvement. When, in 1917, the Canadian government finally made a decision and imposed mandatory conscription, the francophones exploded with anger, and Montréal was shaken by intense inter-ethnic tensions.

The war was followed by a few years of economic readjustment, and then "the roaring twenties," a period of sustained growth stretching from 1921 to 1929. During this time, Montréal continued to develop as it had begun to before the war, while at the same time maintaining its role as Canada's metropolis. Toronto, however, thanks to American investment and the development of Western Canada, was already starting to claim a more important place for itself. Taller and taller buildings with designs reflecting American architectural trends gradually began to appear in Montréal's business centre. The city's population also started growing again, so much so that by the end of the 1920's, there were over 800,000 people living in Montréal, while the population of the island as a whole had already exceeded 1,000,000. Due to both the size of its population and the appearance of its business centre, therefore, Montréal already had all the attributes of a big North American city.

The crisis that struck the world economy in 1929 had a devastating effect on Montréal, a good part of whose wealth was based on exports. For an entire decade, poverty became widespread in the city, where up to a third of the population of working age was unemployed. This dark period did not end until the beginning of World War II in 1939. From the start of this conflict, however, the controversy surrounding the war effort was rekindled, once again dividing the city's francophone and anglophone populations. The mayor of Montréal, Camillien Houde, who was opposed to mandatory conscription, was imprisoned between 1940 and 1944. Finally, Canada became fully involved in the war, putting its industrial production and army of conscripts at Great Britain's disposition.

■ Renewed Growth (1945-1960)

After so many years of rationing and unfavourable upheavals, Montréal's economy, emerging from the war stronger and more diversified than ever, finally gave rise to a prosperous period, during which the population's consumer demands could be met. For more than a decade, unemployment was almost nonexistent in Montréal, and the overall standard of living improved radically. The growth of the Montréal urban area was equally remarkable from a demographic point of view, so much so that between 1941 and 1961, the population literally doubled, going from 1,140,000 to 2,110,000, the population of the city itself passing the 1,000,000 mark in 1951. This population explosion had several causes. First of all, the century-old exodus of rural inhabitants to the city, more widespread than ever, resumed after coming to an almost complete halt during the Great Depression and World War II. Immigration also recommenced, the largest groups now arriving from southern Europe, especially Italy and

Greece. Finally, the increase in Montréal's population was also due to a sharp rise in the number of births, a veritable baby boom, which affected Québec as much as it did the rest of North America. To meet the housing needs of this population, neighbourhoods located slightly on the outskirts of the city were quickly covered with thousands of new homes. In addition, suburbs even further removed from the downtown area emerged, fostered by the popularity of the automobile as an object of mass consumption. Suburbs even began developing off the island on the south shore of the river, around the access bridges, and to the north, on Île Jésus. At the same time, downtown Montréal underwent some important changes, as the business section gradually shifted from Vieux-Montréal to the area around Boulevard René-Lévesque (formerly Boulevard Dorchester), where ever more imposing skyscrapers were springing up.

During this same period, the city was affected by a wave of social reforms aiming, in particular, to put an end to the "reign of the underground". At the time, Montréal had a well-deserved reputation as a place where prostitution and gambling clubs flourished, and this for years, thanks to the blind-eye of some corrupt police officers and politicians. A public inquiry conducted between 1950 and 1954, during which lawyers Pacifique Plante and Jean Drapeau stood out in particular, led to a series of convictions and a significant improvement in the social climate. At the same time the desire for social change, was manifested in the strong protest by Montréal's francophone intellectuals, journalists and artists against the all-powerful Catholic Church and the pervading conservatism of the times. Nevertheless, the most striking phenomenon of this period remained French-speaking Montrealers' nascent awareness of their socioeconomic alienation. Indeed, over the years, save certain exceptions, a very clear socio-economic split had developed between the city's two main groups. Francophones earned lower average incomes than their anglophone colleagues, were more likely to hold subordinate positions and their attempts at climbing the social ladder were mocked. And though the francophone population formed a large majority, Montréal projected the image of an Anglo-Saxon city, due to its commercial signs and the supremacy of the English language in the main spheres of economic activity. Nevertheless, it wasn't until the early 1960's that the desire for change evolved into a series of accelerated transformations.

■ **From 1960 to Today**

The 1960's were marked by an unprecedented reform movement in Québec, a veritable race for modernization and change, which soon became known as the Quiet Revolution. Québec francophones, particularly those in Montréal where the opposition between the two main ethnic groups was strongest, clearly expressed their desire to put an end to the anglophone minority's control over the province's societal development. A battery of changes were initiated with this aim in view. At the same time, the nationalist movement, and its push for independence or increased political sovereignty for Québec, found very fertile ground in Montréal. The most important demonstrations in support of this cause were held there. It was also in Montréal, though, that the *Front de Libération du Québec* (FLQ), a small cell of extremists wishing to "accelerate the

decolonization of Québec," was most active.

Starting in 1963, the FLQ carried out a series of terrorist attacks in the city. Then, in October of 1970, a major political crisis broke out when certain members of the FLQ kidnapped British diplomat James Cross and Québec cabinet minister Pierre Laporte. On the pretext of curbing a dreaded climate of revolt, the federal government, headed by Pierre Elliot Trudeau, reacted quickly, enforcing martial law. The Canadian army took up position in Montréal, thousands of searches were conducted and hundreds of innocent people imprisoned. The crisis finally ended when James Cross's kidnappers obtained a safe-conduct to Cuba - not, however, before Pierre Laporte was found dead. The reaction of the Canadian government was judged very harshly by many, who did not hesitate to accuse it of having used the political context not only to bring the FLQ under control, but above all to try to halt the rise of the nationalist movement in Québec.

Be that as it may, over the years, the francophone majority made its presence felt more and more in Montréal. Furthermore, the image projected by the city changed noticeably when successive provincial governments adopted language laws requiring commercial signs, which had up until then been in English, or at best in both languages, to be written entirely in French. For many anglophones, however, these laws, combined with the rise of nationalism and entrepreneurship in Québec, were changes too difficult to accept, and a number of them left Montréal for good.

At the same time, Montréal, whose mayor in those years was Jean

Drapeau, shone more and more brightly on the international scene by hosting a number of large-scale events, the most noteworthy being the 1967 World Fair, the 1976 Summer Olympic Games and the 1980 Floralies Internationales (International Flower Show).

From an economic point of view, Montréal underwent profound changes with the decline of many branches of activity that had shaped its industrial structure for over a century. These were then partially replaced by massive investments in such leading industries as aeronautics, computers and pharmaceutical products. In the mid 1960's, Montréal was also stripped of its title of Canadian metropolis by Toronto, which had been growing at a faster pace for several decades. The appearance of more and more skyscrapers downtown, however, proved that Montréal's economy was nevertheless continuing to grow.

The city's population also increased, so much so that the number of inhabitants in the Montréal urban area reached about 3,000,000. This growth benefitted the suburbs, however, which were farther and farther removed from the city centre, while the population of the city of Montréal itself stagnated at around 1,000,000. Furthermore, with the influx of immigrants from around the world over the previous decades, Montréal had blossomed into an increasingly complex cultural mosaic. More than ever, it had become a true international crossroads, while at the same time playing the role of the North American metropolis of French culture.

During the summer of 1992, Montrealers enthusiastically celebrated the 350th anniversary of the founding of their city, hoping, no doubt, that the past would ensure the future. For

Montréal, having gone through a number of important changes in the course of its three and a half centuries of existence, has always managed to adapt, while knowing how to distinguish itself and preserve its unique character.

The Language Question

The coexistence of two distinct cultural ideologies is one of the most fundamental and dynamic elements of Montréal's makeup. More than anywhere else in Québec or Canada, two language communities, francophone and anglophone, share the same territory, the same city.

Montréal's language paradox is in fact much more complex than it seems, and has apparently always been that way. Visiting Montréal at the beginning of the 19th century, Alexis de Toqueville was surprised to observe the almost complete absence of the French language in public affairs and commerce. In fact, although francophones have always been in the majority in Montréal, except for a short period in the middle of the last century, the city projected an image almost as typically Anglo-Saxon as London, Toronto or New York for nearly two hundred years. On business signs, in downtown department stores or during encounters, unexpected or not, between anglophones and francophones, the English language triumphed. Eventually, however, a new awareness on the part of francophones, leading to bitter disputes during the 1960's, initiated the process of restoring French to favour in Montréal. Later, when Québec governments instituted a battery of language laws, including the thenceforward famous Bill 101 in 1977, the presence of the French language grew stronger in Montréal. The "Frenchifying" of the city did not, however, take place without offending the feelings of the anglophone minority, whose members viewed it as an attack on their rights. Many anglophones left Montréal in the mid-1970's, while activists began denouncing certain provisions of Québec's language laws, particularly those requiring business signs to be written in French only and the mandatory integration of children of new arrivals into French schools. However, despite appearances, things are far from being as simple as some people would like to believe; the anglophone community feels threatened nowadays, but francophones also find themselves in a fairly precarious situation. Even now, the English language is alive and well in Montréal. Downtown, for example, in the very heart of what people often like to refer to as the second largest francophone city in the world after Paris, English is still very present. You have to venture farther east or north in the city to truly feel the francophones' presence as a majority in Montréal. The anglophone community has also preserved the prestigious institutions and social privileges of a highly pampered minority, and still succeeds in integrating most of the new arrivals into its world, despite the provincial government's efforts to reverse this trend. (According to the 1991 census, this assimilation into the anglophone community takes place in approximately 65% of all cases). That isn't all, however. English, the international language, is also used by 98% of North Americans; its power of attraction as a means of cultural integration into North American society is tremendous.

In their own way, therefore, Montréal's francophones and anglophones share the same fear—that of disappearing. Under circumstances such as these, how can Montréal maintain a balance between French and English that is acceptable to everyone? This question, put forward many times over the past 30 years, has still not been answered, and presumably won't be by means of simple principles. Consequently, until of the magic formula capable of settling all discord is discovered, relations between the two communities will continue to be perpetually called into question.

The Economy and Politics

Harshly affected over the past two decades by the loss of momentum in several primary branches of industry that had long been the driving force behind its growth and wealth, Montréal's economy has neither the panache nor the power it once did. Many factories, some true symbols of Montréal's strength, have been swept away by technological changes or are quite simply only shadows of their former selves. And despite the growth of a number of other industries, particularly those related to high technology, the effects of this massive deindustrialization have not yet been entirely absorbed. This is revealed by statistics relating to the unemployment rate of some neighbourhoods, where almost a quarter of the population is out of work. These difficulties, reinforced by the middle class exodus to the suburbs, a trend which has continued steadily since the 1950's, now project an image of a city leaning toward impoverishment.

Of course, Montréal is not the only city affected by these problems; they are the lot of many big North American centres. The situation, moreover, is not hopeless, since this Québec metropolis has many assets capable of revitalizing its economy: the quality of its workforce, the existing infrastructures and the possibilities of research and development offered by the four universities located within its limits.

On the other hand, before discussing economic recovery, it will be necessary to consider a malaise that has long been affecting Montréal—the impossibility of establishing a consensus between the principal parties involved. On a regional level, Montréal is at daggers drawn more often than it should be with the administrations of the cities on its outskirts, which it regularly accuses of not paying their fair share. Furthermore, despite its size and importance, this city, the seat of neither the federal nor provincial government, is often the victim of politicians' incomprehension and, above all, the prevailing tensions between these two levels of government, leading to the development of plans of action that are frequently incoherent or ineffective. In fact, Montréal, more than anywhere else, is both at the centre of the guerilla war between Québec and Canada and its victim. As pathetic as it might seem, the city now waits for some sort of political direction to establish a more well-defined role and position for it. Should Montréal join the Canadian sphere once and for all, or become the centre of an independent Québec? Time will tell, and the game will probably be played out mainly on the local scene, since greater Montréal contains approximately half of Québec's population and will thus carry a lot of weight when decision time comes.

Montréal's Communities

Saturday night, on Rue Durocher in Outremont, dozens of Hasidic (orthodox) Jews dressed in traditional clothing hurry to the nearby synagogue. A few hours earlier, as usual, a portion of Montréal's large Italian community met at Marché Jean-Talon to negotiate the purchase of products imported directly from Italy or simply to socialize with compatriots and discuss the latest soccer game between Milan and Turin. These scenes, well known to all Montrealers, are only two examples among many of the very vital community life of a number of the city's ethnic groups. In fact, Montréal's different ethnic communities have countless meeting places and associations. And one need only take a brief stroll down Boulevard Saint-Laurent—the Main, which serves as the dividing line between east and west and is lined with restaurants, grocery stores and other businesses with an international flavour, selling specialties from around the world—to be convinced of the richness and diversity of Montréal's population.

Indeed, Montréal often seems like a heterogeneous group of villages which, without being ghettos, are mainly inhabited by members of one or another ethnic community. In fact, this sectioning of the city was initiated back in the last century by Montrealers of French and English descent—a division which still marks the city to a certain degree. The east thus remains to a large extent francophone, while the west is anglophone. The most affluent members of the two communities for the most part live on opposite sides of Mont Royal, in Outremont and Westmount. With the arrival of a growing number of people from different backgrounds, however, a number of new neighbourhoods gradually fit into this puzzle. Very early, a small Chinese community, whose members had come to work in Canada when the railroads were being built, took up residence around Rue de la Gauchetière, west of Boulevard Saint-Laurent. They created a Chinatown which still has a mysterious quality about it. The city's large Jewish community, for its part, first gathered a little higher on Boulevard Saint-Laurent and then settled further west, particularly in certain parts of Outremont, Côte-des-Neiges and Snowdon and in the municipalities of Côte-Saint-Luc and Hampstead, where its institutions flourished. Little Italy, often a very lively and colourful place, with its many cafés, restaurants and shops, occupies a large section in the northern part of the city, near Rue Jean-Talon and the Saint-Léonard area. The Italians, for that matter, make up Montréal's largest ethnic community and add an undeniable energy to the city. Finally, a number of other more recently established communities also tend to gather in certain areas, for example, the Greeks along Avenue du Parc, the Haitians in Montréal-Nord, the Portuguese around Rue Saint-Urbain and the Jamaicans in Griffintown. In Montréal, it seems as if you almost pass from one country to another, from one world to another within the space of a few blocks.

Indeed, what would Montréal be without all its communities, without its famous smoked meat, a specialty developed by Eastern European Jews, or its countless little restaurants serving so-called "Canadian" cuisine, whose owners are, more often than not, Greek?

Four Seasons, As Many Faces

It is common knowledge that Montréal has at least as many different moods and personalities as there are seasons in a year. Indeed, this city truly lives in step with its often capricious climate, to which it has managed to adapt so well as to reap all the possible benefits the weather has to offer. In winter, for example, seeing as that is the season with which people most commonly identify this "Northern" city, the temperature often wavers well below freezing and tons of snow fall upon the city — without ever managing to paralyze it completely. This is because Montréal has become a world leader in "winter management," a veritable point of reference for a multitude of other big "cold" cities around the globe. During the winter months, day and night, 3,000 workers are available on call to remove the approximately 6.5 million cubic metres of snow that, on average, obstruct the city's streets every year. To a large degree, Montrealers have also managed to circumvent the problems that can accompany a severe winter climate, notably by building an incredible underground city, one of the world's largest. Linked to one another by the Métro system, these underground passageways, which cover almost 30 km, make it possible to reach all sorts of office buildings, stores, restaurants, bars, hotels, cinemas, theatres and residential high-rises — without ever having to step outside! In short, be it the snow or the cold, nothing slows this city down. Of course, winter doesn't only bring problems; it also offers its share of pleasures, and helps shape Montréal's character undeniably. Transformed by winter, the urban landscape lacks neither charm nor romanticism. The season's finest days offer an opportunity to enjoy a pleasant outing under the snow-laden trees, or a delightful visit to one of the city's outdoor skating rinks. In addition, winter marks the awakening of a veritable passion, as typical of Montréal as any ever was—the love of hockey. During the professional hockey season, the performance of Montréal's famous team, the Canadiens, is the centre of many conversations. Year after year, Montrealers manage to get through the long winters, sometimes grumbling a little, but also enjoying the marvellous pleasures the season has to offer.

Often abruptly, winter makes way for spring, an exhilarating season when Montréal takes on the appearance of a Mediterranean city. The first days of the season are always unforgettable, when the effect of the climate upon the city's inhabitants is most evident, as Montrealers, transformed by the first rays of spring sun, seem to get back in touch with their Latin roots. It is finally possible to dress in lighter clothing, sit on a terrace or roam idly through the city streets. As if emerging from long months of hibernation, a frenzied crowd storms Rue Saint-Denis, Boulevard Saint-Laurent and Parc du Mont-Royal. This short, buccolic period of the year, when Montrealers are finally able to take advantage of the beautiful parks and main streets of their city, is only a prelude to the summer season—vacation time. Come summer, there is so much to do that Montrealers often choose their own city as a vacation spot. With the warm weather Montréal comes to life, hosting numerous festivals to celebrate jazz, humour and film, not to mention the traditional Saint-Jean-Baptiste Day, leading inevitably to gatherings of hundreds of thousands of people. In summer, Montréal is not exclusive, it is wide open. The festivities continue until September, then slowly autumn settles in, and before fluttering to the ground the leaves change colour, turning brillant yellow, orange and red. But before Montrealers bundle themselves up for another long cold winter, there is a brief respite known as Indian Summer—just to remind them how acutely their lives are lead by Mother Nature.

A Brief Overview of Quebecois Literature

As with much of modern literature in the Americas, Quebecois writing began with accounts of voyages by early explorers. These texts were meant to inform Europeans about the "new" lands, and often described in detail the life of indigenous peoples. Toward the end of the 18th century and the beginning of the 19th century, the oral tradition still dominated literary life. Later, the legends from this era were committed to paper, but there was no true literary movement until the end of the 19th century in Québec. At this point, some of the major themes were survival and praise for a simple, religious, country life. With few exceptions, the novels of this period are mostly of socio-historic interest.

Tradition continued to be the main characteristic of Quebecois literature well into the 1930's, though there were several innovative writers worth noting. Émile Nelligan, a poet in the early 20th century, was influenced by Baudelaire, Rimbaud and Verlaine. Producing much of his work early on in life, he then sank slowly into madness, and remains a mythic figure today. Though country life remained a main feature in novels of the time, it began to be represented more realistically, such as in *Maria Chapdelaine* by **Louis Hémon**.

Literary works began to evolve toward modernism during the economic crisis and the Second World War. Novels set in the city, where the majority of the population now lived, began to appear. One of the most interesting of these is set in Montréal: *Bonheur d'occasion* (The Tin Flute) by **Gabrielle Roy**, a franco-Manitoban. Modernism took hold at the end of the Second World War, in spite of the strict political regime of Maurice Duplessis. Novels of the time were split into two categories: urban or psychological. Poetry flourished, with a number of great writers such as **Alain Grandbois** and **Anne Hébert**. Quebecois theatre was also born, with important works by **Gratien Gélinas** and **Marcel Dubé**.

During the Quiet Revolution, in the sixties, political and social changes affected literary creation in the sixties, and began the "demarginalization" of authors. Novels went through a golden age, and new authors began to be established: **Marie-Claire Blais, Hubert Aquin**, and **Réjean Ducharme**. Theatre also went through an exciting period, with the emergence of **Michel**

Tremblay. Many poets, novelists and playwrights began to use *joual*, which is the spoken, popular form of Quebecois french.

Contemporary literature is becoming richer and more diverse. Important names on the current scene include **Alice Parizeau, Roch Carrier, Yves Beauchemin**, and **Christian Mistral**. In the 1980's, theatre became a far more important genre, with many innovative new directors, such as **André Brassard, Robert Lepage, Lorraine Pintal**, and **René-Richard Cyr**.

Humour has also always been an important part of Quebecois culture, and has been integral to the changes the society has been through. In the sixties, comedy troupe **Les Cyniques** (The Cynics) produced biting criticisms of the clergy and political institutions, and so did their own part for the Quiet Revolution. In the seventies, **Yvon Deschamps** created characters who typified the exploited but nice Quebecois everyman, and brought about painful self-awareness in the province. The years following the referendum in the early eighties produced humour with elements of self-deprecation and the absurd - signs of a disillusioned generation. This type of humour is typified in groups such as **Ding et Dong, Rock et Belles Oreilles**, and **Daniel Lemire**.

Reading Montréal Writing: Tasting Montréal

When I first moved to Montréal, my apartment was on St-Urbain, a busy central street lined in the summer with energetic gardens and tendrils of grape vines looping up the balcony railings and bearing fruit in the fall for Greek and Portuguese wine-making.

To locate myself on the literary map of Montréal I went to the neighbourhood library to check out St-Urbain's Horseman *by* **Mordecai Richler**. *How literary to live on a street with a novel named after it and to actually read the novel. (The library copy was tattered; thousands of other new St-Urbain residents must have had the same idea since it was published in 1971.) In novels like this one and before it in* The Apprenticeship of Duddy Kravitz, *Richler's sharply comic prose, as salty as a smoked meat on rye, depicts life in the cold water flats and Kosher delis of mid-town Montréal in the fifties. These novels portray a neighbourhood whose face is now changed but still recognizable on certain corners such as Clark and Fairmount, home to the hand-mixed cherry Cokes and fried bologna sandwiches of Wilensky's, possibly one of Montréal's dingiest landmarks.*

Richler *is a frequent contributor to the* New Yorker *with his crusty and controversial accounts of Quebec politics, and to out-of-towners he, along with poet* **Irving Layton**, *gravel-throated crooner/poet* **Leonard Cohen**, *and novelist and essayist* **Hugh MacLennan**, *may be the most familiar literary voices of English Montréal. But Montréal is rife with other anglophone writers both new and established whose pages grapple with the texture of Montréal. This is a city where low rent and cheap espresso on every other corner guarantee a high density of writers per capita. What follows is just a sampling of contemporary writers.*

Montréal is a pizza with a thousand toppings, a dinner of a hundred courses. **Joe Fiorito's** *essays on food are flavourful slices of prose about savouring life in Montréal and beyond in sips, gulps and heaping platefuls. These pieces originally appeared in the local weekly* Hour Magazine *and are now collected in* Comfort Me With Apples.

The incendiary arrival of a Montréal spring, the disorienting resonance of a car alarm, the bitterness of a parking lot attendant, are all palpable in The Woman Downstairs, **Julie Bruck's** *collection of poetry.*

Gail Scott *fuses French and English in her lyrical mosaic of Montréal streets, bars, cafes and politics. Her experimental novels* Heroine *and* Main Brides *portray characters in a finely etched atmosphere of architectural and linguistic detail.*

Robert Majzel's Hellman's Scrapbook *is the story of David Hellman, a character who can read people's thoughts and memories by touching their hands, so whenever he touches anyone he is too blisteringly close, and knows too much. The novel is a scrapbook of many lifetimes, bulging with the stories he receives through his palms, stories of humour, beauty and pain.*

In P. Scott Lawrence's *award-winning collection of bittersweet short stories,* Missing Fred Astaire, *characters negotiate their uneasy position in relation to each other and the changing Quebec around them.*

Other fine local writing is listed in the Recommended Reading section, p 223.

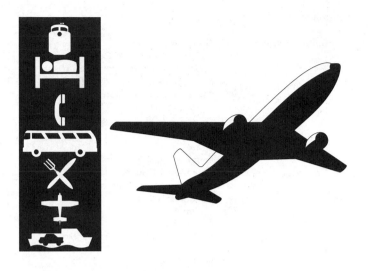

PRACTICAL INFORMATION

I nformation in this section will help visitors from English-speaking countries better plan their trip to Montréal.

Entrance Formalities

■ Passport

A valid passport is usually sufficient for most visitors planning to stay less than three months; visas are not required. A three-month extension is possible, but a return ticket and proof of sufficient funds to cover this extension may be required.

Caution: some countries do not have an agreement with Canada concerning health and accident insurance, so it is advisable to have the appropriate coverage. For more information, see the section entitled "Health" (p 45).

European citizens who want to enter the United States will need a visa. It is best to apply for this visa from the home country, although it is obtainable abroad, usually without problems.

Extended Visits

Visitors must submit their request **in writing** and **before** the expiration of their visa (the date is usually written in your passport) to an Immigration Canada office. To make a request, you must have a valid passport, a return ticket, proof of sufficient funds to cover the stay, as well as the $50 non-refundable filing fee. In some cases (work, study), however, the request must be made **before** arriving in Canada.

Embassies and Consulates

■ **Abroad**

Australia
Canadian Consulate General
Level 5, Quay West
111 Harrington Road
Sydney, N.S.W.
Australia 2000
☎ (612) 364-3000
⇄ (612) 364-3098

Belgium
Canadian Embassy
2, avenue de Tervueren
1040 Brussels
☎ 735.60.40
⇄ 735.60.40
Métro Mérode

Denmark
Canadian Embassy
Kr. Bernikowsgade 1
DK = 1105 Copenhagen K
Denmark
☎ 12.22.99
⇄ 14.05.85

Finland
Canadian Embassy
Pohjos Esplanadi 25 B
00100 Helsinki, Finland
☎ 171-141
⇄ 601-060

Germany
Canadian Consulate General
Internationales Handelzentrum
Friedrichstrasse 95, 23rd Floor
10117 Berlin, Germany
☎ 261.11.61
⇄ 262.92.06

Great Britain
Canada High Commission
Macdonald House
One Grosvenor Square
London W1X 0AB
England
☎ 258-6600
⇄ 258-6384

Netherlands
Canadian Embassy
Parkstraat 25
2514JD The Hague
Netherlands
☎ 361-4111
⇄ 365-6283

Norway
Canadian Embassy
Oscars Gate 20,
Oslo 3, Norway
☎ 46.69.55
⇄ 69.34.67

Sweden
Canadian Embassy
Tegelbacken 4, 7th floor,
Stockholm, Sweden
☎ 613-9900
⇄ 24.24.91

Switzerland
Canadian Embassy
Kirchenfeldstrasse 88
3000 Berne 6
☎ 532.63.81
⇄ 352.73.15

United States
Canadian Embassy
501 Pennsylvania Avenue, N.W.
Washington, DC
20001
☎ (202) 682-1740
⇄ (202) 682-7726

Canadian Consulate General
Suite 400 South Tower
One CNN Center
Atlanta, Georgia
30303-2705
☎ (404) 577-6810 or 577-1512
⇄ (404) 524-5046

Canadian Consulate General
Three Copley Place
Suite 400
Boston, Massachusetts
02116
☎ (617) 262-3760
⇄ (617) 262-3415

Canadian Consulate General
Two Prudential Plaza
180 N. Stetson Avenue, Suite 2400,
Chicago, Illinois
60601
☎ (312) 616-1860
⇄ (312) 616-1877

Canadian Consulate General
St. Paul Place, Suite 1700
750 N. St. Paul Street
Dallas, Texas
75201
☎ (214) 922-9806
⇄ (214) 922-9815

Canadian Consulate General
600 Renaissance Center
Suite 1100
Detroit, Michigan
48234-1798
☎ (313) 567-2085
⇄ (313) 567-2164

Canadian Consulate General
300 South Grande Avenue
10th Floor, California Plaza
Los Angeles, California
90071
☎ (213) 687-7432
⇄ (213) 620-8827

Canadian Consulate General
Suite 900, 701 Fourth Avenue South
Minneapolis, Minnesota
55415-1899
☎ (612) 333-4641
⇄ (612) 332-4061

Canadian Consulate General
1251 Avenue of the Americas
New York, New York
10020-1175
☎ (212) 596-1600
⇄ (212) 596-1793

Canadian Consulate General
One Marine Midland Center
Suite 3000
Buffalo, New York
14203-2884
☎ (716) 852-1247
⇄ (716) 852-4340

Canadian Consulate General
412 Plaza 600
Sixth and Stewart Streets
Seattle, Washington
98101-1286
☎ (206) 442-1777
⇄ (206) 443-1782

■ **In Montréal**

American Consulate General
Place Félix-Martin
1155, rue Saint-Alexandre
Montréal H2Z 1Z2
☎ (514) 398-9695

Australian High Commission
(no office in Montréal)
50 O'Connor Street
Ottawa, Ontario
K1N 5R2
☎ (613) 236-0841

Consulate General of Belgium
999, boul. de
Maisonneuve Ouest
suite 1250
Montréal H3A 3C8
☎ (514) 849-7394

British Consulate General
1155, rue University
suite 901
Montréal H3B 3A7
☎ (514) 866-5863

Consulate General of Denmark
1, Place-Ville-Marie
35th Floor
Montréal H3B 4M4
☎ (514) 871-8977

Consulate General of Finland
800, carré Victoria
suite 3400
Montréal H4Z 1E9
☎ (514) 397-7600

Consulate General of Germany
3455, rue de la Montagne
Montréal H3G 2A3
☎ (514) 286-1820

Consulate General of the Netherlands
1002, rue Sherbrooke Ouest
suite 2201
Montréal H3A 3L6
☎ (514) 849-4247

Consulate General of Norway
1155, boul. René-Lévesque Ouest
suite 3900
Montréal H3B 3V2
☎ (514) 874-9087

Consulate General of Sweden
800, carré Victoria
34th Floor
Montréal H4Z 1E9
☎ (514) 866-4019

Consulate General of Switzerland
1572, avenue Dr Penfield
Montréal H3G 1C4
☎ (514) 932-7181

 Tourist Information

Tourist information is available from *Tourisme Québec* through the offices of the *Délégation Générale du Québec* located abroad, and from the tourist offices in Montréal. See below for the addresses :

Tourisme Québec
Case postale 979
Montréal H3C 2W3

■ **Québec Delegations Abroad**

Belgium
Délégation Générale du Québec
46, avenue des Arts
7e étage
1040 Bruxelles
☎ 512.00.36
Métro Art-Loi

Canada
Bureau du Québec
20 Queen St., West
Suite 1504, Box 13
Toronto, Ontario
M5H 3S3
☎ (416) 977-6060
⇄ (416) 596-1407

Germany
Délégation Générale du Québec
Immermannstrasse 65D
Immermannhof
40210 Düsseldorf
Germany
☎ (211) 17863-0
⇄ (211) 17863-31

Great Britain
Délégation Générale du Québec
59 Pall Mall
London SW1Y 5JH
England
☎ (71) 930-8314
⇄ (71) 930-7938

United States
Délégation Générale du Québec
Exchange Place, 19th Floor
53 State Street
Boston, Massachusetts
02109
☎ (617) 723-3366
⇄ (617) 723-3659

Délégation Générale du Québec
Two Prudential Plaza
180 N. Stetson Avenue, Suite 4300
Chicago, Illinois
60601
☎ (312) 856-0655
⇄ (312) 856-0725

Délégation Générale du Québec
Rockefeller Center
17 West 50th Street
New York, New York
10020-2201
☎ (212) 397-0200
⇄ (212) 757-4753

Bureau du Québec
1300 19th Street N.W., Suite 220
Washington, DC
20036
☎ (202) 659-8991
⇄ (202) 659-5654

■ **Information in Montréal**

Centre Infotouriste
1001, rue du Square-Dorchester
(corner Metcalfe and Square
Dorchester)
Métro Peel
☎ 873-2015
The centre is open from 9 a.m. to
6 p.m. every day during the summer
and from November to April. It provides
detailed information, maps, flyers and
accommodation information for
Montréal and all the tourist regions of
Québec.

Bureau du Vieux-Montréal (Old
Montréal)
174, rue Notre-Dame Est
Métro Champs-de-Mars
Information on the Montréal region
only.

 Finding Your Way Around

There are 28 municipalities on the
island of Montréal, which measures
32 km at its longest point and 16 km
at its widest. Montréal proper, with a
population of about one million, is the
main urban area in the *Communauté
Urbaine de Montréal* (Montréal Urban
Community), which encompasses all of
the boroughs on the island. Greater
Montréal also includes the Rive-Sud
(South Shore), Laval and the Rive-Nord
(North Shore), for a grand total of
3,200,000 inhabitants (1991). The
downtown area runs along the St-
Laurent, south of Mont Royal (234 m),
which is one of the seven hills of the
Montérégie region.

■ **Access**

When coming from Québec City, there are two possible routes - take either Highway 20 West to the Pont Champlain (bridge), then Autoroute Bonaventure (10), which leads directly downtown, or take Highway 40 West to Autoroute Décarie (15), and then follow the signs for downtown *(centre-ville)*.

From Ottawa, take Highway 40 East to Autoroute Décarie (15), and then follow the signs for downtown *(centre-ville)*.

Visitors arriving from Toronto will arrive via Highway 20 East, continue along it and then take Autoroute Ville-Marie (720) and follow the signs for downtown *(centre-ville)*.

From the United States, via either Highway 10 (Eastern Townships) or Highway 15 you will use the Pont Champlain and Autoroute Bonaventure (10).

■ **Airports**

There are two airports near Montréal: **Mirabel** and **Dorval**. Mirabel Airport is intended for international flights whereas the Dorval Airport handles domestic (from Québec and other Canadian provinces) and U.S. air traffic.

Mirabel Airport

Location

This airport is located approximately 50 km north of Montréal, in Mirabel. To reach downtown Montréal from Mirabel, follow the Autoroute des Laurentides (15) South until it intersects with the Autoroute Métropolitaine (40), which you follow for a few kilometres, then continue once again on the 15 South (now called

Autoroute Décarie) until Autoroute Ville-Marie (720). Follow the signs for downtown *(centre-ville, Vieux-Montréal)*. The trip takes 40 to 60 minutes (☎ 514-476-3010 or toll free 1-800-465-1213).

Information

For information on airport services (arrivals, departures, and other information), visit the information counter, which is open every day from 8 a.m. to 11:30 p.m. There is also a 24-hour telephone service (☎ 514-476-3010 or toll free 1-800-465-1213).

Buses

● From Mirabel to downtown Montréal : the Connaisseur Bus Company offers a service (Mon to Fri from 8 a.m. to 8 p.m., departures every 20 min, otherwise departures every 30 min, no departures between 1 a.m. and 7 p.m.; ☎ 514-934-1222). The bus stops at the Hôtel Reine-Elizabeth (Queen Elizabeth Hotel, rue Mansfield, Métro Bonaventure) and at the Voyageur bus terminal (505, boul. de Maisonneuve Est, Métro Berri-UQAM). Cost : $14 one-way, $20 return (free for children under five).

● From Dorval to Mirabel: with the Connaisseur Bus Company (☎ 514-934-1222). Daily departures from 9:20 a.m. to 11:20 p.m. Cost : $12 one-way and $16 return.

Airport Limousine

Limousine service is provided by Limousine Montréal Inc. (☎ 514-333-5466).

Foreign Exchange

The Royal Bank of Canada is open during flight arrivals and departures, but charges a commission. Better exchange rates are available in downtown Montréal (see p 42). This bank, however, has various automatic teller machines that can exchange more common currencies.

Lost and Found

☎ (514) 476-3010

Dorval Airport

Location

Dorval Airport is located approximately 20 km from downtown Montréal, about 20 min by car. To get downtown from here, take Highway 20 East to the junction of Highway 720 (Autoroute Ville-Marie), then follow the signs for downtown *(centre-ville, Vieux-Montréal)*.

Information

A counter is open from 6 a.m. to 10 p.m. seven days a week; ☎ (514) 633-3105 to provide information regarding airport services (arrivals, departures and other information).

Buses

From Dorval to downtown: with the Connaisseur Bus Company (☎ 514-934-1222). Daily departures from 7 a.m. to 11 p.m.; Monday to Friday, departures every 30 min from 7 a.m. to 8 a.m., every 20 min from 8 a.m. to 11 p.m. and every 30 min from 11 p.m. and 1:30 a.m.; Saturday and Sunday from 7 a.m. to 1:30 a.m., departures every 30 min. There are no

departures between 1:30 a.m. and 7 p.m.. The bus stops at the Hôtel Reine-Elizabeth (Queen Elizabeth 900, boul. René-Lévesque Ouest, Métro Bonaventure), the Château Champlain, the Centre Sheraton and the Voyageur Bus Terminal (505, boul. de Maisonneuve Est, Métro Berri-UQAM). Free for children under five. Cost : $8.75 one-way and $16 return.

Foreign Exchange

A Thomas Cook counter is open from 6 a.m. to 11 p.m., but a commission is charged. Better exchange rates are available in downtown Montréal (see p 42).

Lost and Found

☎ (514) 633-3094

■ Taxis

Co-op Taxi : ☎ 725-9885
Diamond : ☎ 273-6331
Taxi Lasalle : ☎ 277-2552

■ Public Transportation

Visitors are strongly advised to take advantage of Montréal's public transportation system which consists of an extensive network of buses and subway trains (the Métro) that service the region well. Métro stations are identifiable by a blue sign with a white arrow pointing downwards and the word "Métro." Bus stops, indicated by a blue and white sign, are usually located at street corners. Smoking is prohibited throughout the system.

A pass entitling the holder to unlimited use of the public transportation services for one month costs $43 (on sale at the beginning of the month only). For shorter stays, visitors can

purchase six tickets for $7, or single tickets at $1.75 each. Children and seniors benefit from reduced fares. Tickets and passes can be purchased at all Métro stations. Take note that bus drivers do not sell tickets and do not give change.

If a trip involves a transfer (from the bus to the Métro or vice versa, for example), the passenger must ask the bus driver for a transfer ticket when getting on, or take one from a transfer machine in the Métro station. Free subway maps are available inside all stations, as are timetables for the buses that stop at that station.

Commuter trains serve the western section of the island. These leave from the Vendôme and Bonaventure Métro stations and provide an efficient means of getting to these areas. However, on weekends, the service is less frequent, so it is a good idea to check the timetables carefully.

On the above Métro map, the dotted lines represent projected stations, the thin lines are commuter train lines, and the circles with squares inside are stations served by both commuter trains and Métros. For more information on the public transportation system, call ☎ 288-6287 (which corresponds to the word *AUTOBUS*, French for bus, on a telephone dial).

■ **By Car**

Since Montréal is well served by public transportation and taxis, having a car is not essential to visiting the city, especially since most of the sights are located relatively close to one another, and all of the suggested tours can be done on foot, except the one of the West Island. Nevertheless, it is quite easy to get around by car. Parking lots, though quite expensive, are numerous in the downtown area. Parking on the street is possible, but be sure to read the signs carefully. Ticketing of illegally-parked cars is strict and expensive.

Things to Consider

Driver's License: As a general rule, foreign driver's licenses are valid for six months from the date of arrival in Canada.

Winter Driving: Although roads are generally in good condition, the dangers brought on by drastic climatic conditions must be taken into consideration.

Driving and the Highway Code: Signs marked *"Arrêt"* or *"Stop"* in white against a red background must always be respected. Come to a complete stop even if there is no apparent danger.

Turning right on a red light and turning from a one-way street onto another on a red light are both forbidden in Québec.

Traffic lights are often located on the opposite side of the intersection, so be careful to stop at the stop line, a white line on the pavement before the intersection.

When a school bus (usually yellow) has stopped and has its signals flashing, you must come to a complete stop, no matter what direction you are travelling in. Failing to stop at the flashing signals is considered a serious offense, and carries a heavy penalty.

Seatbelts must be worn in both the front and back seats at all times.

There are no tolls on Québec highways, and the speed limit on highways *(autoroutes)* is 100 km/h. The speed limit is usually 90 km/h on secondary highways and 50 km/h in urban areas.

Gas Stations : Because Canada produces its own crude oil, gasoline prices are less expensive than in Europe. However, due to hidden taxes, gas prices are considerably higher than those in the United States and in Western Canada. Some gas stations (especially in the downtown area) might ask for payment in advance as a security measure, especially after 11 p.m.

Car Rentals

Vacation packages that include flight, hotel and car, or simply hotel and car are generally less expensive than car rentals on the spot. Many travel agencies have agreements with the major car rental companies (Avis, Budget, Hertz, etc.) and offer good deals; contracts often include added bonuses (reduced show ticket prices for example). Package deals usually prove to be a good deal.

Avis
Mirabel Airport, ☎ 476-3481
Dorval Airport, ☎ 636-1902
1255, rue Metcalfe ☎ 866-7906
Bus Station ☎ 288-9934

Budget
Mirabel Airport, ☎ 476-2687
Dorval Airport, ☎ 636-0052
1240, rue Guy, ☎ 937-9121
Complexe Desjardins, ☎ 842-9931

Discount
607, boul. de Maisonneuve Ouest
☎ 286-1554

Hertz
Mirabel Airport, ☎ 476-3385
Dorval Airport, ☎ 636-9530
1073, rue Drummond, ☎ 938-1717
1475, rue Aylmer, ☎ 842-8537

Tilden
Mirabel Airport, ☎ 476-3460
Dorval Airport, ☎ 636-9030
Place Bonaventure (Train Station) :
☎ 878-1112
1200, rue Stanley, ☎ 878-2771

Via Route
1255, rue Mackay, ☎ 871-1166

When renting a car, find out if:

● the contract includes unlimited kilometres or not;

● the insurance offered provides full coverage (accident, property damage, hospital costs for you and passengers, theft).

Remember :

● To rent a car in Québec, you must be at least 21 years of age and have had a driver's license for **at least** one year. If you are between 21 and 25, certain companies (for example Avis, Thrifty, Budget) will ask for a $500 deposit, and in some cases they will also charge an extra sum for each day you rent the car. These conditions do not apply for those over 25 years of age.

● A credit card is extremely useful for the deposit to avoid tying up large sums of money, and can in some cases (gold cards) cover the insurance.

● Most rental cars have an automatic transmission, however you can request a car with a manual shift.

● Child safety seats cost extra.

Accidents and Emergencies

In case of serious accident, fire or other emergency, dial ☎ **911.**

If an accident occurs, always fill out an accident report. In case of a disagreement as to who is at fault, ask a police officer for assistance. Be sure to alert the car rental agency as soon as possible.

If you are planning a long trip and have decided to buy a car, it is a good idea to become a member of the Canadian Automobile Association, or C.A.A., which offers assistance throughout Québec and Canada. If you are a member of an equivalent association in your home country (U.S.A. : American Automobile Association; Switzerland : Automobile Club de Suisse; Belgium: Royal Automobile Touring Club de

Belgique), you can benefit from some of the services offered. For more information, contact your association or the C.A.A. in Montréal (☎ 514-861-7111).

■ **Cycling in Montréal**

One of the most enjoyable ways to get around in the summer is by bicycle. Bike paths have been set up to allow cyclists to explore various neighbourhoods in the city. To help you find your way around, there is a booklet called *The Great Montréal Bike Path*, which shows all the bike paths in Montréal. A small free map of the paths is also available from the tourist information office. Except during rush hour, bicycles can be taken on the Métro. For more information on the bike paths contact the *Bureau des Loisirs de la Ville de Montréal* (the city's activities office) at ☎ 872-6211.

Since drivers are not always attentive, cyclists should be alert, respect road signs (as is required by law) and be careful at intersections. Bicycle helmets are not mandatory in Montréal, but wearing one is strongly recommended.

The *Vélo-Québec* Association offers extensive information to cyclists.
3575, boul. Saint-Laurent
Bureau 310
Montréal H2X 2T7
☎ (514) 847-8356
⇄ (514) 847-0242

There is another association called *Le Monde à Bicyclette* (The World by Bike), whose horizons stretch a little farther. It publishes a small French-language newsletter of the same name, free-of-charge.
3680, rue Jeanne-Mance
Bureau 341
Montréal
☎ (514) 844-2713

Bicycle Rental

Many bicycle shops also rent out bicycles. We have suggested two. For others (and there are a lot), it is best to check with *Vélo-Québec* or with regional tourist offices. You could also look in the *Yellow Pages* under *"Bicyclettes-Location"* or under "Bicycle-Rental". Purchasing insurance is a good idea. Some places include the insurance in the rental price. Be sure to check when renting.

Cyclotouriste
Centre Infotouriste
1001, rue du Square-Dorchester
Métro Peel
☎ 393-8942
Expect to pay about $22 for a full day, and $16 for a half-day (a $200 deposit is required).

La Cordée
2159, rue Sainte-Catherine Est
Métro Papineau
☎ 524-1515
Expect to pay $20 for a full day (a $400 deposit is required).

Guided Tours of Montréal

Various companies organize tours of Montréal, offering visitors interesting ways to explore the city. Walking tours lead to an intimate discovery of the city's neighbourhoods, while bus tours provide a perspective of the city as a whole. Boat cruises highlight another facet of the city, this time in relation to the river. Though the options are countless, the following companies are worth mentioning:

■ By Foot

Héritage Montréal
☎ 875-2985
These walking tours crisscross various neighbourhoods focusing on architecture, history and town planning. Tours are organized on weekends during the summer. They last about two hours and cost $8 per person.

L'Autre Montréal
2138, rue Rachel
☎ 521-7802
This organization uncovers the hidden face of Montréal, through its hippest neighbourhoods and little known nooks and crannies. Some tours are thematic (for example, women in the city).

■ By Bus

Murray Hill Bus Line
1001, rue du Square-Dorchester
(Centre Infotouriste)
☎ 871-4733
From June 24 to October 10, the Carrousel de Murray Hill city tour stops 14 times to let tourists explore particular areas. For the rest of the year, between October 10 and June 23, Murray Hill offers regular three-hour tours. Each tour costs $23.50.

Connaisseur-Gray Line
1001, rue du Square-Dorchester
(Centre Infotouriste)
☎ 934-1222
Regular city tours aboard comfortable buses. Each outing lasts three hours and costs $22.50. Tours aboard a trolley-style bus are also offered.

■ By Boat

Le Bateau-Mouche
Vieux-Port
Quai Jacques-Cartier
☎ 849-9952
Cruises along the river offer an interesting perspective of Montréal. During the day, a cruise costs $19.75 and lasts an hour and a half. Evening tours during which dinner is served last three hours and cost $58.75.

Croisières du Port de Montréal
Quai Victoria
☎ 842-3871
☎ 1-800-667-3131
Visitors enjoy two-hour cruises along the river for $18.75.

Currency and Banks

■ Exchange Offices

Several banks in the downtown area readily exchange foreign currency, but almost all charge a commission. There are exchange offices, on the other hand, that do not charge commission, but their rates are sometimes less competitive. It is a good idea to shop around. The majority of banks can change American money.

Banque Nationale du Canada
1001, rue Sainte-Catherine Ouest
☎ 281-9640

Banque Nationale du Canada
600, rue de la Gauchetière Ouest
☎ 394-8875

Thomas Cook
625, boul. René-Lévesque Ouest
☎ 397-4029

Automatic teller machines that exchange currency have been installed at Complexe Desjardins (on Sainte-Catherine West, between Jeanne-Mance and Saint-Urbain). They are open every day from 6 a.m. to 2 a.m. Various foreign currencies can be changed into Canadian money. Canadian money can also be changed into American and French money. Similar machines are also located at Mirabel Airport.

■ Traveller's Cheques

Remember that Canadian dollars are different from American dollars. If you do not plan on travelling to the United States on the same trip, it is best to get your traveller's cheques in Canadian dollars. Traveller's cheques are accepted in most large stores and hotels; however, it is easier and to your advantage to change your cheques at an exchange office. Traveller's cheques in American and Canadian dollars can be purchased at most banks in Montréal.

■ Credit Cards

Most credit cards are accepted at stores, restaurants and hotels. While the main advantage of credit cards is that they allow visitors to avoid carrying large sums of money, using a credit card also makes leaving a deposit for car rental much easier and some cards, gold cards for example, automatically insure you when you rent a car. In addition, the exchange rate with a credit card is generally better. The most commonly accepted credit cards are Visa, Master Card, and American Express.

■ Banks

Banks can be found almost everywhere, and most offer the standard services to tourists. Visitors who choose to stay in Québec for a long period of time should note that **non-residents** cannot open bank accounts. If this is the case, the best way to have ready money is to use traveller's cheques. Withdrawing money from foreign accounts is expensive. Visitors who have attained residence status, permanent or not (immigrants, students), can open a bank account. A passport and proof of resident status are required.

Money withdrawals from automatic teller machines are possible across Canada, thanks to the Interac network; and in most other countries (in the U.S. and Europe), thanks to the Cirrus network. Most machines are open at all times. Many machines accept foreign bank cards, so that you can withdraw directly from your account (check before to make sure you have access). Cash advances on your credit card are another option, although interest charges are higher. Money orders are a final alternative for which no commission is charged. This option does, however, take more time.

Banks are open Monday to Friday, from 10 a.m. to 3 p.m.. Many are also open Thursdays and Fridays until 6 p.m., and sometimes until 8 p.m.

A Few Addresses

Banque Canadienne Impériale de Commerce
1155, boul. René-Lévesque Ouest
☎ 876-2290

Banque de Montréal
119, rue Saint-Jacques
☎ 877-7373

Banque Nationale du Canada
600, rue de la Gauchetière Ouest
☎ 394-8875

Banque Royale
1, Place Ville-Marie
☎ 874-7222

■ **Currency**

The monetary unit is the dollar ($), which is divided into cents. One dollar = 100 cents.

Bills come in 2, 5, 10, 20, 50 and 100 dollar denominations, and coins come in 1, 5, 10, 25 cent pieces and in 1 dollar coins.

Francophones sometimes speak of *"piastres"* and *"sous"* which are dollars and cents respectively. On occasion, especially in popular language, you might be asked for a *"trente sous"* (thirty-cent piece), what the person really want is a 25 cent piece. A *"cenne noir"* furthermore, is a one-cent piece! In English, Europeans will be surprised to hear "pennies" (1¢), "nickels" (5¢), "dimes" (10¢), "quarters" (25¢), and "loonies" ($1).

Post Offices

Large post offices are open from 8 a.m. to 5:45 p.m. There are several smaller post offices throughout Québec, located in shopping malls, *dépanneurs*, and even pharmacies; these post offices are open much later than the larger ones.

1250, rue University
☎ 395-4909

1250, rue Sainte-Catherine Ouest
☎ 522-5191

Time Difference

Québec is in the Eastern Standard Time Zone, as is most of the Eastern United States. It is three hours ahead of the west coast of the continent. There is a six-hour time difference between Québec and most continental European countries and five hours between Québec and the United Kingdom. Daylight savings time goes into effect in Québec on the last Sunday in October and ends on the first Sunday in April. All of Québec (except the Îles-de-la-Madeleine) is on the same time.

Business Hours and Public Holidays

■ **Business Hours**

Stores

The law respecting business hours allows stores to be open the following hours:

● Monday to Wednesday from 8 a.m. to 9 p.m., though most stores open at 10 a.m. and close at 6 p.m.
● Thursday and Friday from 8 a.m. to 9 p.m., though most open at 10 a.m.
● Saturday from 8 a.m. to 5 p.m., though most open at 10 a.m.
● Sunday from 8 a.m. to 5 p.m., most open at noon, but not all stores are open Sundays.

Dépanneurs (convenience stores that sell food) are found throughout Québec and are open later, sometimes 24 hours a day.

■ Holidays and Public Holidays

The following is a list of public holidays in Québec. Most administrative offices and banks are closed on these days.

January 1st and 2nd
Easter Monday and\or Good Friday
The Fête de Dollard, also called "Victoria Day" (the 3rd Monday in May)
June 24: Saint-Jean-Baptiste Day (Québec's national holiday)
July 1st: Canada Day
Labour Day (1st Monday in September)
Thanksgiving (2nd Monday in October)
Remembrance Day (November 11; only banks and federal government services are closed)
December 25 and 26

Climate

Québec's seasonal extremes are something that set the province apart from much of the world. Temperatures can climb to above 30°C in summer and drop to - 25°C in winter. Visiting Québec during the two "main" seasons (summer and winter) is like visiting two totally different countries, with the seasons influencing not only the scenery, but also the lifestyles and behaviour of the local population.

Health

■ General Information

Vaccinations are not necessary for people coming from Europe or the United States. On the other hand, it is strongly suggested, particularly for medium or long-term stays, that visitors take out health and accident insurance. There are different types, so it is best to shop around. Bring along all medication, especially prescription medicine. Unless otherwise stated, the water is drinkable throughout Québec.

For Emergencies, dial ☎ 911

 Accommodation

A wide choice of accommodation to fit every budget is available in Montréal. Costs vary depending on the season. Summer is the high season, during which rooms are the most expensive. The weeks of the Grand Prix Molson du Canada Formula 1 races, and the jazz festival are among the busiest of the year; reservations made far in advance are strongly recommended during this period. Furthermore prices are generally lower on weekends than during the week.

Depending on your mode of travel, the choice is extensive. Most places are very comfortable and offer a number of extra services. Prices vary according to the type of accommodation, but remember to add the 7 % G.S.T (federal Goods and Services Tax) and the 6.5 % Québec Services Tax. These taxes are refundable for non-residents (see p 48). When making reservations, which is strongly recommended during the summer months, a credit card is indispensable, as a deposit for the first night is often required in advance.

Accommodation prices listed in this guide are for one night's lodging, double occupancy during the high season.

In Montréal's Infotouriste information centre, there is a service called *Hospitalité Canada* which makes hotel reservations free of charge.
1001, rue du Square-Dorchester
Montréal H3B 4V4
☎ (514) 393-9049

■ Hotels

Hotels rooms abound, ranging from modest to luxurious. Most come equipped with a private bathroom.

■ Bed and Breakfasts

Unlike hotels, rooms in private homes are not always equipped with a private bathroom. There are several bed and breakfasts in Montréal. Take note that credit cards are not always accepted in bed and breakfasts.

In Québec, bed and breakfasts are known as *Gîtes du Passant*. In order to be a *Gîte du Passant*, a bed and breakfast must be a member of the *Fédération des Agricotours du Québec* and must conform to regulations and norms meant to ensure the impeccable quality of your stay. The *Fédération*, in collaboration with Ulysses Travel Publications, produces the guide *Best Bed and Breakfasts in Québec*, which lists, for each region, a variety of accommodations and the services offered by each one. In addition to bed and breakfasts, the guide also lists addresses for farm-stays and country houses for rent.

■ Motels

There are many motels, but they are usually located in the suburbs. Though less expensive, they often lack atmosphere; they are particularly useful when pressed for time.

■ Youth Hostels

Tourisme Jeunesse publishes a list of the addresses of all the youth hostels (called *Auberges de Jeunesse* in Québec), as well as the services offered at each one. This list is available from :

Tourisme Jeunesse
4545, avenue Pierre-de-Coubertin
C.P. 1000, Succ. M
☎ (514) 252-3117

■ University Residences

Due to certain restrictions, this can be a complicated alternative. Residences are only available during the summer (mid-May to mid-August) and making reservations in advance is strongly recommended; these can usually be made by paying the first night with a credit card.

This type of accommodation, however, is less costly than the "traditional" alternatives, making the effort to reserve early worthwhile. Visitors with valid student cards can expect to pay approximately $20 plus tax, while non students can expect to pay around $33. Bedding is included in the price, and there is usually a cafeteria in the building (meals are not included in the price).

Restaurants and Bars

■ Restaurants

Though you may have learned differently in your French classes, Quebecois refer to breakfast as *déjeuner*, lunch as *dîner*, and dinner as *souper*. Many restaurants offer a "daily special" (called *spécial du jour*), a complete meal for one price, which is usually less expensive than ordering individual items from the menu. Served only at lunch, the price usually includes a choice of appetizers and main dishes, plus coffee and dessert. In the evenings, a *table d'hôte* (same formula, but slightly more expensive) is also an attractive possibility.

"Bring Your Own Wine"

At certain restaurants, you can bring your own wine. This interesting phenomenon is a result of the fact that in order to sell alcohol, a restaurant must have an alcohol permit, which is very expensive. Restaurants who want to offer their clientele a less expensive menu opt for a special type of permit that allows their patrons to bring their own bottle of wine. In most cases, a sign in the restaurant window indicates whether alcohol can be purchased on the premises or if you have to bring your own (*Apportez votre vin*). Besides the alcohol permit, there is also a bar permit. Restaurants with only the alcohol permit can sell alcohol, beer and wine, but only accompanied by a meal. Restaurants with both permits can sell customers just a drink, even if they do not order a meal.

■ Cafés

Going out to a café has become a veritable Quebecois "institution" (especially in Montréal). Many restaurants serve only desserts. These places are particularly popular among cheesecake connoisseurs!

■ Québec Cuisine

Although many restaurant dishes are similar to those served in France or the United States, some of them are prepared in a typically Quebecois way making them unique; these should definitely be tasted:

La soupe aux pois (pea soup)
La tourtière (meat pie)
Le pâté chinois (also known as shepherd's pie, layered pie consisting of ground beef, potatoes, and corn)
Les cretons (a type of pâté of ground pork cooked with onions in fat)
Le jambon au sirop d'érable (ham with maple syrup)
Les fèves au lard (baked beans)
Le ragoût de pattes de cochon (pigs' feet stew)
Le cipaille (layered pie with different types of meat)
La tarte aux pacanes (pecan pie)
La tarte au sucre (sugar pie)
La tarte aux bleuets (blueberry pie)
Le sucre à la crème (creamy sugar fudge squares)

■ Bars and Discos

Most bars do not have a cover charge (although in winter there is usually a mandatory coat-check). Expect to pay a few dollars to get into discos on weekends. Québec nightlife is particularly lively - of course, it does not hurt that the sale of alcohol continues until 3 a.m.! Some bars remain open past this hour but serve only soft drinks. Drinking establishments that only have a tavern or brasserie permit must close at midnight.

Happy Hour (two for one)

Bars in the downtown areas often offer two for one specials during "Happy Hour" (usually from 5 p.m. to 7 p.m.). During these hours you can buy two beers for the price of one, and drinks are offered at a reduced price. Some snack bars and dessert places offer the same discounts. A recent Québec law prohibits the advertising of these specials, so if you are interested, ask your waiter or waitress.

Taxes and Tipping

■ Taxes

The ticket price on items usually **does not include tax**. There are two taxes, the GST (federal Goods and Services Tax, TPS in French) of 7 % and the PST (Provincial Sales Tax, TVQ in French) at 6.5 % on goods and services. They are cumulative, so you must add 13.96 % in taxes to the price of most items and to restaurant and hotel bills.

There are some exceptions to this taxation system, such as books, which are only taxed at 7 % and food (except for ready-made meals), which is not taxed at all.

Tax Refunds for Non-Residents

Non-residents can be refunded for taxes paid on purchases made while in Québec. To obtain a refund, it is important to keep your receipts. A separate form for each tax (federal and provincial) must be filled out to obtain a refund. The conditions under which refunds are awarded are different for the GST and the PST.

In Montréal :

● Forms are available at customs (at the airport) and certain department stores.

● For further information, call ☎ 1-800-668-4748 (toll-free for the GST) and ☎ (514) 873-4692 (for the PST).

■ Tipping

In general, tipping applies to all table service: restaurants, bars and nightclubs (no tipping in fast-food restaurants). Tipping is also standard in taxis and hair salons.

The tip is usually about 15 % of the bill before taxes, but varies, of course, depending on the quality of service.

Wine, Beer and Alcohol

In Québec, the sale of alcohol is governed by a state-run agency called the *Société des Alcools du Québec* (S.A.Q.). For a wide selection of liqueurs, wine and beer, visit one of the S.A.Q. branches, which are located throughout the province. Grocery stores are authorized to sell beer and some wines, but the choice is limited and the quality of the wine often mediocre. As a general rule, the S.A.Q. branches are open the same hours as stores. In Montréal, there is also the *Maison des Vins*, which has a much wider and specialized selection than other stores. You must be at least 18 years old to purchase alcohol, which is not sold after 11 p.m. Be careful; in Québec, a *liqueur* is a soft drink, not an alcoholic beverage!

A Few Addresses

4053, rue Saint-Denis (corner Duluth), ☎ 845-5200
1246, rue Sainte-Catherine Ouest, ☎ 861-7908
Maison des Vins, 505, avenue de Président-Kennedy, ☎ 873-2274

Beer

Two huge breweries share the largest share of the beer market in Québec : Labatt and Molson-O'Keefe. They each produce different types of beer, mostly pale beers, with varying levels of alcohol. In bars, restaurants, and discos, beer on tap is cheaper than bottled beer.

Besides these large breweries, some interesting independent micro-breweries have developed in the past few years. The variety and taste of their beers make them quite popular in Québec. However, because these are produced by micro breweries, they are not available everywhere.

Listed below are a few of the micro-brewery beers : Massawippi, Belle-Gueule, Saint-Ambroise, Boréale, Brasal, Maudite (with 8 % alcohol, the strongest in Québec) and Blanche de Chambly.

Wines

Surprising as it may seem, Québec produces a small variety of wines, mostly white. Grapes are grown in the Eastern Townships (Estrie) region.

Apple cider is also produced in Québec, mostly in the Montérégie region.

Advice for Smokers

As in the United-States, cigarette smoking is considered taboo and is being prohibited in more and more public places :

- in most shopping centres;
- in buses and Métros;
- in government offices.

Many public places (restaurants, tearooms) have smoking and non-smoking sections. Cigarettes are sold in bars, grocery stores and newspaper and magazine shops.

Safety

Violence is far less prevalent in Québec than in the United States. A genuine non-violence policy is advocated throughout the province. The city of Montréal even boasts a peace monument built out of 12,700 war toys given up voluntarily by Montréal-area children. The monument, designed by Linda Covit, is on display at Jarry Park (Métro Jarry) in Montréal.

Visitors who take the normal precautions should have no need to be overly worried about personal security. If trouble should arise, remember to call ☎ 911.

Senior Citizens

Older people who would like to meet people their age can do so through the association listed below. It regroups most organizations of people 55 and older, and provides information about activities and local clubs throughout Québec.

For further information:

Fédération de l'Âge d'Or du Québec
4545, av. Pierre-de-Coubertin
C.P. 1000, Succursale M
Montréal H1V 3R2
☎ (514) 252-3017

Reduced transportation fares and entertainment tickets are often available to seniors. Do not hesitate to ask.

Gay and Lesbian Life

Montréal offers many services to the gay and lesbian community. These are mostly concentrated in the part of town known as **The Village**, located on Rue Sainte-Catherine, between Amherst and Papineau streets, as well as on the adjoining streets.

In Montréal there are two telephone lines that provide details on activities in the city : **Gai-Info** (☎ 768-0199), which is bilingual, and **The Gay Line** (☎ 931-8668), in English only. There is also the gay and lesbian bookstore **L'Androgyne**, located at 3636 Boulevard Saint-Laurent and the **Centre Communautaire des Gais et Lesbiennes**, ☎ 528-8424. The latter organizes various activities, such as dances, language courses, music, etc. The **Pa-**rade de la Fierté Gaie et Lesbienne (Gay and Lesbian Pride March) takes place at the end of June on Rue Sainte-Catherine, and ends with various performances at Parc Campbell (information ☎ 987-1774).

Two free magazines called *RG* and *Fugues* are available in bars. They are both monthly publications and contain information concerning the gay and lesbian communities.

Disabled People

The Keroul Association publishes a free guide called *Accès Tourisme*, which lists places accessible to the disabled throughout the province. These places are classed by tourist region. Most of the regions also have associations that organize leisure and sports activities for disabled persons. Contact the *Association Québécoise de Loisir pour Personnes Handicapées* for the addresses of these associations.

For information:

Association Québécoise de Loisir pour Personnes Handicapées
4545, avenue Pierre-de-Coubertin
C.P.1000, Succursale M
Montréal H1V 3R2
☎ (514) 252-3144

KEROUL (tourism for handicapped people)
☎ (514) 252-3104

Children

Children in Québec are treated like royalty. Facilities are available almost everywhere, whether it be transportation or leisure activities. Generally, children under five travel for free, and those under 12 are eligible for fare reductions. The same rules apply for various leisure activities and shows. Find out before you purchase tickets. High chairs and children's menus are available in most restaurants, while a few of the larger stores provide a babysitting service while parents shop.

Pets

Dogs on a leash are permitted in most public parks in the city. Small pets are allowed on the public transportation system, as long as they are in a cage or well controlled by the owner. Pets are generally not allowed in stores, especially not food stores, however many Montrealers tie their pets up near the entrance while they run in. Pets are not allowed in restaurants, although some establishments with terraces permit pets.

Weights and Measures

Although the metric system has been in use in Canada for more than 10 years, some people continue to use the Imperial system in casual conversation. Here are some equivalents:

- 1 pound (lb) = 454 grams
- 1 foot (ft) = 30 centimetres
- 1 mile = 1.6 kilometres
- 1 inch = 2.2 centimetres
- 1 kilometres (km) = 0.63 miles
- 1 kilogram = 2.2 pounds
- 1 metre (m) = 45.4 inches

General Information

Drugs: Drugs are strictly forbidden (even "soft" drugs). Drug users and dealers caught with drugs in their possession risk severe consequences.

Electricity: Voltage is 110 volts throughout Canada, the same as in the United States.

The cycle is not the same as Europe's (60 cycles rather than 50 cycles), and items such as tape recorders, video cassettes, record-players, etc. are not recommended.

Electrical plugs are flat, and adaptors are available here.

Folklore: Québec's rich folklore offers an interesting insight into the history and culture of the province. The organization below regroups various regional committees aimed at the preservation and development of folklore. Various activities are organized depending on the season and location. For more information:

Association Québécoise des Loisirs Folkloriques
4545, Pierre-de-Coubertin
C.P. 1000 Succursale M
Montréal H1V 3R2
☎ (514) 252-3022

Hairdressers: A tip of 15 % before taxes is standard, as in restaurants.

Laundromats: These are found almost everywhere. In most cases, detergent is sold on the spot. Although change machines are sometimes provided, it is best to bring plenty of quarters with you.

Movie Theatres: There are no ushers and therefore no tips in theatres.

Museums: Most museums charge admission, however, permanent exhibits at some museums are free on Wednesday evenings from 6 p.m. to 9 p.m., while reductions are offered for temporary exhibits. Reduced prices are available for seniors, children, and students. Call the museum for further details.

Newspapers: International newspapers can easily be found in Montréal. The major Montréal newspapers are : in French *Le Devoir*, *La Presse* and *Le Journal de Montréal*, and in English *The Gazette*. Three free weekly newspapers are also available : *Hour* and *The Mirror* in English and *Voir* in French.

Pharmacies: Apart from the smaller drug stores, there are large pharmacy chains that sell everything from chocolate to laundry detergent, as well as the more traditional items, such as cough drops and headache medications.

Religion: Almost all religions are represented in Montréal. Unlike English Canada, the majority of the Québec population are Catholic, although most Quebecois are not practising Catholics.

Telegrams: These are sent by private companies, so it is a good idea to consult the *Yellow Pages* under the heading "telegrams". Listed below are two companies :

American Telegram
☎ 1-800-343-7363

Unitel Communications Inc.
☎ (514) 861-7311

Telephones: Much cheaper than in Europe, but more expensive than in the U.S., pay phones can be found everywhere, often in the entrances of some of the larger department stores, and in restaurants. They are easy to use and some even accept credit cards. In Montréal and the surrounding area, a call costs $0.25 for unlimited time. Have a lot quarters on hand if you are making a long distance call. For example, a call to Québec City from Montréal costs $2.50 for the first three minutes, and $0.38 for each additional minute. Calling direct from a private home is less expensive.

Weather: For road conditions, call ☎ (514) 873-4121; for weather forecasts, call ☎ (514) 636-3302.

Language

Quebecois are very proud of their language, and have struggled long and hard to preserve it while surrounded on all sides by English. The accent and vocabulary are different from European French, and can be surprising at first, but have a charm all their own.

When writing a guide to a region where the use and preservation of language are a part of daily life, certain decisions have to be made. We have tried to keep our combined use of English and French consistent throughout the guide. The official language in Québec is French, so when listing attractions and addresses, we have kept the titles in French. This will allow readers to make the connection between the guide and the signs they will be seeing. The terms used in these titles are in the glossary, but we are confident that after a couple of days, you will not even need to check! English style has been used in the text itself, to preserve readability. In Montréal visitors will often hear English almost as much as French, and though English terms for zattractions are common, we have maintained the French nomenclature, in keeping with the rest of the guide.

English-speaking visitors to Montréal will often be able to take a break from practising their French, if they want. Just remember, a valiant effort and a sincere smile go a long way!

A complete list of all the local expressions would be too long to include in the guide. Travellers interested in knowing a bit more on the subject can refer to the *Dictionnaire de la Langue Québécoise* by Léandre Bergeron, published by Éditions VLB, or the excellent *Dictionnaire Pratique des Expressions Québécoises*, published by Éditions Logiques.

Glossary of Unique Québec Expressions

achaler : to bother someone

avoir un flat : (pronounced "flatt") to have a flat tire

blonde : a girlfriend

breuvage : in general, all non-alcoholic beverages

carosse : an airport or store cart

cenne : a penny

c'est pas pire : an expression warning of the banality of a situation or thing; also means: that's not too bad (according to the tone of voice)

char : automobile

chum : friend, buddy, boyfriend; ex: *mon chum* for a male friend and *ma chumme* for a female friend

dépanneur : a convenience store, (to be *en panne* means out of order, not working) *dispendieux* : something that is expensive; ex: a car that is *dispendieux*

donner un bec : to give a friendly kiss. The word *bec* can also mean mouth or beak in a figurative sense; ex: *se sucrer le bec* = to eat sweets

être tanné : to have enough of a situation, at the end of one's rope

jaser : to chat

la valise du char : the trunk of a car

le fun : a good time, to be good or great

liqueur : a flavoured, non-alcoholic drink, a soft drink

plate : used to discribe an unpleasant situation; ex: missing the bus, *c'est plate!*

piastre (pronounced "piasse"): dollar

niaiseux : a stupid person or situation; ex : a person who seems *niaiseuse*, *une situation niaiseuse*

se tasser : to make room for somebody, to move over.

tu viens-tu : The repetition of *tu*, even when the subject is not the second person, is very common. It can cause some confusion until the listener gets used to it, but adds a certain charm: *ça s'en vient tu?, ça marche-tu?, tu veux-tu?, tu m'aimes-tu?, tu travailles-tu?*

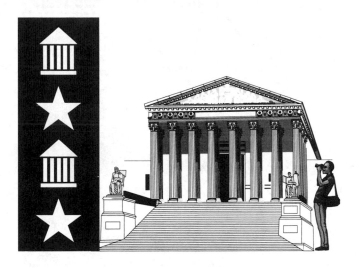

EXPLORING

To discover Montréal and the neighbouring municiplities we have outlined below 16 walking tours and one longer tour that can be done by bike or by car:

 **Tour A:
Vieux-Montréal ★★★**
(two days)

In the 18th century, Montréal was surrounded by stone fortifications, like Québec City. Between 1801 and 1817, these ramparts were demolished following the efforts of the local merchants, who saw them as an obstacle to the city's development. The network of old streets, compressed after nearly a century of confinement,

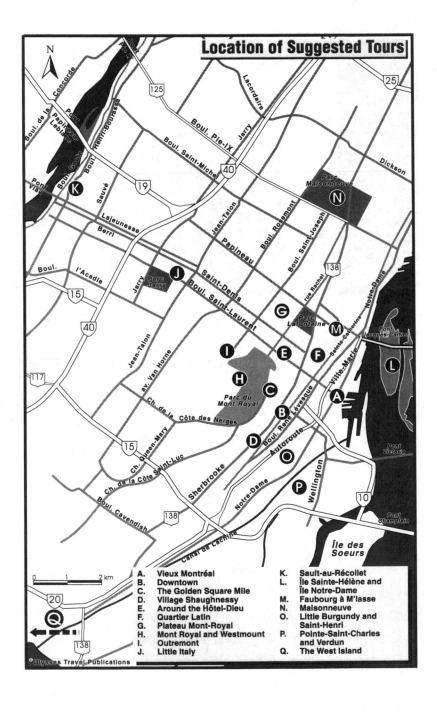

Location of Suggested Tours

A. Vieux Montréal
B. Downtown
C. The Golden Square Mile
D. Village Shaughnessy
E. Around the Hôtel-Dieu
F. Quartier Latin
G. Plateau Mont-Royal
H. Mont Royal and Westmount
I. Outremont
J. Little Italy

K. Sault-au-Récollet
L. Île Sainte-Hélène and Île Notre-Dame
M. Faubourg à M'lasse
N. Maisonneuve
O. Little Burgundy and Saint-Henri
P. Pointe-Saint-Charles and Verdun
Q. The West Island

© Ulysses Travel Publications

nevertheless remained in place. Today's Vieux-Montréal thus corresponds quite closely to the area covered by the fortified city. During the 19th century, this area became the hub of commercial and financial activity in Canada. Banks and insurance companies built sumptuous head offices here, leading to the destruction of almost all buildings erected under the French Regime. The area was later abandoned for nearly 40 years in favour of the modern downtown area of today. Finally, the long process of putting new life into Vieux-Montréal got underway during the preparations for the Expo '67, and continues today with numerous conversion and restoration projects.

The tour begins at the west end of Vieux-Montréal, on Rue McGill, which marks the site of the surrounding wall that once separated the city from the Faubourg des Récollets (Square-Victoria Métro station). Visitors will notice a considerable difference between the urban fabric of the modern downtown area behind them, with its wide boulevards lined with glass and steel skyscrapers, and the old part of the city, whose narrow, compact streets are crowded with stone buildings.

The numbers following the names of attractions refer to the map of Vieux-Montréal.

La Tour de la Bourse ★ (1) *(Place de la Bourse)*, or stock exchange, dominates the surroundings. It was erected in 1964 according to a design by the famous Italian engineers Luigi Moretti and Pier Luigi Nervi, to whom we owe the *Palazzo dello Sport* (Sports Stadium) in Rome and the Exhibition Centre in Turin. The elegant 47-floor black tower houses the offices and trading floor of the *Bourse*. It is one of many buildings in this city designed by

foreign talents. Its construction was intended to breathe new life into the business section of the old city, which was deserted after the stock market crash of 1929 in favour of the area around Square Dorchester. According to the initial plan, there were supposed to be two or even three identical towers.

In the 19th century, **Square Victoria (2)** was a Victorian garden surrounded by Second Empire and Renaissance Revival style stores and office buildings. Only the narrow building at 751 Rue McGill survives from that era. North of Rue Saint-Antoine, visitors will find a **statue of Queen Victoria**, executed in 1872 by English sculptor Marshall Wood, as well as an authentic Art Nouveau style **Parisian Métro railing**. The latter, designed by Hector Guimard in 1900 and given to the city of Montréal by the city of Paris for Expo '67, was installed at one of the entrances to the Square-Victoria Métro station.

Enter the covered passageway of the Centre de Commerce Mondial.

World Trade Centres are exchange organizations intended to promote international trade. Montréal's **Centre de Commerce Mondial ★ (3)** *(Rue McGill)*, completed in 1991 is a new structure hidden behind an entire block of old façades. An impressive glassed-in passageway stretches 180 m through the centre of the building, along a portion of the Ruelle des Fortifications, a lane marking the former location of the northern wall of the fortified city. Alongside the passageway, visitors will find a fountain and an elegant stone stairway, that provide the setting for a statue of Amphitrite, Poseidon's wife, taken from the municipal fountain in Saint-Mihielde-la-Meuse in France. This work dates back to the mid-18th century, it was executed by Barthélémy Guibal, a sculptor from Nîmes (France), who also designed the fountains gracing Place Stanislas in Nancy (France).

Climb the stairway, then walk along the passageway to the modest entrance of the lobby of the Hôtel Inter-Continental. Turn right onto the footbridge leading to the Nordheimer building, which was restored in order to accommodate the hotel's reception halls linked to the Centre de Commerce Mondial. Erected in 1888, the building originally housed a piano store and a small concert hall, where many great artists performed, including Maurice Ravel and Sarah Bernhardt. The interior, with its combination of dark woodwork, moulded plaster and mosaics, is typical of the late 19th century, characterized by exuberant eclecticism and lively polychromy. The façade, located on Rue Saint-Jacques, combines Romanesque Revival elements, as adapted by American architect Henry Hobson Richardson, with elements from the Chicago School, notably the metallic roof with its many windows.

Exit via 363 Rue Saint-Jacques.

Rue Saint-Jacques was the main artery of Canadian high finance for over a century. This role is reflected in its rich and varied architecture, which serves as a veritable encyclopedia of styles from 1830 to 1930. In those years, the banks, insurance companies and department stores, as well as the nation's railway and shipping companies were largely controlled by Montrealers of Scottish extraction, who had come to the colonies to make their fortune.

Begun in 1928 according to plans by New York skyscraper specialists York and Sawyer, the former head office of the **Banque Royale** ★★ (4) *(360 rue Saint-Jacques)*, or Royal Bank, was one of the last buildings erected during this era of prosperity. The 22-floor tower has a base inspired by Florentine palazzos, which corresponds to the scale of the neighbouring buildings. Inside the edifice, visitors can admire the high ceilings of this "temple of finance," built at a time when banks needed impressive buildings to win customers' confidence. The walls of the great hall are emblazoned with the heraldic insignia of eight of the 10 Canadian provinces, as well as those of Montréal (St. George's cross) and Halifax (a yellow bird), where the bank was founded in 1861.

The **Banque Molson** ★ (5) *(288 rue Saint-Jacques)* was founded in 1854 by the Molson family, famous for the brewery established by their ancestor, John Molson (1763-1836), in 1786. The Molson Bank, like other banks at the time, even printed its own paper money—an indication of the power wielded by its owners, who contributed greatly to the city's development. The head office of the family business looks more like a patrician residence than an anonymous bank. Completed in 1866, it is one of the earliest examples of the Second Empire, or Napoleon III style to have been erected in Canada. This French style, modelled on the Louvre and the Paris Opera, was extremely popular in North America between 1865 and 1890. Above the entrance, visitors will see the heads of William Molson and two of his children sculpted out of sandstone. The Molson Bank merged with the Banque de Montréal in 1925.

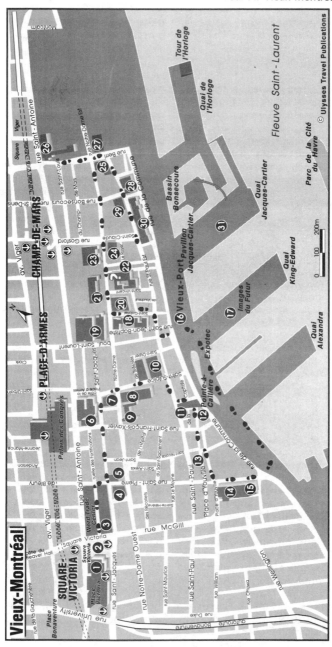

*Walk along Rue Saint-Jacques to quick-
ly come upon Place d'Armes.*

The **Banque de Montréal** ★★ **(6)**
(119 rue Saint-Jacques), founded in
1817 by a group of merchants, is the
country's oldest banking institution. Its
present head office takes up an entire
block on the north side of Place
d'Armes. A magnificent building by
John Wells, built in 1847 and modelled
after the Roman Pantheon, it occupies
the place of honour in the centre of the
block, and offers customer banking. Its
Corinthian portico is a monument to the
commercial power of the Scottish
merchants who founded the institution.
The capitals of the columns, severely
damaged by pollution, were replaced in
1970 with aluminum replicas. The
pediment includes a bas-relief depicting
the bank's coat of arms carved out of
Binney stone in Scotland by Her
Majesty's sculptor, Sir John Steele.

The interior was almost entirely redone
in 1904-05, according to plans by
celebrated New York architects McKim,
Mead and White (Boston Library,
Columbia University in New York City,
etc.). On this occasion, the bank was
endowed with a splendid banking hall,
designed in the style of a Roman
basilica, with green syenite columns,
gilded bronze ornamentation and beige
marble counters. A small **Numismatic
museum** *(free admission; Mon to Fri,
from 10 a.m. to 4 p.m.)* located in the
lobby of the modern building displays
bills from different eras, as well as an
amusing collection of mechanical piggy
banks. Across from the museum,
visitors will find four bas-reliefs carved
out of an artificial stone called *coade*,
which once graced the façade of the
bank's original head office. These were
executed in 1819, after drawings by
English sculptor John Bacon.

Under the French Regime, **Place
d'Armes** ★★ **(7)** was the heart of the
city. Used for military manouevres and
religious processions, it was also the
location of the Gadoys well, the city's
main source of potable water. In 1847,
the square was transformed into a
lovely, fenced-in Victorian garden,
which was destroyed at the beginning
of the 20th century in order to make
room for a tramway terminal. In the
meantime, a **monument to Maisonneuve** was erected in 1895. Executed
by sculptor Philippe Hébert, it shows
the founder of Montréal, Paul de
Chomedey, Sieur de Maisonneuve,
surrounded by prominent figures from
the city's early history, namely Jeanne
Mance, founder of the Hôtel-Dieu
Hospital, Lambert Closse, along with
his dog Pilote, and Charles Lemoyne,
head of a family of famous explorers.
An Iroquois warrior completes the
tableau.

The square, which is in fact shaped
more like a trapezoid, is surrounded by
several noteworthy buildings. The
surprising red sandstone tower at
number 511 was erected in 1888 for
the New York Life insurance company
according to a design by architects
Babb, Cook and Willard. Although it
only has eight floors, it is regarded as
Montréal's first skyscraper. The stone
used for the facing was imported from
Scotland. At the time, this type of
stone was transported in the holds of
ships, where it served as ballast until it
was sold to building contractors at the
pier. The edifice next door (507 Place-
d'Armes) is adorned with beautiful Art
Deco details. It was one of the first
buildings over 10 stories tall to be
erected in Montréal after a regulation
restricting the height of structures was
repealed in 1927.

On the south side of the square, visitors will find the Basilique Notre-Dame and the Vieux Séminaire, which are described below.

In 1663, the seigneury of the island of Montréal was acquired by the Parisian Sulpicians, who remained its undisputed masters up until the British conquest of 1760. In addition to distributing land to colonists and laying out the city's first streets, the Sulpicians were responsible for the construction of a large number of buildings, including Montréal's first parish church (1673). Dedicated to *Notre-Dame* (Our Lady), this church had a beautiful Baroque façade, which faced straight down the centre of the street of the same name, creating a pleasant perspective characteristic of classical French townplanning. At the beginning of the 19th century, however, this rustic little church cut a sorry figure when compared to the Anglican cathedral on Rue Notre-Dame and the new Catholic cathedral on Rue Saint-Denis, neither of which remains today. The Sulpicians therefore decided to make a decisive move to surpass their rivals once and for all. In 1823, to the great displeasure of local architects, they commissioned New York architect James O'Donnell, who came from an Irish Protestant background, to design the largest and most original church north of Mexico.

Basilique Notre-Dame ★★★(8) *(110 rue Notre-Dame Ouest)*, built between 1824 and 1829, is a true North American masterpiece of a Gothic Revival architecture. It should be seen not as a replica of a European cathedral, but rather as a fundamentally neoclassical structure characteristic of the Industrial Revolution, complemented by a medieval-style decor which foreshadowed the historicism of the Victorian era. These elements make the building remarkable.

O'Donnell was so pleased with his work that he converted to Catholicism before dying, in order to be buried under the church. Between 1874 and 1880, the original interior, considered too austere, was replaced by the fabulous polychromatic decorations found today. Executed by Victor Bourgeau, then the leading architect of religious buildings in the Montréal region, along with about 50 artists, it is made entirely of wood, painted and gilded with gold leaf. Particularly noteworthy features include the baptistery, decorated with frescoes by Ozias Leduc, and the powerful electro-pneumatic Casavant organ with its 5,772 pipes, often used during the numerous concerts given at the basilica. Lastly, there are the stained-glass windows by Francis Chigot, a master glass artist from France, which depict various episodes in the history of Montréal. They were installed in honour of the church's 100th anniversary.

To the right of the chancel, a passage leads to the *Chapelle du Sacré-Cœur* (Sacred Heart Chapel), added to the back of the church in 1888. Nicknamed the *Chapelle des Mariages* (Wedding Chapel) because of the countless nuptials held there every year, it was seriously damaged by fire in 1978. The spiral staircases and the side galleries are all that remains of the exuberant, Spanish-style Gothic Revival decor of the original. The architects Jodoin, Lamarre and Pratte decided to tie these vestiges in with a modern design, completed in 1981, and including a lovely sectioned vault with skylights, a large bronze reredos by Charles Daudelin and a Guilbault-Thérien mechanical organ. To the right, on the way out of the chapel, visitors will find the small **Musée de la Basilique** *(admission $1; open on weekends 9:30 a.m. to*

4 p.m.), a museum displaying various treasures, including embroidered liturgical clothing as well as the episcopal throne and personal effects of Monseigneur de Pontbriand, the last bishop of New France.

The **Vieux Séminaire** ★ **(9)** *(116 rue Notre-Dame Ouest)*, or old seminary, was built in 1683 in the style of a Parisian *hôtel particulier*, with a courtyard in front and a garden in back. It is the oldest building in the city. For more than three centuries, it has been occupied by Sulpician priests, who, under the French Regime, used it as a manor, from which they managed their vast seigneury. At the time of the building's construction, Montréal had barely 500 inhabitants, and was constantly being terrorized by Iroquois attacks. Under those circumstances, the seminary, albeit modest in appearance, represented a precious piece of European civilization in the middle of a wild, isolated land. The public clock at the top of the façade was installed in 1701, and may be the oldest one of its kind in the Americas.

Take Rue Saint-Sulpice, which runs alongside the basilica.

Vieux-Montréal contains a large number of 19th century warehouses with stone frames, used to store the goods unloaded from ships at the nearby port. Certain elements of their design—their large glass surfaces, intended to reduce artificial gas lighting and consequently the risk of fire; their wide open interior spaces; the austere style of their facing, given the Victorian context in which they were built; and their cast-iron framed American counterparts - make these buildings the natural precursors of modern architecture.

The immense warehouses of the **Cours Le Royer** ★ **(10)** *(rue Saint-Sulpice)* belonged to the *religieuses hospitalières de Saint-Joseph*. These religious nurses rented them out to importers. Designed between 1860 and 1871 by Michel Laurent and Victor Bourgeau, who seldom worked on commercial structures, they are located on the site of Montréal's first Hôtel-Dieu Hospital, founded by Jeanne Mance in 1643. The warehouses, covering a total of 43,000 m², were converted into apartments and offices between 1977 and 1986. The small Rue Le Royer was excavated to make room for an underground parking lot, now covered by a pleasant pedestrian mall.

Turn right on Rue Saint-Paul, towards Place Royale, which lies on the left-hand side of the street.

Montréal's oldest public square, **Place Royale (11)** dates back to 1657. Originally a market square, it later became a pretty Victorian garden surrounded by a cast iron fence. In 1991, it was raised in order to make room for an archeological observation site. It now links the Musée d'Archéologie de la Pointe-à-Callière to the **Vieille Douane**, the old customs house, on the north side. The latter is a lovely example of British neoclassical architecture transplanted into a Canadian setting. The building's austere lines, accentuated by the facing, made of local grey stone, are offset by the appropriate proportions and simplified references to antiquity. The old customs house was built in 1836 according to drawings by John Ostell, who had just arrived in Montréal.

The **Musée d'Archéologie et d'Histoire de la Pointe-à-Callière** ★★ **(12)** *(adults $7, during winter, Tue to Sun 10 a.m. to 5 p.m.; from Jun 24 on, Tue to Sun*

10 a.m. to 8 p.m.; free on Wed, 5 p.m. to 8 p.m.; 350 Place Royale, Pointe-à-Callière, ☎ 872-9150). This archeology and history museum lies on the exact site where Montréal was founded on May 18, 1642. The Rivière Saint-Pierre used to flow alongside the area now occupied by Place d'Youville, while the muddy banks of the St-Laurent reached almost as far as the present-day Rue de la Commune. The first colonists built Fort Ville-Marie out of earth and posts on the isolated point of land created by these two bodies of water. Threatened by Iroquois flotillas and flooding, the leaders of the colony soon decided to establish the town on *Coteau Saint-Louis*, the hill now bisected by Rue Notre-Dame. The site of the fort was then occupied by a cemetery and the château of Gouverneur de Callière, hence the name.

The museum uses the most advanced techniques available to provide visitors with a survey of the city's history. Attractions include a multimedia presentation, a visit to the vestiges discovered on the site, excellent models showing the different stages of Place Royale's development, holographic conversations and thematic exhibitions. Designed by architect Dan Hanganu, the museum was erected for the celebrations of the city's 350th anniversary (1992).

Head towards Place d'Youville, to the right of the museum.

Place d'Youville (13), which stretches from Place Royale to Rue McGill, owes its elongated shape to its location, on top of the bed of the Rivière Saint-Pierre, canalized in 1832. In the middle of the square stands the **Centre d'Histoire de Montréal** *(adults $4.50; Tue to Sun 10 a.m. to 5 p.m.; 335 place d'Youville, ☎ 872-3207)*, a small, unpretentious museum presenting temporary exhibitions on various themes related to life in Montréal. The building itself is the former fire station number 3, one of only a few examples of Flemish-style architecture in Québec. The Marché Sainte-Anne once lay to the west of Rue Saint-Pierre and was, from 1840 to 1849, the seat of the parliament of United Canada. In 1849, the Orangemen burned the building after a law intended to compensate both French and English victims of the rebellion of 1837-38 was adopted. The event marked the end of Montréal's political vocation.

Turn left on Rue Saint-Pierre.

The *Sœurs de la Charité* (Sisters of Charity) are better known as the *Sœurs Grises* (Grey Nuns), a nickname given these nuns falsely accused of selling alcohol to the Amerindians and thus getting them tipsy (in French, *gris* means both grey and tipsy). In 1747, the founder of the community, Saint Marguerite d'Youville, took charge of the former *Hôpital des Frères Charon*, established in 1693, and transformed it into the **Hôpital Général des Sœurs Grises ★ (14)** *(138 rue Saint-Pierre)*, a shelter for the city's homeless children. The west wing and the ruins of the chapel are all that remains of this complex built during the 17th and 18th centuries in the shape of an "H." The other part, which made up another of the old city's classical perspectives, was torn open when Rue Saint-Pierre was extended through the middle of the chapel. The right transept and a part of the apse, visible on the right, have been reinforced in order to accommodate a work of art representing the text of the congregation's letters patent.

The small **Musée Marc-Aurèle-Fortin** **(15)** *(adults $3; Tue to Sun. 11 a.m. to 5 p.m.; 118 Saint-Pierre, ☎ 845-6108)*, which has only a few rooms, is entirely dedicated to the work of Marc-Aurèle Fortin. Using his own unique style, Fortin painted picturesque Quebecois scenes. Paintings executed on a black background and majestic trees are just a couple of his trademarks. The museum has some lovely pieces.

Head across Rue de la Commune to the Promenade du Vieux-Port, which runs alongside the St-Laurent.

The Port of Montréal is the largest inland port on the continent. It stretches 25 km along the St-Laurent, from Cité du Havre to the refineries in the east end. The **Vieux-Port de Montréal ★★ (16)**, the old port, corresponds to the historic portion of the port, located in front of the old city. Abandoned because of its obsolescence, it was revamped between 1983 and 1992, following the example of various other centrally-located North American ports. The old port encompasses a pleasant park, laid out on the embankments and coupled with a promenade, which runs alongside the piers or *quai*, offering a "window" on the river and the few shipping activities that have fortunately been maintained. The layout accents the view of the water, the downtown area and Rue de la Commune, whose wall of neoclassical, grey stone warehouses stands before the city, one of the only examples of so-called "waterfront planning" in North America. From the port, visitors can set off on an excursion on the river and the *Canal de Lachine* aboard **Le Bateau Mouche** *(Quai Jacques-Cartier; ☎ 849-9952)*, whose glass roof enables passengers to fully appreciate the beauty of the surroundings.

On the right, directly in line with Rue McGill, visitors will find the mouth of the **Canal de Lachine**, inaugurated in 1825. This waterway made it possible to bypass the formidable Rapides de Lachine upriver from Montréal, thus providing access to the Great Lakes and the American Midwest. The canal also became the cradle of the industrial revolution in Canada, since the spinning and flour-mills were able to use it as a source of power, as well as a direct means of taking in supplies and sending out shipments (from the boat to the factory and vice versa). Closed in 1959, when the seaway was opened, the canal was turned over to the Canadian Parks Services. A bicycle path now runs alongside it, continuing on to the old port. The locks, restored in 1991, lie adjacent to a park and a boldly-designed lock-keeper's house. Behind the locks stands the last of the old port's towering **grain silos**. Erected in 1905, this reinforced concrete structure excited the admiration of Walter Gropius and Le Corbusier when they came here on a study trip. It is now illuminated as if it were a monument. In front, visitors will see the strange pile of cubes that form Habitat '67 (see p 128) on the right, and the **Gare Maritime Iberville** *(information: ☎ 496-7678)*, the harbour station for liners cruising the St-Laurent, on the left.

The former warehouses at **Quai King-Edward**, to the east, now house various seasonal expositions, a flea market, a café, and most importantly, the **Cinéma Imax ★ (17)** *(Quai King-Edward)*, a marvel of Canadian technology. The cinema projects truer than life films, shot with a special camera, onto a giant screen (see p 203). At the far end of the pier, there is a lookout, commanding a stunning view of Vieux-

Montréal, framed by the downtown skyline.

Walk along the promenade to **Boulevard Saint-Laurent**, one of the city's main arteries, which serves as the dividing line between east and west not only as far as place names and addresses are concerned, but also from an ethnic point of view. Traditionally, there has always been a higher concentration of English-speakers in the western part of the city, and French-speakers in the eastern part, while ethnic minorities of all different origins are concentrated along Boulevard Saint-Laurent.

Head up Boulevard Saint-Laurent to Rue Saint-Paul. Turn right, then left on to a narrow street named Rue Saint-Gabriel.

It was on this street that Richard Dulong opened an inn in 1754. Today, the **Auberge Saint-Gabriel (18)** *(426 rue Saint-Gabriel)*, the oldest Canadian inn still in operation, is only a restaurant. It occupies a group of 18th-century buildings with sturdy rubble stone walls.

Turn right on Rue Notre-Dame.

Having passed through the financial and warehouse districts, visitors now enter an area dominated by civic and legal institutions, where not less than three courthouses lie clustered along Rue Notre-Dame. Inaugurated in 1971, the massive new **Palais de Justice (19)** *(1 rue Notre-Dame Est)*, or courthouse, dwarfs the surroundings. A sculpture by Charles Daudelin entitled *Allegrocube* lies on its steps. A mechanism makes it possible to open and close this stylized "hand of Justice."

From the time it was inaugurated in 1926 until it closed in 1970, the **Édifice Ernest-Cormier ★ (20)** *(100 rue Notre-Dame Est)* was used for criminal proceedings. The former courthouse was converted.into a conservatory, and was named after its architect, the illustrious Ernest Cormier, who also designed the main pavilion of the Université de Montréal and the doors of the United Nations Headquarters in New York City. The Courthouse is graced with outstanding bronze sconces, cast in Paris at the workshops of Edgar Brandt. Their installation in 1925 ushered in the Art Deco style in Canada. The main hall, faced with travertine and topped by three dome-shaped skylights, is worth a quick visit.

The **Vieux Palais de Justice ★ (21)** *(155 rue Notre-Dame Est)*, the oldest courthouse in Montréal, was built between 1849 and 1856, according to a design by John Ostell and Henri-Maurice Perrault, on the site of the first courthouse, which was erected in 1800. It is another fine example of Canadian neoclassical architecture. After the courts were divided in 1926, the Vieux Palais was used for civil cases, judged according to the Napoleonic Code. Since the opening of the new Palais to its left, the Vieux Palais has been converted into an annex of City Hall, located to the right.

Place Jacques-Cartier ★ (22) was laid out on the site once occupied by the Château de Vaudreuil, which burned down in 1803. The former Montréal residence of the governor of New France was without question the most elegant private home in the city. Designed by engineer Gaspard Chaussegros de Léry in 1723, it had a horseshoe-shaped staircase, leading up to a handsome cut stone portal, two projecting pavilions (one on each side of the main part of the building), and a formal garden, that extended as far as Rue Notre-Dame. After the fire, the property was purchased by local merchants, who decided to give the government a small strip of land, on the condition that a public market be established there, thus increasing the value of the adjacent property, which remained in private hands. It is for this reason that Place Jacques-Cartier is oblong in shape.

Merchants of British descent sought various means of ensuring their visibility and publicly expressing their patriotism in Montréal. They quickly formed a much larger community in Montréal than Québec City, where the government and headquarters of the forces of occupation where located. In 1809, therefore, they were the first in the world to erect a monument to Admiral Horatio Nelson, who defeated the combined French and Spanish fleets in the Battle of Trafalgar. Supposedly, they even got the French Canadian merchants drunk in order to extort a financial contribution from them for the project. The base of the **Colonne Nelson** (Nelson Column) was designed and executed in London, according to plans by architect Robert Mitchell. It is decorated with bas-reliefs depicting the exploits of the famous Admiral at Abukir, Copenhagen, and of course Trafalgar. The statue of Nelson at the top was originally made of *coade* artificial stone, but after being damaged time and time again by protestors, it was finally replaced by a fibre-glass replica in 1981. The column is the oldest extant monument in Montréal. At the other end of Place Jacques-Cartier, visitors will see the **Quai Jacques-Cartier** and the river, while **Rue Saint-Amable** lies tucked away on the right, at the halfway mark. During summer, artists and artisans gather on this little street, selling jewellery, drawings, etchings and caricatures.

Under the French Regime, Montréal, following the example of Québec City and Trois-Rivières, had its own governor, not to be confused with the governor of New France as a whole. The situation was the same under the English Regime. It wasn't until 1833 that the first elected mayor, Jacques Viger, took control of the city. This man, who was passionately interested in history, gave Montréal its motto (*Concordia Salus*) and coat of arms, composed of the four symbols of the "founding" peoples, namely the fleur-de-lys, the Irish clover, the Scottish thistle and the English rose, which could all be substituted by the French Canadian beaver.

After occupying a number of inadequate buildings for decades (a notable example was the Hayes aqueduct, an edifice containing an immense reservoir of water, which cracked one day while a meeting was being held in the council chamber immediately below; it's easy to imagine what happened next), the municipal administration finally moved into its present home in 1878. The **Hôtel de Ville ★ (23)** *(275 rue Notre-Dame Est)*, a fine example of the Second Empire, or Napoléon III style, is the work of Henri-Maurice Perrault, who also designed the neighbouring Palais de Justice. In 1922, a fire (yet another!) destroyed the interior and roof of the building, later restored in 1926, after the model of the city hall in Tours, France. Exhibitions are occasionally presented in the main hall, which is accessible via the main entrance. Visitors may also be interested to know that it was from the balcony of City Hall that France's General de Gaulle cried out his famous *"Vive le Québec libre!"* ("Freedom for Québec!") in 1967, to the great delight of the crowd gathered in front of the building.

Head to the rear of the Hôtel de Ville, by way of the pretty **Place Vauquelin**, the continuation of Place Jacques-Cartier.

The statue of Admiral Jean Vauquelin, defender of Louisbourg at the end of the French Regime, was probably put here to counterbalance the monument to Nelson, a symbol of British control over Canada. Go down the staircase leading to the **Champ-de-Mars**, modified in 1991 in order to reveal some vestiges of the fortifications that once surrounded Montréal. Gaspard Chaussegros de Léry designed Montréal's ramparts, erected between 1717 and 1745, as well as those of Québec City. The walls of Montréal, however, never saw war, as the city's commercial calling and its location ruled out such rash acts. The large, tree-lined lawns are reminders of the Champ-de-Mars' former vocation as a parade ground for military manoeuvres up until 1924. There is a view of the downtown area's skyscrapers through the clearing.

Head back to Rue Notre-Dame.

The humblest of all the "châteaux" built in Montréal, the **Château Ramezay ★★ (24)** (adults $5; Tue to Sun 10 a.m. to 4:30 p.m.; open Mon during summer); 280 rue Notre-Dame Est, ☎ 861-3708), is the only one still standing. It was built in 1705 for the governor of Montréal, Claude de Ramezay, and his family. In 1745, it fell into the hands of the Compagnie des Indes Occidentales (The French West India Company), which made it their North American headquarters. Precious Canadian furs were stored in its vaults awaiting shipment to France. After the conquest (1760), the British occupied the house, before being temporarily removed by American insurgents, who wanted Québec to join the nascent United States. Benjamin Franklin even came to stay at the château for a few months in 1775, in an attempt to convince Montrealers to become American citizens.

After serving as the first building of the Montréal branch of the Université Laval in Québec City, the château was converted into a museum in 1896, under the patronage of the Société d'Histoire et de Numismatique de Montréal (Montréal Numismatic and Antiquarian Society), founded by Jacques Viger. Visitors will still find a rich collection of furniture, clothing and everyday objects from the 18th and 19th centuries here, as well as a large number of Amerindian artefacts. The Salle de Nantes is decorated with beautiful Louis XV-style mahogany panelling, designed by Germain Boffrand, imported from the Nantes office of the Compagnie des Indes (circa 1750).

Walk along Rue Notre-Dame to Rue Berri.

At the corner of Rue Berri lies the **Lieu Historique National George-Étienne-Cartier ★ (25)** (free admission; May to Sep, open every day 10 a.m. to 6 p.m.; Oct. to Apr 10 a.m. to 12 p.m. and 1 p.m. to 5 p.m.; closed Jan.; 458 rue Notre-Dame Est, ☎ 283-2282), composed of twin houses inhabited successively by George-Étienne Cartier, one of the Fathers of Canadian Confederation. Inside, visitors will find a reconstructed mid 19th century French Canadian bourgeois home, complete with sound effects. Temporary exhibitions top off a tour of the premises. The neighbouring building, at number 452, is the former **Cathédrale Schismatique Grecque Saint-Nicolas**, built around 1910 in the Romanesque-Byzantine Revival style.

Rue Berri marks the eastern border of Vieux-Montréal, and thus the fortified city of the French Regime, beyond which extended the Faubourg Québec, excavated in the 19th century to make way for railroad lines, which explains the sharp difference in height between *Coteau Saint-Louis* and the Viger and Dalhousie stations. **Gare Viger (26)**, visible on the left, was inaugurated by the Canadian Pacific in 1895 in order to serve the eastern part of the country. Its resemblance to the Château Frontenac in Québec City is not merely coincidental; both buildings were designed for the same railroad company and by the same architect, an American named Bruce Price. The Château-style station, closed in 1935, also included a prestigious hotel and large stained glass train shed that has been destroyed.

Small **Gare Dalhousie (27)**, located near the Maison Cartier *(514 rue Notre-Dame)* was the first railway station built by Canadian Pacific, a company established for the purpose of building a Canadian transcontinental railroad. The station was the starting point of the first transcontinental train headed for Vancouver on June 28, 1886. Canadian Pacific seems to have had a weakness for foreign architects, since it was Thomas C. Sorby, Director of Public Works in England, who drew up the plans for this humble structure. Today, it is used by the *École Nationale du Cirque* (National Circus School). From the top of Rue Notre-Dame, the port's former refrigerated warehouse is visible, made of brown brick, as well as Île Sainte-Hélène, in the middle of the river. This island, along with Île Notre-Dame, was the site of the Expo '67.

Turn right on Rue Berri, and right again on Rue Saint-Paul, which offers a lovely view of the dome of the former Marché

Bonsecours. Continue straight ahead to Chapelle Notre-Dame-de-Bonsecours.

This site was originally occupied by another chapel, built in 1657 upon the recommendation of Saint Marguerite Bourgeoys, founder of the congregation of Notre-Dame. The present **Chapelle Notre-Dame-de-Bonsecours ★ (28)** *(400 rue Saint-Paul Est)* dates back to 1771, when the Sulpicians wanted to establish a branch of the main parish in the eastern part of the fortified city. In 1890, the chapel was modified to suit contemporary tastes, and the present stone façade was added, along with the "aerial" chapel looking out on the port. Parishioners asked God's blessing on ships and their crews bound for Europe from this chapel. The interior, redone at the same time, contains a large number of votive offerings from sailors saved from shipwrecks. Some are in the form of model ships, hung from the ceiling of the nave. At the back of the chapel, the little **Musée Marguerite-Bourgeoys** *(adults $2; May to Oct., Tue to Sun 9 a.m. to 4:30 p.m.; Nov to Apr 10:30 a.m. to 4:30 p.m.)* displays mementos of the Saint. From there, visitors can reach a platform adjoining the "aerial" chapel, which offers an interesting view of the old port.

The **Maison Pierre-du-Calvet**, at the corner of Rue Bonsecours (number 401), is representative of 18th century French urban architecture adapted to the local setting, with thick walls made of rubble stone embedded in mortar, storm windows doubling the casement windows with their little squares of glass imported from France, and high firebreak walls, then required by local regulations as a means of limiting the spread of fire from one building to the next.

A little higher on Rue Bonsecours, visitors will find the **Maison Papineau (29)** *(440 rue Bonsecours)* inhabited long ago by Louis-Joseph Papineau (1786-1871), lawyer, politician and head of the French-Canadian nationalist movement up until the insurrection of 1837. Built in 1785 and covered with a wooden facing made to look like cut stone, it was one of the first buildings in Vieux-Montréal to be restored (1962).

The **Marché Bonsecours ★★ (30)** *(350 rue Saint-Paul Est)* was erected between 1845 and 1850. The lovely grey stone neoclassical edifice with sash windows, was erected on **Rue Saint-Paul**, for many years Montréal's main commercial artery. The building is adorned with a portico supported by cast iron columns moulded in England, and topped by a silvery dome, which for many years served as the symbol of the city at the entrance to the port. In addition to a large market, set up both inside and outside, the building originally accommodated both the city council and a concert hall. It is presently undergoing major renovations.

Walk to Place Jacques-Cartier, then turn left, toward the Vieux-Port.

The **Grand Chapiteau du Cirque du Soleil ★ (31)** *(Quai Jacques-Cartier)*, the *Cirque du Soleil's* big top displays its blue and yellow stripes alongside the St-Laurent with well-deserved pride. This new-style Quebecois circus troupe is world-renowned for the quality of its productions and the great physical dexterity of its performers. The 50 m Grand Chapiteau will be set up here in spring 1994, when the circus puts on its shows. The rest of the time, the troupe travels with it on tour.

To return to the Métro, walk back up Place Jacques-Cartier, cross Rue Notre-Dame, Place Vauquelin and lastly Champ-de-Mars, to the station of the same name.

**Tour B:
Downtown ★★★**
(two days)

The downtown skyscrapers give Montréal a typically North-American look. Nevertheless, unlike most other cities on the continent, there is a certain Latin spirit here, which seeps in between the towering buildings, livening up this part of Montréal both day and night. Bars, cafés, department stores, shops and head offices, along with two universities and numerous colleges, all lie clustered within a limited area at the foot of Mont Royal.

At the beginning of the 20th century, Montréal's central business district gradually shifted from the old city to what was up until then a posh residential neighbourhood known as The Golden Square Mile, inhabited by upperclass Canadians. Wide arterial streets such as Boulevard René-Lévesque were then lined with palatial residences surrounded by shady gardens. The city centre underwent a radical transformation in a very short amount of time (1960-1967), marked by the construction of Place Ville-Marie, the Métro, the underground city, Place des Arts, and various other infrastructures which still exert an influence on the area's development.

Walk uphill on Rue Guy (at the exit of the Guy-Concordia Métro station), then turn right on Rue Sherbrooke.

The numbers following the names of attractions refer to the map of the downtown area.

In addition to being invaded by the business world, the Golden Square Mile also underwent profound social changes that altered its character—the exodus of the Scottish population, the shortage of servants, income taxes, World War I, during which the sons of many of these families were killed, and above all the stock market crash of 1929, which ruined many businessmen. Consequently, numerous mansions were demolished and the remaining population had to adjust to more modest living conditions. **The Linton ★ (1)** *(1509 rue Sherbrooke Ouest)*, a prestigious apartment building erected in 1907, provided an interesting alternative. It was built on the grounds of the house of the same name still visible in the back, on little Rue Simpson. The façade of the Linton is adorned with lavish Beaux-Arts details made of terra cotta and a beautiful cast iron marquee.

The lovely presbyterian **Church of St. Andrew and St. Paul ★★ (2)** *(at the corner of Rue Redpath)* was one of the most important institutions of the Scottish elite in Montréal. Built in 1932 according to plans by architect Harold Lea Fetherstonhaugh, as the community's third place of worship, it illustrates the endurance of medieval-style design in religious architecture. The stone interior is graced with magnificent commemorative stained glass windows. Those along the aisles came from the second church and are for the most part significant British pieces, such as the windows of Andrew Allan and his wife, produced by the workshop of William Morris after sketches by the famous English Pre-Raphaelite painter, Edward Burne-Jones. The Scottish-Canadian Black Watch Regiment has been affiliated with the church ever since it was created in 1862.

The **Musée des Beaux-Arts de Montréal ★★★ (3)** *(adults $4.50 for the permanent collection, a little more for special exhibitions; Tue to Sun 11 a.m. to 6 p.m., Wed and Sat until 9 p.m.; 1380 rue Sherbrooke Ouest, ☎ 285-1600)*, Montréal's Museum of Fine Arts, the oldest and most important museum in Québec, was founded in 1860 by the Art Association of Montreal, a group of Anglo-Saxon art lovers. The Pavillon Beniah-Gibb, on the north side of Rue Sherbrooke (1379 rue Sherbrooke Ouest), opened its doors in 1912. Its façade, made of white Vermont marble, is the work of the Scottish merchants' favourite architects, the prolific Edward and William Sutherland Maxwell. The building became too small for the museum's collection, and was enlarged towards the back on three different occasions. Finally, in 1991, architect Moshe Safdie designed the Pavillon Jean-Noël-Desmarais, just opposite on the south side of Rue Sherbrooke. This new wing includes the red brick façade of a former apartment building, and is linked to the original building by tunnels under Rue Sherbrooke. The museum's main entrance is now in the new wing, at the corner of Rue Crescent.

The museum houses a variety of collections, most of which belonged to the great families of the Golden Square Mile. The Pavillon Gibb contains Canadian art, while the Pavillon Desmarais houses the largest portion of the permanent collection (American, European, African and pre-Columbian pieces, among others), and also hosts international exhibitions. The rooms

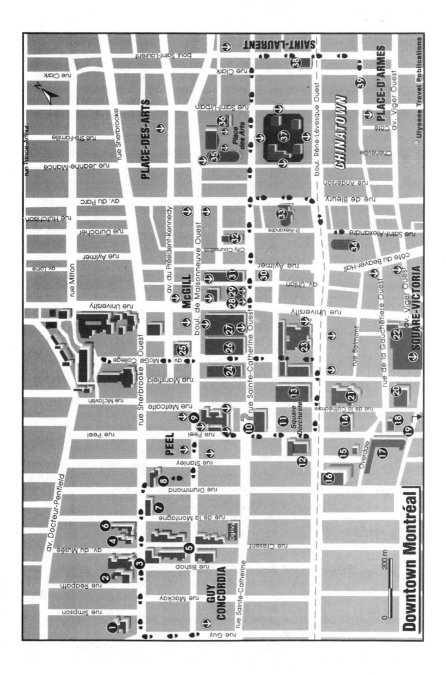

Downtown Montréal

devoted to miniatures, the Middle Ages and the Renaissance, as well as those containing Canadian paintings from the first half of the 20th century, are definitely among the most interesting in the museum. The surprising interior spaces of the new wing are also worth careful examination.

When the Unitarian church at the corner of Rue Simpson burned down, its congregation turned to **Erskine & American United Church** ★ **(4)** *(at the corner of avenue du Musée)*. Erected in 1892, this church is an excellent example of the Romanesque Revival style as interpreted by American architect Henry Hobson Richardson. The textured sandstone, large arches flanked by either squat or disproportionately elongated columns, and sequences of small, arched openings are typical of the style. The auditorium-shaped interior was remodeled in the style of the Chicago School in 1937. The lower chapel (along Avenue du Musée), contains lovely, brilliantly coloured Tiffany stained-glass windows.

Rue Crescent ★ **(5)**, located immediately east of the museum, has a split personality. To the north of Boulevard de Maisonneuve, the street is lined with old row houses, that now accommodate antique shops and luxury boutiques, while to the south, it is crowded with night clubs, restaurants and bars, most with sunny terraces lining the sidewalks. For many years, Rue Crescent was known as the English counterpart of Rue Saint-Denis. Though it is still a favourite among American visitors, its clientele is more diversified now.

A symbol of its era, **Le Château** ★ **(6)** *(1321 rue Sherbrooke Ouest)*, a handsome Château-style building, was erected in 1925 for a French Canadian

businessman by the name of Pamphile du Tremblay, owner of the French-language newspaper *La Presse*. Architects Ross and Macdonald designed what was at the time the largest apartment building in Canada. The Royal Institute awarded these same architects a prize for the design of the fashionable **Holt-Renfrew** store built across the street *(1300 rue Sherbrooke Ouest)* in 1937. With its rounded, horizontal lines, the store is a fine example of the streamlined version of the Art Deco style.

The last of Montréal's old hotels, the **Ritz-Carlton** ★ **(7)** *(1228 rue Sherbrooke Ouest)* was inaugurated in 1911 by César Ritz himself. For many years, it was the favourite gathering place of the Montréal bourgeoisie. Some people even stayed here year-round, living a life of luxury among the drawing rooms, garden and ballroom. The building was designed by Warren and Wetmore of New York City, the well-known architects of Grand Central Station on New York's Park Avenue. Many celebrities have stayed at this sophisticated luxury hotel over the years. Richard Burton and Elizabeth Taylor were even married here in 1964.

Continue along Rue Sherbrooke to the entrance of Maison Alcan. Three noteworthy buildings lie across the street. **Maison Baxter** *(1201 rue Sherbrooke Ouest)*, on the left, now serves as the head office of Corby Distilleries. **Maison Forget** *(1195 rue Sherbrooke Ouest)*, in the centre, was built in 1882 for Louis-Joseph Forget, one of the only French Canadian magnates to live in this neighbourhood during the 19th century. Today, it is occupied by the United Services Club, a private club for retired army officers. The building on the right is the Mount Royal Club, another private club, this one is for business people. Built in 1905, it is the work of Stanford White of the famous New York firm McKim, Mead and White, architects of the head office of the Banque de Montréal on Place d'Armes.

Maison Alcan ★ **(8)** *(1188 rue Sherbrooke Ouest)*, head office of the Alcan aluminum company, is a fine example of historical preservation and inventive urban restructuring. Five buildings along Rue Sherbrooke, including the lovely **Maison Atholstan** *(1172 rue Sherbrooke Ouest)*, the first Beaux-Arts style structure erected in Montréal (1894), have been carefully restored, and then joined in the back to an atrium, which is linked to a modern aluminum building. The garden running along the south wall of the modern part provides a little-known passageway between Rue Drummond and Rue Stanley.

Enter the atrium through the Sherbrooke entrance, which used to lead into the lobby of the Berkeley Hotel. Exit through the garden and head south on Rue Stanley. Turn left on Boulevard de Maisonneuve, then right on Rue Peel.

Montréal has the most extensive underground city in the world. Greatly appreciated in bad weather, it provides access to over 2,000 shops and restaurants, as well as movie theatres, apartment and office buildings, hotels, parking lots, train stations, the bus station, Place des Arts and even the Université du Québec à Montréal (UQAM) via tunnels, atriums and indoor plazas. **Les Cours Mont-Royal** ★★ **(9)** *(1455 rue Peel)* are duly linked to this sprawling network, which centres around the various Métro stations. A multi-purpose complex, it consists of four levels of stores, offices and apart-

ments laid out inside the former Hôtel Mont-Royal. With its 1,100 rooms, this Jazz Age palace, inaugurated in 1922, was the largest hotel in the British Empire. Aside from the exterior, all that was preserved during the 1987 remodelling was a portion of the ceiling of the lobby, from which the former chandelier of the Monte Carlo casino is suspended. The four 10-story *cours* (inner courts) are definitely worth a visit, as is a stroll through what may be the most well-designed shopping centre in the downtown area. The building that looks like a small Scottish manor across the street is in fact the head office of the Seagram Company (Barton & Guestier wines).

Head south on Rue Peel to Square Dorchester.

At the **Centre Infotouriste (10)**, visitors will find representatives from a number of tourist-related enterprises, such as tourist offices, Greyhound Bus Lines, the Le Réseau hotel-reservation service and Ulysses Travel Bookshop.

From 1799 to 1854, **Square Dorchester** ★ **(11)** was occupied by Montréal's Catholic cemetery, which was then moved to Mont Royal, where it is still located. In 1872, the city turned the free space into two squares, one on either side of Rue Dorchester (now Boulevard René-Lévesque). The northern portion is called Square Dorchester, while the southern part was renamed Place du Canada to commemorate the 100th anniversary of the Confederation (1967). A number of monuments adorn Square Dorchester. In the centre, there is an equestrian statue dedicated to Canadian soldiers who died during the Boer War in South Africa, while a handsome statue of Scottish poet Robert Burns, a sculpture styled after Bartholdi's Roaring Lion, donated by the Sun Life insurance company, and Émile Brunet's monument to Sir Wilfrid Laurier, prime minister of Canada from 1896 to 1911, stand around the perimeter. The square also serves as the starting point for guided bus tours.

The Windsor ★ (12) (1170 rue Peel), the hotel where royal family members used to stay during their visits to Canada, no longer in exists. The prestigious Second Empire style edifice, built in 1878 by architect W. W. Boyinton of Chicago, was claimed by fire in 1957. All that remains of it is an annex erected in 1906, that was converted into an office building in 1986. The ballrooms and lovely Peacock Alley have, however, been preserved. An impressive atrium, visible from the upper floors, has been constructed for the building's tenants. The handsome Tour CIBC, designed by Peter Dickinson (1962), stands on the site of the old hotel. Its walls are faced with green Lancashire slate, which blends harmoniously with the dominant colours of the buildings around the square, namely the greyish beige of stone and the green of oxidized copper.

The Édifice Sun Life ★★(13) (1155 rue Metcalfe), erected between 1913 and 1933 for the powerful Sun Life insurance company, was for many years the largest building in the British Empire. It was in this "fortress" of the Anglo-Saxon establishment, with its colonnades reminiscent of ancient mythology, that the British Crown Jewels were hidden during World War II. In 1977, the company's head office was moved to Toronto, in protest against provincial language laws favouring French. Fortunately, the chimes that ring at 5 p.m. every day are still in place and remain an integral part of the neighbourhood's spirit.

Place du Canada ★ (14), the southern portion of Square Dorchester, is the location of the annual Remembrance Day ceremony (November 11th) in honour of Canadian soldiers killed in the two World Wars. Veterans reunite around the War Memorial, which occupies the place of honour in the centre of the square. A more imposing monument to Sir John A. Macdonald, Canada's first prime minister, elected in 1867, stands alongside Boulevard René-Lévesque.

A number of churches clustered around Square Dorchester before it was even laid out in 1872. Unfortunately, only two of the eight churches built in the area between 1865 and 1875 have survived. One of these is the beautiful Gothic Revival style St. George's Anglican Church ★★(15) (at the corner of rue de la Gauchetière and rue Peel). Its delicately sculpted sandstone exterior conceals an interior covered with lovely, dark woodwork. Particularly noteworthy are the remarkable ceiling, with its exposed framework; the woodwork in the chancel, and the tapestry from Westminster Abbey, used during the coronation of Elizabeth II.

The elegant 47-story Tour IBM-Marathon ★ (16) (1250 boulevard René-Lévesque Ouest), forming part of the backdrop of St. George's, was completed in 1991 according to a design by the famous New York architects Kohn, Pedersen and Fox. Its winter bamboo garden is open to the public.

In 1887, the head of Canadian Pacific, William Cornelius Van Horne, asked his New York friend Bruce Price (1845-1903) to draw up the plans for Gare Windsor ★ (17) (at the corner of rue de la Gauchetière and rue Peel), a modern train station, which would serve as the terminus of the transcontinental railroad, completed the previous year. At the time, Price was one of the most prominent architects in the eastern United States, where he worked on residential projects for high society clients, as well as skyscrapers like the American Surety Building in Manhattan. Later, he was put in charge of building the Château Frontenac in Québec City, thus establishing the Château style in Canada.

Massive-looking Gare Windsor, with its corner buttresses, Roman arches outlined in the stone, and series of arcades, is Montréal's best example of the Romanesque Revival style as interpreted by American architect Henry Hobson Richardson. Its construction established the city as the country's railway centre and initiated the shift of commercial and financial activity from Vieux-Montréal to the Golden Square Mile. Abandoned in favour of the Gare Centrale after World War II, Gare Windsor was used only for commuter trains up until 1993. Construction of the new Forum, future home of the Montréal Canadiens hockey team, now makes it impossible for trains to reach the station because it interrupts the railine. A new role will have to be found for the station.

Built in 1966, the **Hôtel Château Champlain** ★ **(18)** *(1 Place du Canada)*, nicknamed the "cheese grater" by Montrealers, due to its many arched, convex openings, was designed by Quebecois architects Jean-Paul Pothier and Roger D'Astou. The latter is a disciple of American architect Frank Lloyd Wright, with whom he studied for several years. The hotel is not unlike some of the master's late works, characterized by rounded, fluid lines.

The **Planétarium Dow (19)** *(adults $5; Jun to Sep, open every day; Sep to Jun, Tue to Sun 8:30 a.m. to 12 p.m. and 1 p.m. to 4 p.m.; 45 min presentation from Mon to Fri at 1:30 p.m. and 8:30 p.m.; Sat and Sun. and holidays at 3:30 p.m.; 1000 rue Saint-Jacques Ouest,* ☎ *872-4530)* projects astronomy films onto a 20 m hemispheric dome. The universe and its mysteries are explained in a way that makes this marvelous, often poorly understood world accessible to all. Guest lecturers provide commentaries on the presentations. The show lasts more than an hour.

Tour 1000 (20) *(1000 rue de la Gauchetière)*, a 50-story skyscraper, was completed in 1992. It houses the terminus for buses linking Montréal to the south shore, as well as the Amphithéâtre Bell an indoor skating rink open year-round *(adults $6.50, skate rentals $4; Mon to Fri 11:30 a.m. to 2:30 p.m. and 4 p.m. to 5:30 p.m.; Sat and Sun 1:30 p.m. to 5:30 p.m.)*. The architects wanted to set the building apart from its neighbours by crowning it with a copper-covered point. Its total height is the maximum allowed by the city, namely the height of Mont Royal. The ultimate symbol of Montréal, the mountain may not surpassed under any circumstances.

In 1852, a terrible fire destroyed the Catholic cathedral on Rue Saint-Denis. The ambitious Monseigneur Ignace Bourget (1799-1885), who was bishop of Montréal at the time, seized the opportunity to work out a grandiose scheme to outshine the Sulpicians' Basilique Notre-Dame and ensure the supremacy of the Catholic Church in Montréal. What could accomplish these goals better than a replica of Rome's St. Peter's, right in the middle of the Protestant neighbourhood? Despite reservations on the part of architect Victor Bourgeau, the plan was carried out. The bishop even made Bourgeau go to Rome to measure the venerable building. Construction began in 1870 and was finally completed in 1894. Copper statues of the 13 patron saints of Montréal's parishes were installed in 1900. **Cathédrale Marie-Reine-du-Monde** ★★ **(21)** *(Boulevard René-Lévesque Ouest)* is the seat of the archdiocese of Montréal and a reminder of the tremendous power wielded by the clergy up until the Quiet Revolution. It is exactly one third the size of St. Peter's.

Modernized during the 1950's, the interior is no longer as harmonious as it once was. Nevertheless, there is a lovely replica of Bernini's baldaquin, executed by sculptor Victor Vincent. The bishops and archbishops of Montréal are interred in the mortuary chapel on the left, where the place of honour is occupied by the recumbent statue of Monseigneur Bourget. A monument outside reminds visitors yet again of this individual, who did so much to strengthen the bonds between France and Canada.

An immense, grooved concrete block with no façade, **Place Bonaventure** ★ **(22)** *(1 Place Bonaventure)*, which was completed in 1966, is one of the most revolutionary works of modern architecture of its time. Designed by Montrealer Raymond Affleck, it is a multi-purpose complex built on top of the railway lines leading into the Gare Centrale, containing a parking area, a two-level shopping centre linked to the Métro and the underground city, two large exhibition halls, wholesalers, offices, and an intimate 400-room rooftop hotel laid out around a charming hanging garden, worth a short visit.

Place Bonaventure is linked to the Métro station of the same name, designed by architect Victor Prus (1964). With its brown brick facing and bare concrete vaults, the station looks like an early Christian basilica. The Montréal Métro system has a total of 65 stations divided up among four lines used by trains running on rubber wheels. Each station has a different design, some very elaborate. For more information, consult the French-language Ulysses travel guide entitled *Montréal en Métro*.

A railway tunnel leading under Mont Royal to the downtown area was built in 1913. The tracks ran under Avenue McGill College, then multiplied at the bottom of a deep trench, which stretched between Rue Mansfield and Rue University. In 1938, the subterranean **Gare Centrale** was built, marking the true starting point of the underground city. Camouflaged since 1957 by the **Hôtel Reine-Elizabeth** (the Queen Elizabeth), it has an interesting, streamlined Art Deco waiting hall. **Place Ville-Marie** ★★★ **(23)** *(1 place Ville-Marie, Métro Bonaventure)*, was erected above the northern part of the formerly open-air trench in 1959. The famous Chinese-American architect Ieoh Ming Pei (Louvre Pyramid, Paris; East Building of the National Gallery, Washington, D.C.) designed the multi-purpose complex built over the railway tracks and containing vast shopping arcades now linked to most of the surrounding edifices. It also encompasses a number of office buildings, including the famous cruciform aluminum tower, whose unusual shape enables natural light to penetrate all the way into the centre of the structure, while at the same time symbolizing Montréal, the Catholic city dedicated to the Virgin Mary.

In the middle of the public area, made of granite a compass card indicates true north, while **Avenue McGill College**, which leads straight toward the mountain, indicates "north" as perceived by Montrealers in their everyday life. This artery, lined with multicoloured skyscrapers, was still a narrow residential street in 1950. It now offers a wide view of Mont Royal, crowned by a metallic cross, erected in 1927 to commemorate the gesture of Paul Chomedey de Maisonneuve, founder of Montréal, who climbed the mountain in January 1643 and placed a wooden cross at its summit to thank the Virgin Mary for having spared Fort Ville-Marie from a devastating flood.

Cross Place Ville-Marie, then take Avenue McGill College up to Rue Sherbrooke.

Avenue McGill College was widened and entirely redesigned during the 1980's. Walking along it, visitors will see several examples of eclectic, polychromatic postmodern architecture composed largely of granite and reflective glass. **Place Montréal Trust (24)** *(at the corner of rue Sainte-Catherine)* is one of a number of Montréal shopping centres topped by an office building and linked to the underground city as well as the Métro by corridors and private plazas. Children often visualize "transformers" from outer space in the building's pink and green façade.

The **Tour BNP ★ (25)** *(1981 avenue McGill College)*, certainly the best designed building on Avenue McGill College, was built for the Banque Nationale de Paris in 1981, by the architectural firm Webb, Zerafa, Menkès, Housden Partnership (Tour Elf-Aquitaine, Paris; Royal Bank, Toronto). Its bluish glass walls set off a sculpture entitled *La Foule Illuminée* (The Il-

luminated Crowd), by the Franco-British artist Raymond Mason.

Head back to Rue Sainte-Catherine Ouest.

Rue Sainte-Catherine is Montréal's main commercial artery. It stretches 15 km, changing in appearance several times along the way. Around 1870, it was still lined with row houses; by 1920, however, it had already become an integral part of life in Montréal. Since the 1960's, a number of shopping centres linking the street to the adjacent Métro lines have sprouted up among the local businesses. The **Centre Eaton (26)** *(rue Sainte-Catherine Ouest)* is the most recent of these. It is composed of a long, old-fashioned gallery lined with five levels of shops, restaurants and movie theatres, and is now linked to Place Ville-Marie by a pedestrian tunnel.

The **Eaton** department store ★★ **(27)** *(677 rue Sainte-Catherine Ouest)* is one of the main "institutions" on Rue Sainte-Catherine. The Art Deco dining room on the 9th floor is well worth a visit. It is the work of Jacques Carlu, who designed the Palais de Chaillot in Paris, as well as the decor of a number of ocean liners. The restaurant, for that matter, is reminiscent of a first-class dining room on the French Line ships. Miraculously, the place has been kept fully intact since its opening in 1931, from the furniture, lights, utensils and wall lamps by Denis Gélin to the frescoes by Anne Carlu, entitled *Amazones* (Amazons) and *Dans un Parc* (In a Park).

The first Anglican cathedral in Montréal stood on Rue Notre-Dame, not far from Place d'Armes. After a fire in 1856, **Christ Church Cathedral ★★ (28)** *(at the corner of rue University)* was relocated nearer the community it served, in the heart of the nascent Golden Square Mile. Using the cathedral of his home town, Salisbury, as his model, architect Frank Wills designed a flamboyant structure, with a single steeple rising above the transepts. The soberness of the interior contrasts with the rich ornamentation of the Catholic churches included in this walking tour. A few beautiful stained glass windows from the workshops of William Morris provide the only bit of colour.

The steeple's stone spire was destroyed in 1927 and replaced by an aluminum replica; otherwise, it would have eventually caused the building to sink. The problem, linked to the instability of the foundation, was not resolved, however, until a shopping centre, the **Promenades de la Cathédrale ★★ (29)**, was constructed under the building in 1987. Christ Church Anglican Cathedral thus rests on the roof of a shopping mall. On the same occasion, a postmodern glass skyscraper topped by a "crown of thorns" was erected behind the cathedral. There is a pleasant little garden at the foot of it.

It was around **Square Phillips ★ (30)** *(at the corner of rue Union, on either side of rue Sainte-Catherine)* that the first stores appeared along Rue Sainte-Catherine, which was once strictly residential. Henry Morgan moved Morgan's Colonial House, now **La Baie** (The Bay) **(32)**, here after the floods of 1886 in the old city. Henry Birks, descendant from a long line of English jewellers, arrived soon after, establishing his famous shop in a handsome beige sandstone building on the west side of the square. In 1914, a monument to King Edward VII, sculpted by Philippe Hébert, was erected in the centre of Square Phillips. Department store

customers and people attending the August film festival at the nearby Cinéma Parisien enjoy relaxing here.

A former Methodist church designed in the shape of an auditorium, **St. James United Church (32)** *(463 rue Sainte-Catherine Ouest)* originally had a complete façade looking out onto a garden. In 1926, in an effort to counter the decrease in its revenue, the community built a group of stores and offices along the front of the building on Rue Sainte-Catherine, leaving only a narrow passageway to the church. Visitors can still see the two Gothic Revival style steeples set back from Rue Sainte-Catherine. Across the street is the **Cinéma Parisien**, which hosts part of Montréal's *Festival des Films du Monde* (World Film Festival), the only competitive film festival held in North America.

Turn right on Rue de Bleury.

After a 40-year absence, the Jesuits returned to Montréal in 1842 at Monseigneur Ignace Bourget's invitation. Six years later, they founded Collège Sainte-Marie, where several generations of boys would receive an outstanding education. **Église du Gesù ★★ (33)** *(1202 rue de Bleury)* was originally designed as the college chapel. The grandiose project begun in 1864 according to plans drawn up by architect Patrick C. Keely of Brooklyn, New York was never completed, due to a lack of funds. Consequently, the church's Renaissance Revival style towers remain unfinished. The *trompe-l'œil* decor inside was executed by artist Damien Müller. Of particular interest are the seven main altars and surrounding parquetry, all fine examples of cabinet work. The large paintings hanging from the walls were commissioned from the Gagliardi brothers of Rome. The Jesuit college, erected to the south of the church, was demolished in 1975, but the church was fortunately saved, and then restored in 1983.

Visitors can take a short side-trip to St. Patrick's Basilica. To do so, head south on Rue de Bleury. Turn right on Boulevard René-Lévesque, then left on little Rue Saint-Alexandre. Go into the church through one of the side entrances.

Fleeing misery and potato blight, a large number of Irish immigrants came to Montréal between 1820 and 1860, and helped construct the Canal de Lachine and Pont Victoria. **St. Patrick's Basilica ★★ (34)** *(rue Saint-Alexandre)*, was thus built to meet a pressing new demand for a church to serve the Irish Catholic community. When it was inaugurated in 1847, St. Patrick's dominated the city below. Today, it is well hidden by the skyscrapers of the business centre. Architect Pierre-Louis Morin and Père Félix Martin, the Jesuit superior, designed the plans for the edifice, built in the Gothic Revival style favoured by the Sulpicians, who financed the project. One of the many paradoxes surrounding St. Patrick's is that it is more representative of French than Anglo-Saxon Gothic architecture. The high, dark interior encourages prayer. Each of the pine columns that divide the nave into three sections is a tree trunk, carved in one piece.

Head back to Rue Sainte-Catherine Ouest.

Formerly located at Cité du Havre, the **Musée d'Art Contemporain ★★ (36)** *(adults $4.75; Tue to Sun 11 a.m. to 6 p.m., free on Wed 6 p.m. to 9 p.m.; 185 rue Sainte Catherine Ouest, at the corner of rue Jeanne-Mance, ☎ 847-6212)*, Montréal's modern art museum, was moved to this site in 1992. The long, low building, erected on top of the Place des Arts parking lot, contains eight rooms, where post-1940 works of art from both Québec and abroad are exhibited. The interior, which has a decidedly better design than the exterior, is laid out around a circular hall. On the lower level, an amusing metal sculpture by Pierre Granche entitled *Comme si le temps... de la rue*, shows Montréal's network of streets crowded with helmeted birds, in a sort of semicircular theatre.

Inspired by cultural complexes like New York's Lincoln Center during the rush of the Quiet Revolution, the government of Québec built **Place des Arts ★ (36)** *(rue Sainte-Catherine Ouest)*, a collection of five halls for the performing arts. Salle Wilfrid Pelletier, in the centre, was inaugurated in 1963 (2,982 seats). It accommodates both the Montreal Symphony Orchestra and the Opéra de Montréal. The cube-shaped Théâtre Maisonneuve, on the right, contains three theatres, Théâtre Maisonneuve (1,460 seats), Théâtre Jean-Duceppe (755 seats) and the intimate little Café de la Place (138 seats). The Cinquième Salle (350 seats) was built in 1992 in the course of the construction of the Musée d'Art Contemporain. Place des Arts is linked to the governmental section of the underground city, which stretches from the Palais des Congrès Convention Centre to Avenue du Président-Kennedy. Developed by the various levels of government, this portion of the underground network distinguishes itself from the private section, centred round Place Ville-Marie, further west.

Since 1976, the head office of the *Fédération des Caisses Populaires Desjardins* has been located in the vast **Complexe Desjardins ★ (37)** *(rue*

Sainte-Catherine Ouest), which houses a large number of government offices as well. The building's large atrium, surrounded by shops and movie theatres, is very popular during the winter months. A variety of shows are presented in this space, also used for recording television programmes.

The tour leaves the former Golden Square Mile and enters the area around **Boulevard Saint-Laurent**. At the end of the 18th century, the Faubourg Saint-Laurent grew up along the street of the same name, which led inland from the river. In 1792, the city was officially divided into east and west sections, with this artery marking the boundary. Then, in the early 20th century, the addresses of east-west streets were assigned so that they all began at Boulevard Saint-Laurent. Meanwhile, around 1880, the French Canadian high society came up with the idea of turning the boulevard into the "Champs-Élysées" of Montréal. The west side was destroyed in order to make the street wider and to reconstruct new buildings in Richardson's Romanesque Revival style, which was in fashion at the end of the 19th century. Populated by the successive waves of immigrants arriving at the port, Boulevard Saint-Laurent never attained the heights of glory anticipated by its developers. The section between Boulevard René-Lévesque and Boulevard de Maisonneuve did, however, become the hub of Montréal nightlife in the early 20th century. The city's big theatres, like the *Français*, where Sarah Bernhardt performed, were located around here. During the Prohibition era (1919-1930), the area became run-down. Every week, thousands of Americans came here to frequent the cabarets and brothels, which abounded in this neighbourhood up until the end of the 1950's.

Turn right on Boulevard Saint-Laurent.

Erected in 1893 for the Société Saint-Jean-Baptiste, which is devoted to protecting the rights of French-speakers, the **Monument National ★ (38)** *(1182 boulevard Saint-Laurent)* was intended to be a cultural centre dedicated to the French Canadian cause. It offered business courses, became the favourite platform of political orators, and presented shows of a religious nature. However, during the 1940's, it also hosted cabaret shows and plays, launching the careers of a number of Quebecois performers, including Olivier Guimond senior and junior. The building was sold to the National Theatre School of Canada in 1971. As Canada's oldest theatre, it was artfully restored on its 100th anniversary.

Cross Boulevard René-Lévesque, then turn right on Rue de la Gauchetière.

Montréal's **Chinatown ★ (39)** may be rather small, but it is nonetheless a pleasant place to walk around. A large number of the Chinese who came to Canada to help build the transcontinental railroad, completed in 1886, settled here at the end of the 19th century. Though they no longer live in the neighbourhood, they still come here on weekends to stroll about and stock up on exotic products. Rue de la Gauchetière has been converted into a pedestrian area lined with restaurants and framed by lovely Chinese-style gates.

To return to the starting point of the tour, walk back up Boulevard Saint-Laurent to the Place-des-Arts Métro station (at the corner of Boulevard de Maisonneuve). Take the subway west to the Guy-Concordia station.

Tour C:
The Golden Square Mile ★
(four hours)

The Golden Square Mile was the residential neighbourhood of the Canadian upper class between 1850 and 1930. Since the early 20th century, the shady streets lined with sumptuous Victorian houses have gradually given way to the city's modern business centre. At its apogee, around 1900, the Golden Square Mile was bordered by Avenue Atwater to the west, Rue de Bleury to the east, Rue de la Gauchetière to the south and the mountain, Mont Royal to the north. In those years, an estimated 70% of the country's wealth lay in the hands of local residents, who were mainly of Scottish descent. Only a few houses from this era remain, most of which are clustered north of Rue Sherbrooke, the Golden Square Mile's luxurious main street.

From the McGill Métro station, head north on Avenue McGill College toward the campus of McGill University. The tour starts on Rue Sherbrooke.

The numbers following the names of attractions refer to the map of the Golden Square Mile.

The **Maison William Alexander Molson (1)** *(888 rue Sherbrooke Ouest, McGill Métro)* provides a good idea of Rue Sherbrooke's modest scale and residential character back in the early 20th century. It was built in 1906 according to a design by Robert Findlay, favourite architect of the famous Molsons, a name associated with the brewing of beer for two centuries. William Alexander Molson chose a different path, however, for he

became an eminent doctor. After his death in 1920, this Neo-Elizabethan style house served first as the head office of the Anglin-Norcross construction company and was then used by McGill University's Institute of Space Research. The Banque Commerciale Italienne du Canada took over the building in 1993.

The **Musée McCord d'Histoire Canadienne ★★(2)** *(adults $5, children under 12 free; Sat and Sun 10 a.m. to 5 p.m., closed Mon, Tue, Wed and Fri 10 a.m. to 6 p.m., Thu 10 a.m. to 9 p.m., free admission Thu 6 p.m. to 9 p.m.; 690 rue Sherbrooke Ouest, McGill Métro)* occupies a building formerly used by the McGill University Students' Association. Designed by architect Percy Nobbs (1906), this handsome building of English baroque inspiration was enlarged toward the back in 1991. Along Rue Victoria, visitors can see an interesting sculpture by Pierre Granche entitled *Totem Urbain/Histoire en Dentelle* (Urban Totem/History in Lace). For anyone interested in Amerindians and daily life in Canada in the 18th and 19th centuries, this is *the* museum to see in Montréal. It houses a large ethnographic collection, as well as collections of costumes, decorative arts, paintings, prints and photographs, including the famous Notman collection, composed of 700,000 glass negatives and constituting, a veritable portrait of Canada at the end of the 19th century.

McGill University ★★ (3) *(805 rue Sherbrooke Ouest, McGill Métro)* was founded in 1821, thanks to a donation by fur trader James McGill. It is the oldest of Montréal's four universities. Throughout the 19th century, the institution was one of the finest jewels of the Golden Square Mile's Scottish bourgeoisie. The university's main campus lies nestled in greenery at the foot of Mont Royal. The entrance is located at the northernmost end of Avenue McGill College, at the Roddick Gates, which contain the university's clock and chimes. On the right are two Romanesque Revival style buildings, designed by Sir Andrew Taylor to house the physics (1893) and chemistry (1896) departments. The Faculty of Architecture now occupies the second building. A little farther along, visitors will see the Macdonald Engineering Building, a fine example of the English Baroque Revival style, with a broken pediment adorning its rusticated portal (Percy Nobbs, 1908). At the end of the drive stands the oldest building on campus, the Arts Building (1839). For three decades, this austere neoclassical structure by architect John Ostell was McGill University's only building. It houses Moyse Hall, a lovely theatre dating back to 1926, with a design inspired by antiquity (Harold Lea Fetherstonaugh, architect).

The unusual **Redpath Museum** *(815 rue Sherbrooke Ouest, McGill Métro)* stands out in profile to the left. It is a protorationalist openwork building concealed behind a composite façade, the work of architects Hutchison and Steele. Precious objects relating to archeology, botany, geology and palaeontology, accumulated by the university's researchers and professors, have been assembled here. This was the first building in Québec designed specifically as a museum, and also serves as a rare example of a building with iron and stone framework, but intended for neither industrial nor commercial purposes. South of the museum, visitors will see the library and Redpath Hall, equipped with a French style mechanical organ.

Concerts of baroque music are often held in this lovely hall dominated by its visible wooden frame. On the way past, take note of the gargoyles and lavishly sculpted columns of the library, among the most sophisticated examples of the Romanesque Revival style in Canada.

Take the lane leading to Rue McTavish. On the north side stands Morrice Hall *(3485 rue McTavish)*, a Gothic Revival style building erected in 1881, that once housed the Presbyterian Theological College of Montréal.

The **Maison Baumgarten (4)** *(3450 rue McTavish, McGill Métro)*, located a little lower on Rue McTavish, serves as the McGill Faculty Club. It houses a restaurant, reading rooms and a pool room containing pool tables from former residences of the Golden Square Mile now owned by McGill University. The house was built in stages between 1887 and 1902 for Alfred Friedrich Moritz Baumgarten, son of the personal physician of King Frédéric-Auguste of Saxony, chemist, inspector of German sugar refineries and founder of the Saint-Laurent sugar refinery in Montréal. His house stands out from the other bourgeois residences in the Golden Square Mile because of its exterior sobriety and the distribution of reception rooms over three levels. On the first floor of the stairwell, the privileged individuals offered access into the club will see a bird's-eye view of the Battle of Arras (17th century), brought back from France by Sir Arthur Currie, rector of the University.

Walk uphill on Rue McTavish. Visitors can enjoy a view of "Ravenscrag" on the hillside before turning left on Avenue Docteur-Penfield, then right onto Rue Peel.

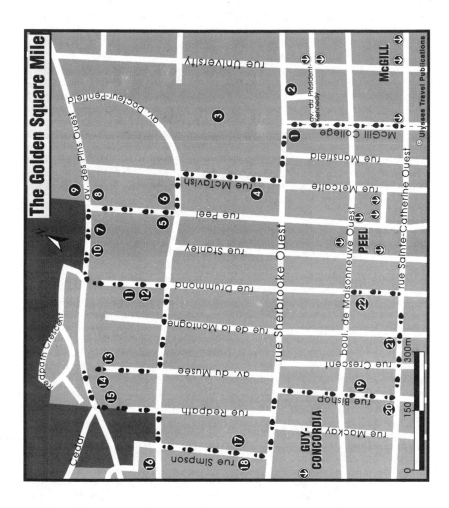

The **Maison James Ross ★ (5)** *(3644 rue Peel, Peel Métro)* was constructed in 1890 according to a design by American architect Bruce Price (Gare Windsor, Château Frontenac in Québec City) for the head engineer of Canadian Pacific. Enlarged on several occasions, it was once the scene of glittering receptions. With its resemblance to a medieval castle, it contributes to the charm of the Golden Square Mile. Particularly noteworthy is the combination of colours of its exterior, made up of a mixture of buff-coloured sandstone, pink granite and red slate. James Ross owned an exceptional collection of paintings, including works by Rembrandt, Rubens, Reynolds,

Courbet, Corot, Millet, Rossetti and Edward Burne-Jones. In 1948, the house became the McGill University Faculty of Law. It lost a considerable portion of its large garden when Avenue Docteur-Penfield was laid out in 1957.

The **Maison John Kenneth L. Ross (6)** *(3647 rue Peel, Peel Métro)* was originally the residence of James Ross's son, who lived in grand style for several years, accumulating yachts and race horses and travelling extensively. Once his father's fortune was exhausted, he had to sell the precious family collection of paintings at Christie's in London, a useless sacrifice in the end, since the economic crisis of 1929 ruined him anyway. His house (1909), a fine example of the Beaux-Arts style, is the work of brothers Edward and William Sutherland Maxwell, the favourite architects of Montréal's Scottish bourgeoisie. It is now an annex of the McGill University Faculty of Law.

Go up Rue Peel to Avenue des Pins. In another era, children used to toboggan down Rue Peel, which, like all of the city's streets during the long winter months, was covered with a thick layer of snow and was therefore perfect for tobogganing.

The **Maison Henry V. Meredith ★ (7)** *(1110 avenue des Pins Ouest)* is perhaps Montréal's best example of the trend toward eclecticism, polychromy and the picturesque that swept through North America in the last two decades of the 19th century. In fact, visitors will discover on its façades a mixture of styles ranging from the Romanesque to the late 18th century, as well as strong hues, and a marvellous jumble of towers, inlays, bay windows and chimneys. The house was built in 1894

for Henry Vincent Meredith, who was president of the Bank of Montréal at the time.

The **Maison Mortimer B. Davis ★ (8)** *(1020 avenue des Pins Ouest)* was once the residence of the founder of the Imperial Tobacco Company, Mortimer Barnett Davis. It was later occupied by Sir Arthus Purvis, and then sold to McGill University. Purvis was responsible for the secret shipment of North American-made arms to Europe during World War II, enabling Great Britain to avoid a Nazi invasion. The Davis house was designed in the Beaux-Arts style, recognizable by the balustrade along the top, the wrought iron balconies supported by brackets and the grandiose, symmetrical design.

Ravenscrag ★★ (9) *(1025 avenue des Pins Ouest)*. Montréal is not a political capital. It is above all a commercial city endowed with an important port. Its castle is not that of a king, but rather that of a financial and commercial magnate. "Ravenscrag" could indeed be labelled the castle of Montréal, due to its prominent location overlooking the city, its exceptional size (originally over 60 rooms) and its history, which is rich in memorable receptions and prestigious hosts. This immense residence was built in 1861-1864 for the extremely wealthy Sir Hugh Allan, who at the time had a near monopoly on sea transport between Europe and Canada. From the central tower of his house, this "monarch" could keep a close eye on the comings and goings of his ships in and out of the port.

Sir Hugh Allan's house is one of the best North American examples of the Renaissance Revival style, inspired by Tuscan villas and characterized, notably, by an irregular plan and an observation tower. The interior, almost entirely destroyed when the building was converted into a psychiatric institute (1943), used to include a Second Empire style ballroom able to accommodate 200 polka dancers. Interesting aspects around the building include the cast iron entry gate, the gate house and the luxurious stables now used as offices.

Head west on Avenue de Pins.

The **Maison Hamilton ★ (10)** *(1132 avenue des Pins Ouest)* has a unique and personal design by the Maxwell brothers, who had developed their own style, characterized by a gradual widening of their structures toward the base and whimsical little openings distributed in a carefully studied disorder. The Hamilton house (1903) has Arts & Crafts elements, as well as features foreshadowing the Art Deco style, such as the zigzag pattern of the brick on the first floor.

Go down the stairway leading to Rue Drummond.

The **Maison James Thomas Davis ★ (11)** *(3654 rue Drummond)* originally belonged to a building contractor, who equipped his house with a reinforced concrete structure. The design for this Elizabethan "manor" was also drawn up by the Maxwells (1908). Those who enter the house will find the lovely original tapestries still in place, in addition to remounted paintings by Canadian artist Maurice Cullen. Like so many old residences in the neighbourhood, the Davis house now belongs to McGill University.

The **Maison Hosmer ★ (12)** *(3630 rue Drummond)* is without question the most exuberant Beaux-Arts style home in Montréal. Thick mouldings, twin columns and cartouches, all carved in red sandstone imported from Scotland were sure to impress both visitors and business rivals. Edward Maxwell drew up the plans while his brother William was studying at the École des Beaux-Arts in Paris. The sketches sent from across the Atlantic clearly had a great influence on the design of this house, erected in 1900 for Charles Hosmer, who had ties with Canadian Pacific and 26 other Canadian companies. Each room was designed in a different style, in order to serve as a showcase for the Hosmer family's diverse collection of antiques. The family lived here until 1968, at which time the house became part of McGill University's Faculty of Medicine.

Turn right on Avenue Docteur-Penfield, then right again on Avenue du Musée.

The **Maison Rodolphe-Forget ★ (13)** *(3685 avenue du Musée)*. Few residences in the Golden Square Mile were built for members of the French Canadian elite. These individuals, generally less affluent than their Anglo-Saxon colleagues, preferred the area around Square Saint-Louis. Rodolphe Forget (1861-1919) was thus regarded as an exception. This distinguished Francophile founded the Banque Internationale du Canada, was a member of the council of the Société Générale and took part in the founding of the Franco-Canadian Crédit Foncier. His house, inspired by Parisian *hôtels particuliers* of the Louis XV era, was designed in 1912 by Jean Omer Marchand, the first French Canadian graduate of the Paris École des Beaux-Arts. The famous Québec suffragette Thérèse Casgrain, daughter of Rodolphe Forget, spent her early childhood here. The building is now part of the Russian consulate.

Climb the Avenue du Musée stairs. There is a lovely view of the downtown area and the river at the top.

The **Maison Clarence-de-Sola** ★ **(14)** *(1374 avenue des Pins Ouest)* is an extremely exotic Hispano-Moorish style residence, which stands out clearly against the urban landscape of Montréal. The contrast is even more amusing the day after a snow storm. The house was erected in 1913 for Clarence de Sola, son of a rabbi of Portuguese Jewish descent.

Head west on Avenue des Pins.

The **Maison Cormier** ★★ **(15)** *(1418 avenue des Pins Ouest)* was designed in 1930 for his personal use by Ernest Cormier, architect of the Université de Montréal and the Supreme Court in Ottawa. He experimented with the house, giving each side a different look—Art Deco for the façade, monumental for the east side and distinctly modern for the back. The interior was planned in minute detail. Cormier created most of the furniture, while the remaining pieces were acquired at the 1925 Exposition des Arts Décoratifs in Paris. Though the façade on Avenue des Pins appears quite small, the house actually has four above-ground floors on the other side, due to the pronounced slope of the terrain south of the avenue. The entire building, now listed as a historical monument, has been carefully restored by its present owner.

Go down the stairs on the left, which lead to Avenue Redpath.

The **Maison Raymond (16)** *(1507 avenue Docteur-Penfield, Guy-Concordia Métro)* was one of the last single-family residences to be erected in the Golden Square Mile (1930), and is still lived in today. It belongs to the family of businessman Aldéric Raymond, who owned the Forum in the 1950's, as well as several big hotels in Montréal. It is another excellent example of the French Beaux-Arts style.

Go down Rue Simpson toward Rue Sherbrooke Ouest.

Chelsea Place ★ **(17)** *(on the east side of rue Simpson, Guy-Concordia Métro)* is a subtle grouping of Neo-Georgian style residences built on a more modest scale than the homes seen thus far. It was erected in 1926 according to plans by architect Ernest Isbell Barott, in the years when Montréal's bourgeoisie of Scottish descent was starting to decline. Decimated by the Great War, burdened by taxes (which were practically nonexistent before 1914) and suffering from a shortage of servants that forced many businessmen had to sell their "palaces" and move into more practical dwellings. Of particular interest is the lovely central garden, giving Chelsea Place a unique style, both communal and refined. Summerhill Terrace, located on the west side of Rue Simpson, is a similar grouping built by the same architect.

The **Maison Linton** ★ **(18)** *(3424 rue Simpson, Guy-Concordia Métro)* is one of the most well-executed examples of the Second Empire style in Montréal. Do not be fooled by the exterior; the façade on Rue Simpson is in fact the east side of the house, whose main façade originally looked out onto a vast lawn stretching all the way to Rue Sherbrooke. The portico and staircase were dismantled, then reconstructed facing Rue Simpson when the apartment building *Le Linton* was erected in 1907 (see p 70). The little cartouches, the openings with segmented arches and above all the mansard roof are all characteristic of the Second Empire, or Napoleon III, style. The house was erected in 1867 according to a design by Cyrus P. Thomas. An underground garage was built all around it in 1990, but its interior remains just as it was at the end of the 19th century, from the fireplaces to the embossed wall paper and lavish mouldings on the ceilings.

Turn left on Rue Sherbrooke, then right on Rue Bishop, which runs alongside the main campus of Concordia University, Montréal's second English-language university and the most recently founded of the city's four universities (1974). The Maison Lyall lies south of Boulevard de Maisonneuve.

The **Maison Lyall** (19) *(1445 rue Bishop, Guy-Concordia Métro)*. Throughout the 19th century, a large number of Scots emigrated to the British colonies. The market in their own land was controlled by the London upper class who prevented the Scots from expanding their modest businesses. In those years, Montréal was the primary destination of these merchants, industrialists and inventors from Glasgow and Inverness. They were anxious to open stores or factories in this new country, which, with its rapidly growing population, needed everything. Peter Lyall was one of these immigrants. Immediately after his arrival from Castletown in 1870, he founded a construction company, which prospered and was even commissioned to reconstruct the Canadian Parliament after the fire in 1916. His eclectic, polychrome, delightfully picturesque residence looks like a big gingerbread house. It has been converted into business and office space. The entrance hall, graced with a

lovely fireplace inlaid with various types of marble, is open to the public.

The **Church of St. James The Apostle** (20) *(1439 rue Sainte-Catherine Ouest, Guy-Concordia Métro)* was built in 1864. At the time, it was located in the middle of a field, not far from where local cricket games were played, thus earning it the nickname St. Cricket in the Fields. Before long, Rue Sainte-Catherine was lined with row houses. These have since made way for commercial buildings.

Turn left on Rue Sainte-Catherine, at 15 km long, it is Montréal's most important commercial artery.

Ogilvy's department store (21) *(1307 rue Sainte-Catherine Ouest, Peel Métro)* the most Scottish of Montréal's department stores, was purchased several years ago by a group of French-Canadian businessmen. The new owners have striven to preserve the original character of this Montréal institution, whose atmosphere is enlivened each day at noon by a bagpipe player. The store sells Scottish wool sweaters, and other typically Anglo-Saxon products, as well as *haute couture* fashions. The Tudor room on the top floor is often used for concerts and receptions. Across the street is a group of neoclassical houses dating back to 1864 (groupings such as these are known as Terraces), among the last houses on the street that have survived to the present day.

Turn left on Rue Drummond.

The **Maison Stephen** ★★ (22) *(1440 rue Drummond, Peel Métro)*. Lord Mount Stephen, born in Stephen Croft, Scotland, was a determined man. Co-founder and first president of Canadian Pacific, he realized the construction of a transcontinental railroad stretching over 5,000 km from New Brunswick to British Columbia. His house is a veritable monument to Montréal's Scottish bourgeoisie. It was built in 1883 according to plans by William Tutin Thomas at a cost of $600,000, an astronomical sum at the time. Stephen called upon the best artisans in the entire world, who covered the interior walls with marble, onyx and woodwork made of such rare materials as English walnut, Cuban mahogany and satinwood from Ceylon. The ceilings are so high that the house seems to have been built for giants. Since 1925, it has been owned by the Mount Stephen Club, a private club for business people. Tours of the house are occasionally organized during summer.

To return to the starting point of the tour, head east on Boulevard de Maisonneuve or Rue Sainte-Catherine, the more pleasant of the two. The entrance to the McGill Métro station is located near the corner of Avenue McGill College.

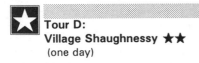

**Tour D:
Village Shaughnessy ★★**
(one day)

When the Sulpicians took possession of the island of Montréal in 1663, they kept a portion of the best land for themselves, then set up a farm and an Amerindian village there in 1676. Following a fire, the Amerindian village was relocated several times before being permanently established in Oka. A part of the farm, corresponding to the area now known as Westmount, was then granted to French settlers. The Sulpicians planted an orchard and a vineyard on the remaining portion.

Starting around 1870, the land was separated into lots. Part of it was used for the construction of mansions, while large plots were awarded to Catholic communities allied with the Sulpicians. It was at this time that Maison Shaughnessy was built—hence the name of the neighbourhood. During the 1970's, the number of local inhabitants increased considerably, making Village Shaughnessy the most densely populated area in Québec.

From Rue Guy (Guy-Concordia Métro station), turn left on Rue Sherbrooke.

The numbers following names of attractions refer to the map of Village Shaughnessy.

Masonic lodges, which had already existed in New France, increased in scale with British immigration. These associations of free-thinkers were not favoured by the Canadian clergy, who denounced their liberal views. Ironically, the **Masonic Temple ★ (1)** *(1850 rue Sherbrooke Ouest)* of the Scottish lodges of Montréal stands opposite the Grand Séminaire, where Catholic priests are trained. The edifice, built in 1928, enhances the secret, mystical character of Freemasonry with its impenetrable, windowless façade, equipped with antique vessels and double-headed lamps.

The Sulpicians' farmhouse was surrounded by a wall linked to four stone corner towers, earning it the name Fort des Messieurs. The house was destroyed when the **Grand Séminaire ★★ (2)** (1854-1860) *(2065 rue Sherbrooke Ouest)* was built, but two towers, erected in the 17th century according to plans by François Vachon de Belmont, superior of the Montréal Sulpicians, can still be found in the

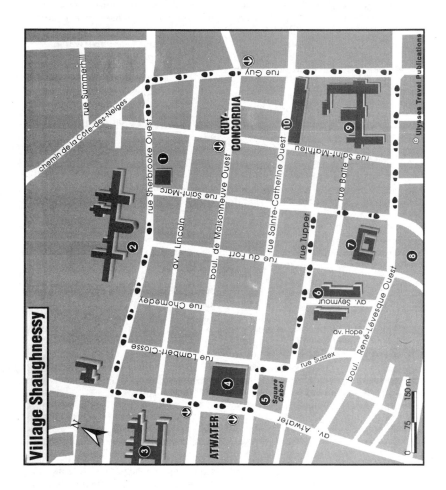

institution's shady gardens. It was in one of these that Saint Marguerite Bourgeoys taught young Amerindian girls. Around 1880, the long neoclassical buildings of the Grand Séminaire, designed by architect John Ostell, were topped by a mansard roof by Henri-Maurice Perrault. Information panels, set up on Rue Sherbrooke, directly in line with Rue du Fort, provide precise details about the farm buildings.

It is well worth entering the Seminary to see the lovely Romanesque Revival style chapel, designed by Jean Omer Marchand in 1905. The ceiling beams are made of cedar from British Columbia, while the walls are covered with stones from Caen. The nave, which stretches 80 m, is lined with 300 hand-carved oak stalls. Sulpicians who have died in Montréal since the 18th century are interred beneath it. The Sulpician order was founded in Paris by Jean-Jacques Olier in 1641, and its main church is Paris's Saint-Sulpice, which stands on the square of the same name.

The *Congrégation de Notre-Dame*, founded by Saint Marguerite Bourgeoys in 1671, owned a convent and a school in Vieux-Montréal. Reconstructed in the 18th century, these buildings were expropriated by the city at the beginning of the 20th century, as part of a plan to extend Boulevard Saint-Laurent all the way to the port. The nuns had to resign themselves to leaving the premises and settling into a new convent. The congregation thus arranged for a convent to be built on Rue Sherbrooke, according to a design by Jean Omer Marchand (1873-1936), the first French Canadian architect to graduate from the École des Beaux-Arts in Paris. The immense complex now bears witness to the vitality of religious communities in Québec before the Quiet Revolution of 1960.

The decline of religious practices and lack of new vocations forced the community to move into more modest buildings. **Collège Dawson ★ (3)** *(3040 rue Sherbrooke Ouest)*, an English-language *CÉGEP (collège d'enseignement général et profession-nel)*, has been located in the convent since 1987. The yellow brick building, set on luxuriant grounds is probably the most beautiful *CÉGEP* in Québec. It is now directly linked to the subway and underground city. The Romanesque Revival style chapel in the centre has an elongated copper dome reminiscent of Byzantine architecture. It now serves as a library and has been barely altered.

Head south on Avenue Atwater, then turn left on Rue Sainte-Catherine Ouest.

Though it looks like a warehouse covered with sheet-metal and aggregate, the **Forum (4)** *(2313 rue Sainte-Catherine Ouest)* occupies a very special place in the hearts of Montrealers. Regarded as the North American shrine of hockey, it is the home ice of the Canadiens, a team which, ever since 1917, has been inspiring the most unusual outbursts imaginable from its passionate fans. Rock concerts and variety shows are also presented here. Across the street, on Avenue Atwater, stands **Place Alexis-Nihon**, a multi-purpose complex containing a shopping mall, offices and apartments. It is linked to the underground city. **Square Cabot (5)**, south of the Forum, used to be the terminal for all buses serving the western part of the city.

Turn right on Rue Lambert-Closse, then left on Rue Tupper.

Between 1965 and 1975, Village Shaughnessy witnessed a massive wave of demolition. A great many Victorian row houses were replaced by high-rises, whose rudimentary designs, characterized by an endless repetition of identical glass or concrete balconies, are often referred to as "chicken coops". **Avenue Seymour ★ (6)** is one of the only streets in the area to have escaped this wave, which has now been curbed. Here, visitors will find charming houses made of brick and grey stone, with Queen Anne, Second Empire or Romanesque Revival details.

Turn right on Rue Saint-Marc, then left on Boulevard René-Lévesque.

Founded in 1979 by Phyllis Lambert, the **Centre Canadien d'Architecture** ★★★ *(7) (adults $5; Jun to Sep, Tue to Sun 11 a.m. to 6 p.m., Thu to 8 p.m.; Oct to May Tue to Fri 11 a.m. to 6 p.m., Thu to 8 p.m.; Sat and Sun 11 a.m. to 5 p.m.,* ☎ *939-7026)* is both a museum and a centre for the study of world architecture. Its collections of plans, drawings, models, books and photographs are the most important of their kind in the entire world. The Centre, erected between 1985 and 1989, has six exhibition rooms, a bookstore, a library, a 217-seat auditorium and a wing specially designed for researchers, as well as vaults and restoration laboratories. The main building, shaped like a "U," was designed by Peter Rose, with the help of Phyllis Lambert. It is covered with grey limestone from the Saint-Marc quarries near Québec City. This material, which used to come from the Plateau Mont-Royal and Rosemont quarries in Montréal, adorns the façades of many of the city's houses.

The centre surrounds the **Maison Shaughnessy**, whose façade looks out on Boulevard René-Lévesque Ouest. This house is in fact a pair of residences, built in 1874 according to a design by architect William Tutin Thomas. It is representative of the mansions that once lined Boulevard René-Lévesque (formerly Boulevard Dorchester). In 1974, it was at the centre of an effort to salvage the neighbourhood, which had been torn down in a number of places. The house, itself threatened with demolition, was purchased at the last moment by Phyllis Lambert. She set up the offices and reception rooms of the Canadian Centre for Architecture inside. The building

was named after Sir Thomas Shaughnessy, a former president of Canadian Pacific, who lived in the house for several decades. The inhabitants of the neighbourhood, grouped together in an association, subsequently chose to name the entire area after him.

The amusing **architecture garden (8)**, by artist Melvin Charney, lies across from Maison Shaughnessy, between two highway on-ramps. It illustrates the different stages of the neighbourhood's development, using a portion of the Sulpicians' orchard on the left, stone lines to indicate borders of 19th century properties and rose bushes reminiscent of the gardens of those houses. A promenade along the cliff that once separated the wealthy neighbourhood from working-class sections, offers a view of the lower part of the city (Little Burgundy, Saint-Henri, Verdun) and the Fleuve St-Laurent. Some of the highlights of this panorama are represented in a stylized manner, atop concrete posts.

Like the *Congrégation de Notre-Dame*, the *Sœurs Grises* had to relocate their convent and hospital, which used to be situated on Rue Saint-Pierre in Vieux-Montréal (see p 63). They obtained part the Sulpicians' farm, where a vast convent, designed by Victor Bourgeau, was erected between 1869 and 1874. The **Couvent des Sœurs Grises** ★★ *(9) (1185 rue Saint-Mathieu)* is the product of an architectural tradition developed over the centuries in Québec. The chapel alone reveals a foreign influence, namely the Romanesque Revival style favoured by the Sulpicians, as opposed to the Renaissance and Baroque Revival styles preferred by the church.

In the northwest wing, visitors will find the **Musée Marguerite-d'Youville** *(free admission; Wed to Sun 1:30 to 4:30;* ☎ *937-9501)*, named after the founder of the community, which displays objects relating to the daily life of the nuns, as well as paintings, furniture, Amerindian, Inuit and missionary art, and some beautiful liturgical clothing. Upon request, it is possible to enter the Chapelle de l'Invention-de-la--Sainte-Croix, in the centre of the convent. Its stained glass windows come from Maison Champigneule in Bar-le-Duc, France. In 1974, the convent was supposed to be demolished and replaced by high-rises. Fortunately, Montrealers protested, and the buildings were saved. Today, the convent is listed as a historical monument.

Turn left on Rue Saint-Mathieu, then right on Rue Sainte-Catherine Ouest.

At the **Faubourg Sainte-Catherine ★ (10)** *(1616 rue Sainte-Catherine Ouest)*, a converted garage, visitors will find movie theatres, a market made up of small specialty shops selling local and foreign products, and a fast-food area with a long glass roof.

To return to the Guy-Concordia Métro station, turn left on Rue Guy.

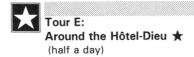

Tour E:
Around the Hôtel-Dieu ★
(half a day)

In 1860, the *religieuses hospitalières de Saint-Joseph*, or nuns who were nurses, left the Hôtel-Dieu Hospital founded by Jeanne Mance (see p 63) in Vieux-Montréal, and moved to Avenue des Pins. Victor Bourgeau designed the plans for the new hospital, located in what was then open country. In the following years, the nuns gradually sold off the remaining property in lots, laying streets soon to be lined with Victorian rowhouses. A number of these row houses were threatened with demolition after the unveiling of a gigantic real-estate development project in 1973. However, neighbourhood residents fought against the developers, who in the end only succeeded in tearing down a few of the coveted buildings. The houses that were saved are now part of the Milton Park project, the largest housing cooperative in Canada.

For this guide, the Hôtel-Dieu area tour also covers the McGill ghetto, a neighbourhood inhabited by many students from that English-language university, whose main campus lies to the west of Rue University (see p 78). The anglophone students who attend McGill in large numbers have converted some of the ghetto's houses into fraternities, typical of those depicted in Hollywood movies. These are identifiable by the large letters of the Greek alphabet that adorn their exteriors.

The tour starts at the exit of the McGill Métro station. Head north on Rue University. The former Royal Victoria College, affiliated with McGill University, is located at the corner of Rue Sherbrooke Ouest and Rue University.

The numbers following the names of attractions refer to the map of the Hôtel-Dieu neighbourhood.

Royal Victoria College (1) *(555 rue Sherbrooke Ouest, McGill Métro)* was once a professional school for young

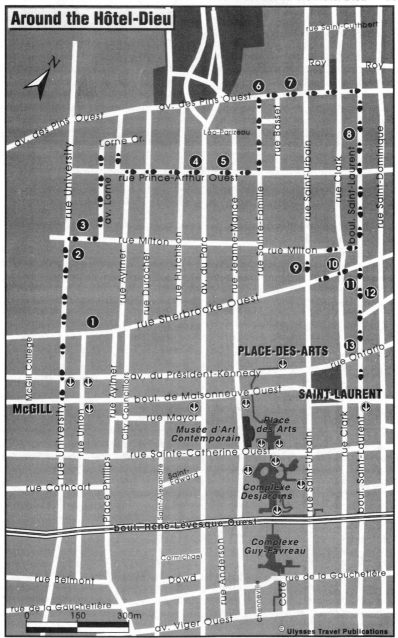

Around the Hôtel-Dieu

women from good families. Today, it houses McGill University's Faculty of Music, as well as the 300-seat Pollack Hall, a perfect place for chamber music. On the front steps of the building, designed by American architect Bruce Price (1899) is a lovely bronze statue of Queen Victoria, executed by her daughter, the talented Princess Louise. Walking up Rue University, visitors will see **Montreal High School**, a pale yellow brick building.

The **Montreal Diocesan Theological College ★ (2)** *(3473 rue University, McGill Métro)* is dedicated to the training of Anglican priests. With its densely ornamented walls of beige sandstone and red brick, the Gothic Revival style building, from 1896, is representative of the picturesque, polychrome period of the end of the Victorian era.

Turn right on Rue Milton.

The **Maison Hans Selye (3)** *(659 rue Milton, McGill Métro)* is at the corner of Rue University. The famous Dr. Hans Selye, a specialist in researching stress, lived and worked here during the 1940's and 1950's.

Turn left on Avenue Lorne. Continue across Rue Prince-Arthur to Lorne Crescent, a residential street little known even to Montrealers.

On this street, visitors will find some interesting semi-detached Victorian houses (circa 1875). During the Vietnam War, American protesters dodging the draft in their country took refuge in this neighbourhood. Turn right on Rue Aylmer, then left on Rue Prince-Arthur. The Montréal *Auberge de Jeunesse* (Youth Hostel) is located immediately to the south *(3541 rue Aylmer)*.

The **La Cité complex (4)** *(at the corner of avenue du Parc)* was renamed "Place du Parc" a few years ago. Distributed over four blocks on either side of Rue Prince-Arthur, it is the only completed portion of an extensive urban renewal project involving the destruction of most of the Victorian buildings on Rue Hutchison, Rue Jeanne-Mance and Rue Sainte-Famille. La Cité, erected between 1974 and 1976, is one of the only complexes of this size in the world to have been designed by a woman, architect Eva Vecsei. It includes high-rise apartment buildings, a hotel, a shopping centre, a movie theatre and a large health club.

Cross Avenue du Parc, which links Rue de Bleury to downtown Montréal and the Mile End ethnic neighbourhood, located north of Parc Jeanne-Mance. This part of the avenue is known for its handful of renowned restaurants and for the very busy Pâtisserie Belge.

The **former First Presbyterian Church (5)** *(3666 rue Jeanne-Mance)*, at the corner of Rue Prince-Arthur was erected in 1910 for American Presbyterians. It underwent a radical transformation in 1986 when apartments were laid out under the nave and all the way to the top of its steeple. Behind the church lies the former Strathearn School, now occupied by local community organizations, while the little German Lutheran Église Saint-Jean stands across the street. East of Rue Jeanne-Mance, there is an opening offering a view of an alley that was given a complete face-life in 1982. After the creation of a residential cooperative, the numerous sheet metal sheds and wooden walkways were replaced by small grassy yards enclosed by fences.

Turn left on Rue Sainte-Famille, which offers two interesting perspectives, one on the chapel of the Hôtel-Dieu on Avenue des Pins to the north and the other on the UQAM School of Design on Rue Sherbrooke to the south. The street is thus reminiscent of classical French town-planning, several examples of which could once be found in Vieux-Montréal. Celebrated physicist Ernest Rutherford lived at 3702 Rue Sainte-Famille while he was teaching at McGill. A little farther up the street, visitors will find six residential buildings with vaguely Art Nouveau style details. These were erected by the sisters in 1910 to house the doctors working at the Hôtel-Dieu (3705 to 3739 rue Sainte-Famille).

The **Hôtel-Dieu** ★ (6) (215 avenue des Pins Ouest, Place-des-Arts Métro and bus #80) is still one of Montréal's main hospitals. The institution and the city were founded almost simultaneously, as part of a project initiated by a group of devout Parisians led by Jérôme Le Royer de La Dauversière. Thanks to the wealth of Angélique Faure de Bullion, wife of the superintendent of finances under Louis XIV, and the devotion of Jeanne Mance, from Langres, the institution grew rapidly on Rue Saint-Paul in Vieux-Montréal. However, the lack of space, polluted air and noise in the old city forced the nuns to move the hospital to their farm in Mont-Sainte-Famille in the mid-19th century. The complex has been enlarged many times and is centred around a lovely neoclassical chapel with a dome and a façade reminiscent of urban churches in Québec under the French Regime. The interior, simplified in 1967, has, however, been divested of several interesting remounted paintings.

The **Musée des Hospitalières** ★ (7) (adults $5; Wed to Sun 1 p.m. to

5 p.m.; 21 avenue des Pins Ouest, Place-des-Arts Métro and bus #80, ☎ 849-2919) is located in the former chaplain's lodgings, next door to the chapel of the Hôtel-Dieu. It provides a detailed account of both the history of the Filles Hospitalières de Saint-Joseph, a community founded at the Abbaye de La Flèche (Anjou, France) in 1636, and the evolution of medicine over the last three centuries. Visitors can see the former wooden stairway of the Abbaye de La Flèche (1634), given to the City of Montréal by the department of Sarthe in 1963. The piece was skillfully restored by the *Compagnons du Devoir* and incorporated into the museum's beautiful entrance hall, the work of architects d'Anjou, Bernard and Mercier(1992).

Head east on Avenue des Pins to Boulevard Saint-Laurent. Turn right on this long street, which divides the city between east and west. Montréal's multi-ethnic businesses are concentrated here. The portion of the boulevard located within the limits of the Hôtel-Dieu area is lined with an assortment of specialty food shops selling products from Eastern Europe, bookstores, second-hand shops, and fashionable restaurants and cafés.

Cinéma Parallèle (8) (3682 boulevard Saint-Laurent, Saint-Laurent Métro and bus #55) occupies a rusticated grey stone building, one of a group of edifices erected in 1892 as part of an urban renewal project aiming to transform Boulevard Saint-Laurent into a prestigious street. The minuscule theatre (83 seats) located at the back of the Café Méliès (see p 185), opened in 1978 in order to present *cinéma d'auteur* to an informed audience. The next street is Rue Prince-Arthur, reserved for pedestrians east of Boulevard Saint-Laurent. Here, visitors will find a cluster of family restaurants, with terraces stretching all the way to the middle of the street. On summer evenings, a dense crowd gathers between the buildings to applaud street performers. Rue Prince-Arthur also provides access to Square Saint-Louis and Rue Saint-Denis *(Sherbrooke Métro)*.

Turn right on Rue Milton. The **Nouvel Élysée**, a repertory theatre located at the corner of Rue Clark, was originally an Austro-Hungarian synagogue. Turn left on Rue Saint-Urbain.

The **Conseil des Arts de la CUM (9)** *(3460 rue Saint-Urbain, Place-des-Arts Métro)* occupies the former École d'Architecture de Montréal, erected in 1922. Ernest Cormier's former studio (1923), a small red brick building with stained glass, stands on the grounds of the school. The Conseil rents it to Quebecois artists wishing to withdraw from the world for a certain period of time in order to create a specific work. At the corner of Rue Sherbrooke stands the former École des Beaux-Arts, now used by the department of maps of the Archives Nationales du Québec.

Turn left on Rue Sherbrooke.

Montréal photographer William Notman, known for his Canadian scenes and portraits of the 19th century bourgeoisie, lived in the **Maison Notman ★ (10)** *(51 rue Sherbrooke Ouest, Place-des-Arts Métro)* from 1876 to 1891. The inexhaustible Notman photographic archives may be viewed at the Musée McCord (see p 81). The house, erected in 1844 according to a design by John Wells, is a fine example of the Greek Revival style as it was interpreted in Scotland in those years. Its extreme austerity is broken only by some small, decorative

touches, such as the palmettes and rosettes of the portico. From 1894 to 1990, the residence served as a hospital providing extended care for the elderly, St. Margaret's Home for the Incurables.

The neighbouring service station has a prime location at the corner of two of the city's main streets, Boulevard Saint-Laurent and Rue Sherbrooke. The residence of the Molson family, famous brewers and bankers, once stood here. Unfortunately, none of the plans to build libraries, opera houses and concert halls on this prestigious site have been realized.

Head south on Boulevard Saint-Laurent.

The **Édifice Godin ★ (11)** *(2112 boulevard Saint-Laurent, Saint-Laurent Métro)*, located at the corner of Rue Sherbrooke, is quite certainly the most daring example of early 20th century modern architecture in Canada (1914). With its visible reinforced concrete structures, the building is evidence of the experiments of Auguste Perret and Paul Guadet, while the addition of a few subtle Art Nouveau curves gives it a very Parisian appearance. The building, designed by architect Joseph-Arthur Godin, to whom we also owe the Saint-Jacques (see p 100), was originally intended as housing, but its novelty frightened off potential renters—so much so that it remained empty for a number of years after being completed, and was finally converted into a clothing factory.

Set up inside the former buildings of the Ekers brewery, the **Nouveau Musée pour Rire ★★ (12)** *(adults $11; Tue to Fri 12 p.m. to 3:30 p.m., Sat 12 p.m. to 8:30 p.m., Sun 12 p.m. to 4:30 p.m.; 2111 boulevard Saint-Laurent, Saint-Laurent Métro, ☎ 845-*

4000), or International Museum of Humour, opened in 1993. This museum, the only one of its kind, explores the different facets of the world of humour, using a variety of film clips and sets. Visitors are equipped with infrared headphones, which enable them to follow the presentation. The building itself was renovated and redesigned by architect Luc Laporte, and has some 3,000 m² of exhibition space.

Édifice Grothé (13) *(2000 boulevard Saint-Laurent, Saint-Laurent Métro).* Boulevard Saint-Laurent changes appearance several times from one end to the other. For a brief while, it takes on an industrial air and then regains its busy commercial look. Located at the corner of Rue Ontario, the former Grothé cigar factory is an austere red brick edifice dating back to 1906, which has been converted into housing. In the early 20th century, when transportation, energy and the big banks were controlled by Anglo-Saxon magnates, French-Canadian strength, as the Grothé company proves, lay in the food and tobacco industries.

The tour of the Hôtel-Dieu neighbourhood ends at the Saint-Laurent Métro station, at the corner of Boulevard de Maisonneuve.

**Tour F:
Quartier Latin ★★**
(three hours)

People come to this university neighbourhood, centred around Rue Saint-Denis, for its theatres, cinemas and countless outdoor cafés, which offer a view of the heterogeneous crowd of students and revelers. The area's origins date back to 1823, when Montréal's first Catholic cathedral, Église Saint-Jacques, was inaugurated on Rue Saint-Denis. This prestigious edifice quickly attracted the cream of French Canadian society—mainly old noble families who had remained in Canada after the conquest—to the area. In 1852, a fire ravaged the neighbourhood, destroying the cathedral and Monseigneur Bourget's bishop's palace in the process. Painfully reconstructed in the second half of the 19th century, the area remained residential until the Université de Montréal was established here in 1893, marking the beginning of a period of cultural turmoil, that would eventually lead to the Quiet Revolution of the 1960's. The Université du Québec, founded in 1974, has since taken over from the Université de Montréal, now located on the north side of Mont Royal. The prosperity of the quarter has thus been ensured.

This tour starts at the west exit of the Sherbrooke Métro station.

The numbers following names of attractions refer to the map of the Quartier Latin.

The **Institut de Tourisme et d'Hôtellerie du Québec (1)** *(3535 rue Saint-Denis),* a school devoted to the tourism and hotel industries, ironically occupies what many people consider the ugliest building in Montréal. Set on the east side of Square Saint-Louis, on Rue Saint-Denis, it is part of a uninspiring group of buildings designed between 1972 and 1976, on the eve of the Olympics. The institute's courses in cooking, tourism and hotel management are nevertheless excellent.

Go across Rue Saint-Denis to Square Saint-Louis.

After the great fire of 1852, a reservoir was built at the top of Côte-à-Barron. In 1879, it was dismantled and the site was converted into a park by the name of **Square Saint-Louis ★★ (2)**. Developers built beautiful Second Empire style residences around the square making it the nucleus of the French-Canadian bourgeois neighbourhood. These groups of houses give the area a certain harmonious quality rarely found in Montréal's urban landscape. To the west, **Rue Prince-Arthur** extends west from the square. In the 1960's, this pedestrian mall (between Boulevard Saint-Laurent and Avenue Laval) was the centre of the counterculture and the hippie movement in Montréal. Today, it is lined with numerous restaurants and terraces. On summer evenings, street performers liven up the atmosphere.

Turn left onto **Avenue Laval**, one of the only streets in the city where the Belle Époque atmosphere is still very tangible. Abandoned by the French-Canadian bourgeoisie from 1920 on, the houses were converted into rooming houses before attracting the attention of local artists, who began restoring them one by one. Poet Émile Nelligan (1879-1941) lived at number 3688 with his family at the turn of the century. The *Union des Écrivains Québécois* (Québec Writers' Association) occupies number 3492, the former home of filmmaker Claude Jutra, who directed such films as *Mon Oncle Antoine*. A number of other artists, including singer Pauline Julien, writers Michel Tremblay and Yves Navarre and pianist André Gagnon, live or have lived in the area around Square Saint-Louis and Avenue Laval.

Mont-Saint-Louis ★ (3) *(244 rue Sherbrooke Est)*, a former boys' school run by the brothers of the Écoles Chrétiennes, was built facing straight up Avenue Laval in 1887. The long façade punctuated with pavilions, grey stone walls, openings with segmental arches and mansard roof make this building one of the most characteristic examples of the Second Empire style as adapted to suit Montréal's big institutions. The school closed its doors in 1970, and the edifice was converted into an apartment building in 1987, at which time an unobtrusive parking lot was built under the garden.

Maison Fréchette (4) *(306 rue Sherbrooke Est)*. Journalist, poet and deputy Louis Fréchette (1839-1908) lived in this Second Empire style house. Sarah Bernhardt stayed here on several occasions during her North American tours.

Turn right on Rue Saint-Denis and walk down "Côte-à-Barron" toward the Université du Québec à Montréal.

Montée du Zouave, the hill on the right known today as **Terrasse Saint-Denis**, was the favourite meeting place of Québec's poets and writers at the turn of the century. The group of houses was built on the site of the home of Sieur de Montigny, a proud papal Zouave.

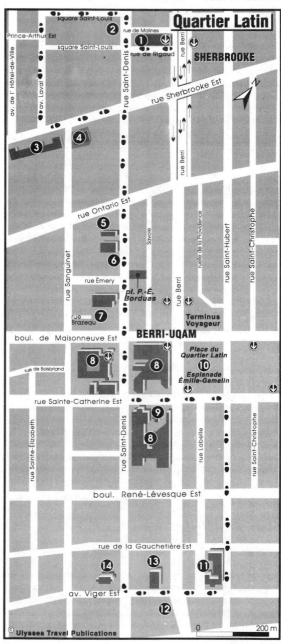

Montréal architect Joseph-Arthur Godin's work was one of the precursors of modern architecture in North America. In 1914, he began construction on three apartment buildings with visible reinforced concrete frames in the Quartier Latin area. One of these is the **Saint-Jacques ★ (5)** *(1704 rue Saint-Denis)*. Godin blended this avant-garde concept with subtle Art Nouveau curves, giving the buildings a light, graceful appearance. The venture was a commercial failure, however, leading Godin to bankruptcy and ending his career as an architect.

The **Bibliothèque Nationale ★ (6)** *(1700 rue Saint-Denis)* was originally built for the Sulpicians, who looked unfavourably on the construction of a public library on Rue Sherbrooke. Even though many works were still on the Index, and thus forbidden reading for the clergy, the new library was seen as unfair competition. Known in the past as Bibliothèque Saint-Sulpice, this branch of the Bibliothèque Nationale du Québec was designed in the Beaux-Arts style by architect Eugène Payette in 1914. This style, a synthesis of classicism and the French architecture of the Renaissance, was taught at the Paris École des Beaux-Arts, hence its name in North America. The interior is graced with lovely stained glass windows created by Henri Perdriau in 1915.

The **Théâtre Saint-Denis (7)** *(1594 rue Saint-Denis)* is made up of two theatres, among the most popular in the city. During summer, the *Festival Juste pour Rire* (Just for Laughs) comedy festival is presented here. The theatre opened in 1914, it has since welcomed all the big names in show business from both France and Québec. Modernized several times over the years, it was completely renovated yet again in 1989. As visitors can see, the top of the original theatre is higher than the recently added pink granite façade.

The screening room and rental service of the **Office National du Film du Canada (ONF) (National Film Board of Canada)** are located at the corner of Boulevard de Maisonneuve. The ONF has the world's only *cinérobothèque*, enabling about 100 people to watch different films at once. Movie lovers can also visit the **Cinémathèque Québécoise** *(335 boulevard de Maisonneuve Est)*, a little further west, which has a collection of 25,000 Canadian, Quebecois and foreign films, as well as hundreds of pieces of equipment dating back to the early history of film. UQAM's new concert hall, **Salle Pierre-Mercure**, is across the street.

Unlike most North American universities, with buildings contained within a specific campus, the campus of the **Université du Québec à Montréal (UQAM) ★ (8)** *(405 rue Sainte-Catherine Est, at the corner of rue Saint-Denis)* is integrated into the city fabric like French and German universities built during the Renaissance. It is also linked to the underground city and the Métro. The university is located on the site once occupied by the buildings of the Université de Montréal and the Église Saint-Jacques, which was reconstructed after the fire of 1852. Only the wall of the right transept and the Gothic Revival steeple were integrated into Pavillon Judith-Jasmin (1979), and have since become the symbol of the university. UQAM is part of the Université du Québec, founded in 1969 and established in different cities across Québec. Every year, over 40,000 students attend this flourishing institution of higher learning.

Turn left on Rue Sainte-Catherine Est.

Artist Napoléon Bourassa lived in a large house on Rue Saint-Denis. **Chapelle Notre-Dame-de-Lourdes** ★ (9) *(430 rue Sainte-Catherine Est)*, erected in 1876, was his greatest achievement. It was commissioned by the Sulpicians, who wanted to secure their presence in this part of the city. Its Roman-Byzantine style is in some way a summary of its author's travels. The little chapel's recently restored interior, adorned with Bourassa's vibrantly coloured frescoes, is a must-see.

Square Berri ★ (10) *(at the corner of rue Berri and rue Sainte-Catherine)*, laid out in 1992 for Montréal's 350th anniversary, is the city's newest public space. In 1994, the area along Rue Sainte-Catherine was renamed **Esplanade Émilie-Gamelin**, while the northern section was renamed **Place du Quartier Latin**. At the far end, visitors will find some curious metal sculptures by Melvin Charney, who also designed the garden of the Centre Canadien d'Architecture (see p 91). Across the street lies the bus terminal (Terminus Voyageur), built on top of the Berri-UQAM Métro station, where three of the city's four metro lines converge. To the east, the Galeries Dupuis and the Atriums, two shopping centres containing a total of about 100 stores, are located on the site of the former Dupuis Frères department store. A few businesses dear to Montrealers, such as the Archambault record shop, still grace Rue Sainte-Catherine Est. The part of this street between Rue Saint-Hubert and Avenue Papineau is regarded as Montréal's "gay village" (see p 132) because it is lined with a large number of bars, discotheques and specialty shops frequented mainly of gay men and women.

Turn right on Rue Saint-Hubert, then right again on Avenue Viger.

A symbol of the social ascent of a certain class of French-Canadian businessmen in the early 20th century, the former **École des Hautes Études Commerciales** ★ (11) *(535 avenue Viger)*, a business school, profoundly altered Montréal's managerial and financial circles. Prior to the school's existence, these circles were dominated by Canadians of British extraction. This imposing building's (1908) very Parisian Beaux-Arts architecture, characterized by twin columns, balustrades, a monumental staircase and sculptures, bears witness to the Francophile leaning of those who built it. In 1970, this business school, known as HEC, joined the campus of the Université de Montréal on the north side of Mont Royal.

Before moving to the Square Saint-Louis area around 1880, members of the French-Canadian bourgeoisie settled around **Square Viger (12)** *(Avenue Viger)* during the 1850's. Marred by the underground construction of Autoroute Ville-Marie (1977-79), it was redesigned in three sections by an equal number of artists, who opted for an elaborate design, as opposed to the sober style of the original 19th century square. In the background, visitors will see the castle-like former Gare Viger (see p 68)

The **Union Française (13)** *(429 avenue Viger Est)*, Montréal's French cultural association, has occupied this old, aristocratic residence since 1909. Lectures and exhibitions on France and its various regions are held here. Every year, Bastille Day (July 14) is celebrated in Square Viger, across the street. The house, attributed to architect Henri-Maurice Perrault, was built in 1867 for shipowner Jacques-Félix

Sincennes, founder of the Richelieu and Ontario Navigation Company. It is one of the oldest examples of Second Empire architecture in Montréal.

At the corner of Rue Saint-Denis is the **Église Saint-Sauveur (14)** *(329 avenue Viger)*, a Gothic Revival church built in 1865, according to a design by architects Lawford and Nelson. Since 1922, it has been the seat of Montréal's Syrian Catholic community. The church has a semicircular chancel, adorned with lovely stained glass windows by artist Guido Nincheri.

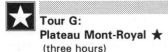

**Tour G:
Plateau Mont-Royal ★**
(three hours)

If there is one neighourhood typical of Montréal, it is definitely this one. Thrown into the spotlight by writer Michel Tremblay, one of its illustrious sons, the "Plateau," as its inhabitants refer to it, is a neighbourhood of penniless intellectuals, young professionals and old Francophone working-class families. Its long streets are lined with duplexes and triplexes adorned with amusingly contorted exterior staircases leading up to long, narrow apartments that are so typical of Montréal. Flower-decked balconies made of wood or wrought iron provide box-seats for the spectacle of the street below. The Plateau is bounded by Mont Royal to the west, the Canadian Pacific railway tracks to the north and east, and Rue Sherbrooke to the south. It is traversed by a few major streets lined with cafés and theatres, such as Rue Saint-Denis and Avenue Papineau, but is a tranquil area on the whole. A visit to Montréal would not be complete without an excursion in this area for a stroll along the

sidewalk to truly grasp the spirit of Montréal. This tour starts at the exit of the Mont-Royal Métro station. Turn right on Avenue du Mont-Royal, the neighbourhood's main commercial artery.

The numbers following names of attractions refer to the map of Plateau Mont-Royal.

The **Monastère des Pères du Très-Saint-Sacrement ★ (1)** *(500 avenue du Mont-Royal Est)* and its church, Église Notre-Dame-du-Très-Saint-Sacrement, were built at the end of the 19th century for the community of priests *(Père* is the French word for Father) of the same name. The somewhat austere façade of the church conceals an extremely colourful interior with an Italian-style decor designed by Jean-Zéphirin Resther. This sanctuary, dedicated to the "eternal Exhibition and Adoration of the Eucharist," is open for prayer and contemplation every day of the week. Concerts of baroque music are occasionally presented here.

Continue heading east on Avenue du Mont-Royal Est, blending in with the neighbourhood's widely varied inhabitants on their way in and out of an assortment of businesses, ranging from the chic *Pâtisserie Bruxelloise* (a Belgian pastry shop) to stores selling knick-knacks for a dollar and used record shops. Turn right on Rue Fabre, for some good examples of Montréal-style housing. Built between 1900 and 1925, the houses contain between two and five apartments, all with a private entry from outside. Decorative details vary from one building to the next. Visitors will see Art Nouveau stained-glass, parapets, cornices made of brick or sheet metal, balconies with Tuscan columns, and ornamental ironwork shaped in ringlets and cables.

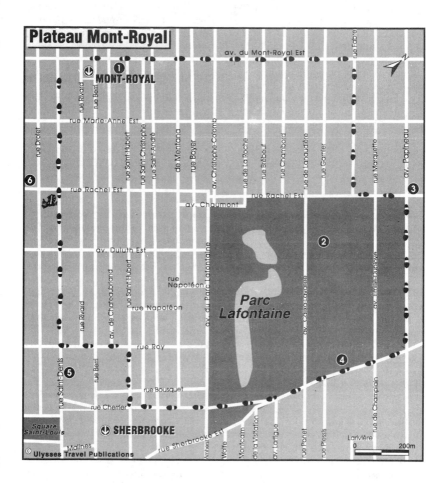

Turn left on Rue Rachel Est.

At the end of Rue Fabre, visitors will find **Parc Lafontaine (2)**, the Plateau's main green space, laid out in 1908 on the site of an old military shooting range. Monuments to Sir Louis-Hippolyte Lafontaine, Félix Leclerc and Dollard des Ormeaux have been erected here. The park covers an area of 40 ha, and is embellished with two artificial lakes and shady paths for pedestrians and bicyclists. There are tennis courts and bowling greens for summer sports enthusiasts, in the winter, the frozen lakes form a large rink, which is illuminated at night. The *Théâtre de Verdure* (Open-Air Theatre) is also located here. Every weekend, the park is crowded with people from the neighbourhood, who come here to make the most of beautiful sunny days.

The parish churches on Plateau Mont-Royal, designed to accommodate large French-Canadian working-class families, are enormous. The Romanesque Revival style **Église de l'Immaculée-Conception (3)** *(at the corner of avenue Papineau)*, designed by Émile Tanguay, was built in 1895. The interior, decorated with plaster statues and remounted paintings, is typical of that period. The stained-glass windows come from the Maison Vermont in France.

Turn right on Avenue Papineau, and right again on Rue Sherbrooke Est.

An obelisk dedicated to General de Gaulle, by French artist Olivier Debré, towers over the long **Place Charles-de-Gaulle (4)** *(at the corner of avenue Émile-Duployé)*, located alongside Rue Sherbrooke. The monument, made of blue granite from the quarries of Saint-Michel-de-Montjoie in Normandy, stands 17 m high. It was given to the City of Montréal by the City of Paris in 1992, on the occasion of Montréal's 350th anniversary.

Hôpital Notre-Dame, one of the city's major hospitals, lies across the street. The attractive **École Le Plateau** (1930) is located a little further west, at 3700 Avenue Calixa-Lavallée. This Art Deco building, designed by architects Perrault and Gadbois, also houses the hall used by the Montréal Symphony Orchestra in its early days. A trail to the north of the school provides access to the lakes in Parc Lafontaine. Back on Rue Sherbrooke Est, visitors will find the **Bibliothèque Municipale de Montréal**, the city's public library inaugurated in 1917 by Maréchal Joffre *(1210 rue Sherbrooke Est)*. Even back in the early 20th century, the edifice

was of modest size, given the number of people it was intended to serve, a result of the clergy's reservations about a non-religious library being opened in Montréal. Today, fortunately, the library has a network of 27 neighbourhood branches. Inside, an entire room is devoted to the genealogy of French-Canadian families (Salle Gagnon, in the basement).

The monument to Sir Louis-Hippolyte Lafontaine (1807-1864), after whom the park was named, is located on the other side of the street. Regarded as the father of responsible government in Canada, Lafontaine was also one of the main defenders of the French language in the country's institutions. Take **Rue Cherrier**, which branches off from Rue Sherbrooke Est across from the monument. This street, along with Square Saint-Louis, located at its west end, once formed the nucleus of the French Canadian bourgeois neighbourhood. At number 840, visitors will find the **Agora de la Danse**, where the studios of a variety of dance companies are located. The red brick building, completed in 1919, originally served as the Palestre Nationale, a sports centre for the neighbourhood youth and the scene of many tumultuous public gatherings during the 1930's.

Turn right on Rue Saint-Hubert, lined with fine examples of vernacular architecture. Turn left on Rue Roy to see **Église Saint-Louis-de-France,** *built in 1936 as a replacement for the original church, destroyed by fire in 1933.*

At the corner of **Rue Saint-Denis** stands the former **Institut des Sourdes-Muettes (5)** *(3725 rue Saint-Denis)*, a large, grey stone building made up of numerous wings and erected in stages between 1881 and 1900. Built in the Second Empire style, it covers an entire

The Pull of Montréal

I arrived here from Calgary, didn't know a soul, and ran into my best friend from kindergarten on St-Laurent four days after I got here. What can I say? Montréal is a magnetic city.

I have no statistics, but Montréal's vibrant reputation moves a huge crowd of young people from across the country to come and soak up their own part of the ethnic mix. Though the prospect of learning and re-learning French puts some people off, a surprising number of English Canadians seek out Montréal, eager to experience another culture and language. The good thing about the city is you can do both - spend the day putting the accents on your e's, and the evening watching movies made in Toronto. This co-habitation survives, running along the usual love-hate roller coaster, sending out sparks from Vancouver to Halifax.

We all unpack our bags here, but after that, similarities are difficult to define. I would say Anglos who choose Montréal have a penchant for diversity, and a love of things exotic. We are travellers at heart, but need to feel at home - many of us are clustered in the Plateau. We are willing to accept a small English-speaking community, in exchange for a city with soul. We are glad political, linguistic and cultural debates are part of everyday conversation - life would be so boring without them!

Something about Montréal fascinates those of us from the more homogeneous parts of Canada, makes us want to try living in a city where everyone from symphony conductors to grocery store clerks must speak a few words in at least two languages. Something about the kaleidoscope of equally adamant points of view being expressed simultaneously on any given day brings curious minds pouring on to the island. And then sometimes, not always, something about the contradictions and quirks of our adopted home makes us stay.

- Carol Wood

block, and is typical of institutional architecture of that period in Québec. It once took in the region's deaf-mutes. The strange chapel with cast iron columns, as well as the sacristy, with its tall wardrobes and surprising spiral staircase, may be visited upon request from the entrance on Rue Berri.

Head north on Rue Saint-Denis. Between Rue Sainte-Catherine, to the south, and Boulevard Saint-Joseph, to the north, this long artery is lined with numerous outdoor cafés and beautiful shops, established inside Second Empire style former residences built during the second half of the 19th century. Visitors will also find many bookstores, tea rooms and restaurants, which have become veritable Montréal institutions over the years.

Take a brief detour left onto Rue Rachel Est in order to see Église Saint-Jean-Baptiste and the institutional buildings around it.

Église Saint-Jean-Baptiste ★★ (6) *(309 rue Rachel Est)*, dedicated to the patron saint of French Canadians, is a gigantic symbol of the solid faith of Catholic working-class inhabitants of Plateau Mont-Royal at the turn of the 20th century, who, despite their poverty and large families, managed to amass considerable amounts of money for the construction of sumptuous churches. The exterior was built in 1901, according to a design by architect Émile Vanier. The interior was redone after a fire, and is now a veritable Baroque Revival masterpiece designed by Casimir Saint-Jean that is not to be missed. The pink marble and gilded wood baldaquin in the chancel (1915) shelters the altar, made of white Italian marble, which faces the large Casavant organs—among the most powerful in the city— in the jube.

Concerts are frequently given at this church. It can seat up to 3,000 people.

Collège Rachel, built in 1876 in the Second Empire style, stands across the street from the church. Finally, west of Avenue Henri-Julien, visitors will find the **former Hospice Auclair** (1894), with its semi-circular entrance on Rue Rachel. On Rue Drolet, south of Rue Rachel, are several good examples of the working-class architecture of the 1870's and 1880's on the Plateau, before the advent of vernacular housing, namely duplexes and triplexes with exterior staircases like those found on Rue Fabre.

Go back to Rue Saint-Denis, and continue walking up it to Avenue du Mont-Royal. Turn right in order to return to the Mont-Royal Métro station.

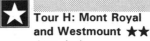

Tour H: Mont Royal and Westmount ★★
(one day)

Montréal's central neighbourhoods are distributed around Mont Royal, an important landmark in the cityscape. Known simply as "the mountain" by Montrealers, this squat mass, measuring 234 m at its highest point, is composed of intrusive rock. It is in fact one of the seven hills studding the St-Laurent plain in the Montérégie region. A "green lung" rising up at the far end of downtown streets, it exerts a positive influence on Montrealers, who, as a result, never lose touch with nature. The mountain actually has three summits; the first is occupied by Parc du Mont-Royal, the second by the Université de Montréal, and the third by Westmount, a separate city with lovely English-style homes. In addition to

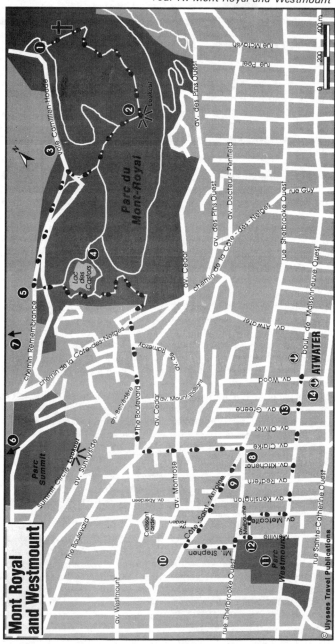

Mont Royal
and Westmount

© Ulysses Travel Publications

these areas, there are the Catholic, Protestant and Jewish cemeteries, which, considered as a whole, form the largest necropolis on the North American continent.

To reach the starting point of the tour, take bus #11 from the Mont-Royal Métro station, located on the Plateau Mont-Royal, and get off at the Observatoire de l'Est.

The numbers following attractions refer to the map of Mont Royal and Westmount.

From the **Observatoire de l'Est** ★★ (1) *(Voie Camilien-Houde)*, a lovely scenic viewpoint, visitors can look out over the entire eastern portion of Montréal. The Plateau Mont-Royal lies in the foreground, a uniform mass of duplexes and triplexes, pierced in a few places by the oxidized copper bell towers of parish churches, while the Rosemont and Maisonneuve quarters lie in the background, with the Olympic Stadium towering over them. In clear weather, the oil refineries in the east-end are visible in the distance. The Fleuve St-Laurent, visible on the right, is actually 1.5 km wide at its narrowest point. The Observatoire de l'Est is Montréal's version of Inspiration Point and a favourite gathering place of sweethearts with cars.

Climb the stone staircase at the south end of the parking lot, and follow the paths leading up to the Chalet du Mont Royal, on the left.

Pressured by the residents of the Golden Square Mile (see tour p 81), who saw their favourite playground being deforested by various firewood companies, the City of Montréal created Parc du Mont-Royal in 1870 (see p 165). Frederick Law Olmsted

(1822-1903), the celebrated designer of New York's Central Park, was commissioned to design the park. He decided to preserve the site's natural character, limiting himself to a few lookout points linked by winding paths. Inaugurated in 1876, the park, which covers 101 ha on the southern part of the mountain, is cherished by Montrealers as a place to enjoy the fresh air.

The **Chalet du Mont Royal** ★★★ (2) *(Mon to Fri 9 a.m. to 5 p.m., Parc du Mont-Royal, ☎ 844-4928)*, located in the centre of the park, was designed by Aristide Beaugrand-Champagne in 1932, as a replacement for the original structure, which was threatening to collapse. During the 1930's and 1940's, big bands gave moonlit concerts on the steps of the building. The interior is decorated with remounted paintings depicting scenes from Canada's history. These were commissioned from some of Québec's great painters, such as Marc-Aurèle Fortin and Paul-Émile Borduas. Still, people go to the chalet mainly to stroll on its esplanade and take in the exceptional view of downtown, best in the late afternoon and in the evening, when the skyscrapers are lit up.

Take the paved road leading to the parking lot of the chalet and Voie Camilien-Houde. One of the entrances to the Mount Royal Cemetery lies on the right.

The **Mount Royal Cemetery** ★★ (3) *(Voie Camilien Houde)*, is a protestant cemetery that ranks among the most beautiful parks in the city. Designed as an Eden for the living visiting the deceased, it is laid out like a landscape garden in an isolated valley, giving visitors the impression that they are a thousand miles from the city, though

The wide variety of hardwood and fruit trees attract species of birds found nowhere else in Québec. Founded by the Anglican, Presbyterian, Unitarian and Baptist churches, the cemetery opened in 1852. Some of its monuments are true works of art, executed by celebrated artists.

The families and eminent personalities buried here include the Molson brewers, with the most impressive and imposing mausoleum, shipowner Sir Hugh Allan, and numerous other figures from the footnotes and headlines of history, such as Anna Leonowens, governess of the King of Siam in the 19th century, who inspired the play *The King and I*. On the left, on the way to Lac aux Castors, visitors will see the last of the mountain's former farmhouses.

Continue along Voie Camilien Houde, then head west on Chemin Remembrance. Take the road leading to Lac aux Castors (see map).

Small **Lac aux Castors (4)** *(alongside chemin Remembrance)* was created in 1958 in what used to be a swamp. In winter, it becomes a pleasant skating rink. This part of the park also has grassy areas and a sculpture garden. It is laid out in a more conventional manner than the rest, violating Olmsted's purist directives.

The **Cimetière Notre-Dame-des-Neiges (5)** and **Oratoire Saint-Joseph (6)** ★★ *(free admission; open every day 10 a.m. to 5 p.m.; 3800 chemin Queen Mary)*. Montréal's largest cemetery is a veritable city of the dead, as more than a million people have been buried here since its inauguration in 1854. It replaced the cemetery in Square Dominion, which was deemed too close to the neighbouring houses. Unlike the Protestant cemetery, it has a conspicuously religious character, clearly identifying it with the Catholic faith. Accordingly, two heavenly angels flanking a crucifix greet visitors at the main entrance on Chemin de la Côte-des-Neiges. The "two solitudes" (Canadians of French Catholic and Anglo-Saxon Protestant extraction) thus remain separated even in death. The tombstones read like a Who's Who in the fields of business, arts, politics and science in Québec. An obelisk dedicated to the *Patriotes* of the rebellion of 1837-38 and numerous monuments executed by renowned sculptors lie scattered alongside the 55 km of roads and paths crisscrossing the cemetery.

Both the cemetery and the roads leading to it offer a number of views of the Oratoire Saint-Joseph, whose entrance is located at 3800 Chemin Queen Mary. The enormous building topped by a copper dome, the second largest dome in the world after that of St Peter's in Rome, stands on a hillside, accentuating its mystical aura even more. From the gate at the entrance, there are over 300 steps to climb to reach the oratory. Small buses are also available for worshippers who do not want to climb the steps. It was built between 1924 and 1956, thanks to the efforts of the blessed Frère André, porter of Collège Notre-Dame (across the street), to whom many miracles are attributed. A veritable religious complex, the oratory is dedicated to both Saint Joseph and its humble creator. It includes the lower and upper basilicas, the crypt of Frère André and two museums, one dedicated to Frère André's life, the other to sacred art. Visitors will also find the porter's first chapel, built in 1910, a cafeteria, a hostelry and a store selling devotional articles.

The oratory is one of the most important centres of worship and pilgrimage in North America. Every year, it attracts some 2,000,000 visitors. The building's neoclassical exterior was designed by Dalbé Viau and Alphonse Venne, while the essentially modern interior is the work of Lucien Parent and French Benedictine monk Dom Paul Bellot, the author, notably, of Saint-Benoît-du-Lac in Estrie. It is well worth visiting the upper basilica to see the stained glass windows by Marius Plamondon, the altar and crucifix by Henri Charlier, and the astonishing gilded chapel at the back. The oratory has an imposing Beckerath style organ, which can be heard on Wednesday evenings during the summer. Outside, visitors can also see the chimes, made by Paccard et Frères, originally intended for the Eiffel Tower, as well as the beautiful *Chemin de Croix* by Louis Parent and Ercolo Barbieri, in the gardens on the side of the mountain. Measuring 263 m, the Oratory's observatory, which commands a sweeping view of the entire city, is the highest point on the island.

After many attempts, Québec City's Université Laval, aiming to preserve its monopoly on French-language university education in Québec, finally opened a branch of its institution in the Château Ramezay. A few years later, it moved to Rue Saint-Denis, giving birth to the Quartier Latin (see p 97). The **Université de Montréal ★ (7)** *(2900 boulevard Édouard-Montpetit)* finally became autonomous in 1920, enabling its directors to develop grandiose plans. Ernest Cormier (1885-1980) was approached about designing a campus on the north side of Mont Royal. This architect, a graduate of the École des Beaux-Arts in Paris, was one of the first to acquaint North Americans with the Art Deco style.

The plans for the main building evolved into a refined, symmetrical Art Deco structure faced with pale yellow bricks and topped by a central tower, visible from Chemin Remembrance and Cimetière Notre-Dame-des-Neiges. Begun in 1929, construction on the building was interrupted by the stock market crash, and it wasn't until 1943 that the first students entered the main building on the mountain. Since then, a whole host of pavilions have been added, making the Université de Montréal the second largest French-language university in the world, with a student body of over 58,000. Since the entrance to the university is somewhat removed from the present route, a visit to the campus constitutes an additional excursion, which takes about an hour.

Next, follow the trails through Parc du Mont-Royal to the exit leading to Westmount (see map of this tour). This wealthy residential city of 20,239 inhabitants, enclosed within the territory of Montréal, has long been regarded as the bastion of the Anglo-Saxon elite in Québec. After the Golden Square Mile was invaded by the business centre, Westmount assumed its role. Its shady, winding roads, on the southwest side of the mountain, are lined with Neo-Tudor and Neo-Georgian residences, most of which were built between 1910 and 1930. The heights of Westmount offer some lovely views of the city below.

Take The Boulevard to Avenue Clarke (near the small triangular park), then turn left to reach Rue Sherbrooke Ouest.

Erected in 1928, Westmount's English Catholic church, **The Church of the Ascension of Our Lord** ★ (8) *(at the corner of avenue Kitchener)* is evidence of the staying power of the Gothic Revival style in North American architecture and the historical accuracy, ever more apparent in the 20th century, of buildings patterned after ancient models. With its rough stone facing, elongated lines and delicate sculptures, it looks like an authentic church from a 14th century English village.

Westmount is like a piece of Great Britain in North America. Its **City Hall** ★ (9) *(4333 rue Sherbrooke Ouest)* was built in the Neo-Tudor style, inspired by the architecture of the age of Henry VIII and Elizabeth I, which was regarded during the 1920's as the national style of England, because it issued exclusively from the British Isles. The style is characterized, in part, by horizontal openings with multiple stone transoms, bay windows and flattened arches. The impeccable green of a lawn-bowling club lies at the back, frequented by members wearing their regulation whites.

Take Chemin de la Côte-Saint-Antoine to Parc Murray. In Québec, the term *côte*, which translates literally as "hill," usually has nothing to do with the slope of the land, but is a leftover of the seigneurial system of New France. The roads linking one farm to the next ran along the sides of the long rectangles of land distributed to colonists. As a result, these plots of land gradually became known as *côtes*, from the French word for "side," *côté*. Côte Saint-Antoine is one of the oldest roads on the island of Montréal. Laid out in 1684 by the Sulpicians on a former Amerindian trail, it is lined with some of Westmount's oldest houses.

At the corner of Avenue Forden is a **milestone** dating back to the 17th century, discreetly identified by the pattern of the sidewalk, which radiates out from it. This is all that remains of the system of road signs developed by the Sulpicians for their seigneury on the island of Montréal.

For those who would like to immerse themselves in a Mid-Atlantic atmosphere, composed of a blend of England and America, **Parc Murray (10)** *(north of avenue Mount Stephen)* offers the perfect combination—a football field and tennis courts in a country setting. Here, visitors will find the remains of a natural grouping of acacias, an extremely rare species at this latitude, due to the harsh climate. The tree's presence is an indication that this area has the mildest climate in Québec. This mildness is a result of both the southwest slant of the land and the beneficial influence of the nearby Rapides de Lachine.

Go down Avenue Mount Stephen to return to Rue Sherbrooke Ouest.

Parc Westmount (11) and the **Westmount Library (12)** ★ *(4575 rue Sherbrooke Ouest)*. The park was laid out on swampy land in 1895. Four years later, Québec's first public library was erected on the same site. The province was somewhat behind in this area since up until then, religious communities had been the only ones to develop this type of cultural facility. The red brick building is the product of the trends toward eclecticism, picturesqueness and polychromy that characterized the two last decades of the 19th century.

From the park, head east on Avenue Melbourne, where there are some fine examples of Queen Anne style houses.

Turn right on Avenue Metcalfe, then left on Boulevard de Maisonneuve Ouest. At the corner of Avenue Clarke stands **Église Saint-Léon ★**, the only French-language Catholic parish in Westmount. The sober, elegant Romanesque Revival façade conceals an exceptionally rich interior decor begun in 1928 by artist Guido Nincheri, who also painted the frescoes in Château Dufresne (see Maisonneuve tour, p 138). Nincheri was provided with a large sum of money to decorate the church using no substitutes and no tricks. Accordingly, the floor and the base of the walls are covered with the most beautiful Italian and French marble available, while the upper portion of the nave is made of Savonnières stone and the chancel, of the most precious Honduran walnut, hand-carved by Alviero Marchi. The complex stained-glass windows depict various scenes from the life of Jesus Christ, including a few personages from the time of the church's construction, whom visitors will be amused to discover among the Biblical figures. Finally, the entire Christian pantheon is represented in the chancel and on the vault in vibrantly coloured frescoes, executed in the traditional manner, using egg. This technique, used, notably by Michelangelo, consists in making pigment stick to a wet surface with a coating made of egg, that becomes very hard and resistant when dry.

Growing up in English in Montreal

Montreal is my home, not Montréal, and when I think of this city and its sights I think of the Olympic Stadium, the Botanical Gardens, the Montreal Museum of Fine Arts, Old Montreal, Mount Royal, Beaver Lake and St. Joseph's Oratory. I know the names of these places should technically be in French, but as an anglophone they have different names because they are part of my city.

As a Montrealer of Anglo-Saxon descent, I grew up in the Anglo stronghold of Montreal and by extension of Québec, that former cottage-country we affectionately call the West Island. I was at an English elementary school when Bill 101 was announced, and thought he was a newscaster! My parents had the good sense to enroll me in French immersion, yet my existence was decidedly anglophile. After English high school, I moved downtown, this time we made our home in Westmount, another of the few anglophone enclaves. I attended an English CÉGEP, and then went on to McGill University for a degree in English Literature.

Ironically it was during these years that I began to have francophone friends. Initially I realized how different we were when they insisted on greeting me with kisses all the time (called la bise *by the way). Then I tried to get them to explain Bill 101. Why was it necessary to deny me what I thought was a basic right and why did I detect fear amongst them? They explained that they were here before us, so naturally they want to preserve their distinct culture, and surrounded by a sea of English, measures had to be taken. Yet my anglophone heritage has been greatly enhanced by its location within a francophone environment, and I also intend to preserve the distinct culture that has resulted. To me Montreal is a unique city because we are both here, and I do not wish that either group be forced out.*

Visitors to Montreal always wonder what I am doing here. Why do I choose to live in a city where signs in my language used to be illegal, where the locals refer to me as a tête-carrée, *(square-head) where the sights and spots I cherish have names that I no longer understand? Well, I live here at the tender age of 23 because I was born and raised here. I choose to live here because, although I am not francophone, I understand those signs and at least some of the politics behind them, and because I understand why they call me a* tête-carrée; *it is the same reason I call them frogs and peppers. I cannot say we do not have our differences, so naturally we have our silly names for each other. Fundamentally we are all Quebecois and we are defined by these differences. I am a Canadian, yet I can not imagine having to live in any other province or to identify with any other provincial mind set. I am a Canadian, a Quebecois, but most of all a Montrealer. I relish the warm welcome of shop keepers when my accent betrays me and they think I am a tourist. I am proud when people cannot detect my English accent, or when I return to the West Island and see that I could still exist exclusively in English. It is then that I know I fit in, that I am at home in both English and French. You see I love Schwartz's Deli just as much as I love the Binerie Mont Royal! I eat both* tourtière *and plum pudding at Christmas! I paint* fleur de lys *on my cheeks on June 24th and maple leaves on July 1st!*

- Jennifer McMorran

Continue along Boulevard de Maisonneuve, which leads through the former French section of Westmount before intersecting with Avenue Greene.

On **Avenue Greene (13)**, a small street with a typically English Canadian character, visitors will find several of Westmount's fashionable shops. In addition to service-oriented businesses, there are art galleries, antique shops and bookstores filled with lovely coffee table books.

Architect Ludwig Mies van der Rohe (1886-1969), one of the leading masters of the modernist movement and the head of Bauhaus in Germany, designed **Westmount Square ★★ (14)** *(at the corner of avenue Wood and boulevard de Maisonneuve Ouest)* in 1964. The complex is typical of the architect's North American work, characterized by the use of black metal and tinted glass. It includes an underground shopping centre, topped by three towers containing offices and apartments. The public areas were originally covered with veined white travertine, one of Mies's favourite materials, which was replaced by a layer of granite, more resistant to the harsh effects of freezing and thawing.

An underground corridor leads from Westmount Square to the Atwater Métro station.

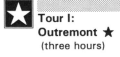

**Tour I:
Outremont ★**
(three hours)

On the other side of the Mont Royal *(oultre mont)*, is the municipality of Outremont, which, like Westmount (its anglophone counterpart on the south side), clings to the slope of the mountain and has, over the course of its development, welcomed a fairly well-off population including many influential Quebecois.

Outremont has long been a sought-after residential area. In fact, recent research suggests that the mysterious Amerindian village of Hochelaga, which disappeared between the voyages of Jacques Cartier and de Maisonneuve (16th and 17th centuries), was probably situated in this region. Furthermore, Chemin de la Côte-Sainte-Catherine, the main road around which Outremont developed, supposedly bears witness to Native activity in the area and follows a former communication route cleared by Amerindians to enable them to skirt the mountain.

The Europeans first used the territory known today as Outremont for market gardening during the 17th and 18th centuries. It was later used for horticultural purposes and, being a rural area close to the city, as a vacation spot for middle-class Montrealers in the 19th century. Agricultural goods produced here at the time were well respected, and served at important tables in the American Northeast. Montréal's urban expansion brought an end to Outremont's agricultural vocation near the close of the 19th century, and led to the development of the essentially residential municipality found today.

Our suggested tour of Outremont is organized around Chemin de la Côte-Sainte-Catherine and begins at the intersection with Avenue Mont-Royal.

The numbers following the names of attractions refer to the map of Outremont.

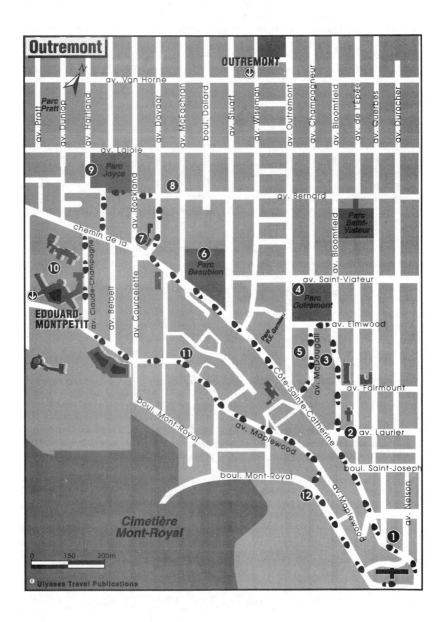

A means of circling the mountain, **Chemin de la Côte-Sainte-Catherine (1)** curves for a good part of its length, and is at an angle to the overall network of local streets. The *côte*, or slope, serves as the border between two types of terrain, while at the same time separating what has come to be known as *"Outremont-en-haut"* (Upper Outremont), perched atop the mountain, from the rest of the municipality. Initially, many imposing residences were built along this large boulevard in order to take advantage of the sharp incline of the south side *(homes of the heirs of the famous cigar manufacturer Grothé at numbers 96 and 98)*. Accordingly, the land all along the road has been laid out in response to this slope. For example some entrances and façades face Avenue Maplewood, located in the back, yards are terraced, wooded areas are left intact to prevent erosion and low retaining walls have been constructed. For the past 20 years, however, the sporadic and controversial development of prestigious high-rises on the north side of the street has somewhat altered the general appearance of the street, or at least the section between Boulevard Mont-Royal and Avenue Laurier. Relatively unoriginal in style, these high-rises, which the municipality hoped would make the street look something like New York's Fifth Avenue, have often replaced older, more interesting residences, such as those of the Berthiaume-Du Tremblay group, owner of the French-language newspaper *La Presse*, which stood at the corner of Avenue Bloomfield *(replaced by the Le Tournesol building, at number 205)*.

Walk to the corner of Bloomfield and Laurier.

Avenue Laurier ★ (2) is one of the three trendy shopping streets in the municipality popular among well-off Outremontais and Montrealers. Over the past few years, the avenue has been given a face-lift, contributing a certain stylishness to the local specialty shops. At the corner of Laurier and Bloomfield visitors will find Église Saint-Viateur, which dates back to the second decade of this century. Its remarkable interior, inspired by the Gothic Revival style was decorated by artists renowned in the fields of painting (Guido Nincheri), glass-working (Henri Perdriau), cabinet-making (Philibert Lemay) and sculpting (Médard Bourgault and Olindo Gratton). The ceiling vaults, covered with paintings depicting the life of St. Viateur, are quite exceptional.

Walk alongside the church on Avenue Bloomfield.

Avenue Bloomfield (3) *(Outremont Métro)* is believed to have been named after a farm once located here, where the harvest would have been typical of the market gardening and fruit growing of the time. Today, the avenue serves as a reminder of the first urban-style lots that would eventually line the city streets from east to west. The overall lay-out of this winding street is very pleasant, with large trees, spacious front yards and distinctive architecture. Several buildings are worth a look. The **Académie Querbes**, at numbers 215 to 235 was built in 1915-1916. The architectural detail - monumental entrance and stone galleries reaching all the way up to the third floor - is quite original for the period. As well, the facilities were ahead of their time, including a swimming pool, bowling alley and gymnasium. The canopy-shaped balconies over the entrances of numbers 249 and 253 have been unusually styled as loggias. The building at number 261 was designed by the same architect as the latter two houses. It was once lived in by Canon Lionel Groulx, a priest, writer, history professor and prominent Québec nationalist. The building now houses a foundation bearing his name. Number 262 stands out because of its façade, made of alternating red brick and grey stone. A little farther, in front of Parc Outremont, at number 345 is a house built in 1922 by and for architect Aristide Beaugrand-Champagne, distinguished by its cathedral roof and white stucco.

Turn left on Avenue Elmwood.

Parc Outremont (4) *(Outremont Métro)* is one of the municipality's many much-appreciated parks, used for both sports and leisure activities. Laid out at the beginning of the century on swamplands supplied with water by a stream flowing from the neighbouring hills, it gives the area a serene beauty. Set in the place of honour in the centre of the Bassin McDougall is a fountain inspired by the *Groupes d'Enfants*, which adorns the grounds of the Château de Versailles. A monument to the citizens of Outremont who died during World War I faces the street.

Turn left on Avenue McDougall.

Avenue McDougall (5) *(Outremont Métro)* is particularly interesting, in part because of the house at numbers 221 and 223 that occupies a very important place in the history of Outremont: the "Ferme Outre-Mont," built for L.-T. Bouthillier between 1833 and 1838. From 1856 to 1887, the farm was the family residence of a financier named McDougall. It later became a horticultural school for deaf-mutes run by the clergymen of Saint-Viateur. This was the scene of the first Mass ever celebrated in Outremont, on April 21, 1887. The house is believed to be the third oldest residence in the city. Henri Bourassa, founder of the newspaper *Le Devoir*, was supposedly once a tenant here. The white section (now divided into two dwellings) still has most of its original characteristics, namely the large porch topped with a gallery, the dormer window wedged between the two chimneys and the small windows. Number 268, designed by a Toronto architect named Ralston for an architecture competition, is a good example of the international Bauhaus style. This influential school of thought from the 1920s emphasized functionalism, and greatly affected the art and science of architecture.

Turn right on Chemin de la Côte-Sainte-Catherine.

Chemin de la Côte-Sainte-Catherine becomes once again lined with residences, some of undeniable architectural interest in this area. This is the case, notably, with number 325, which has a very large gallery and numerous ornamental details, and number 356, home of architect Roger d'Astous, who has added an aviary. D'Astous, a student of celebrated architect Frank Lloyd Wright, conceived the idea for Montréal's Olympic Village.

Parc Beaubien (6) *(Outremont Métro or Édouard-Montpetit Métro)* is located on the site of a farming estate once owned by the important Beaubien family of Outremont, which included several important figures on the Québec scene. The members of the Beaubien clan lived right near each other on the side of the hill, overlooking their land (part of which is now occupied by the Terrasses Les Hautvilliers). Among the family members were Madame Justine Lacoste Beaubien, founder of the renowned Hôpital Sainte-Justine for children; Louis Beaubien, federal and provincial deputy and his wife, Lauretta Stuart. Louis Riel, the Métis chief from Manitoba whose trial and execution became famous, supposedly worked on the Beaubien's land between 1859 and 1864.

Walk to Avenue Davaar and turn right.

The municipal administration is believed to occupy one of the oldest buildings in Outremont (1817). The **Hôtel de Ville (7)** *(Édouard-Montpetit Métro)* served, notably, as a warehouse for the Hudson's Bay Company, a school and a prison. A tollbooth used to stand here on Chemin de la Côte-Sainte-Catherine to collect a fee intended to finance the upkeep of the road, which, like many others in those years, was administered by a private company.

Go down Avenue Davaar to Avenue Bernard.

Avenue Bernard (8) ★ *(Outremont Métro)* is lined with shops, offices, apartment buildings and houses. This wide avenue with large, grassy medians, curbside landscaping and stately buildings appears quite imposing and reflects the will of an era to affirm clearly the growing municipality's prestige. The **Théâtre Outremont** *(numbers 1234-1248)*, once a very popular repertory theatre, whose future use presently remains uncertain is located on the street. Its interior was designed by Emmanuel Briffa. The former post office at number 1145 and the **Clos Saint-Bernard**, a large garage now converted into condominiums at numbers 1167 to 1175 are also interesting. Another highlight on this street is the first large-scale grocery

store opened by the Steinberg family, who later came to own more than 190 such stores across Québec, but nevertheless went bankrupt in 1992. Several residential buildings along Avenue Bernard are architecturally beautiful as well, including the **Montcalm** *(numbers 1040 to 1050)*, the **Garden Court** *(numbers 1058 to 1066)*, the **Royal York** *(numbers 1100 to 1144)* and the **Parkland** *(number 1360)*.

Head west on Avenue Bernard to Avenue Rockland to reach the park located along this avenue.

Parc Joyce (9) *(Outremont Métro or Édouard-Montpetit Métro)* was laid out on a vast piece of property formerly owned by James Joyce, a Canadian of British descent, who was a confectioner by profession. The buildings, of great architectural interest, were demolished, since no one could find a use for them after the land was transferred to the City in 1926. The resulting park has gentle hills and mature vegetation dating back to the time of the estate.

It is worth taking the time to see two residences in particular on Avenue Ainslie, which stops at the park. Numbers 18 and 22 are especially impressive, as much for the size of the lots of land upon which they were built as for the dimensions of the buildings and the majesty of their Victorian-inspired design. Number 7, for its part, was built in 1936, and represents one of the first attempts at modernism in this country.

Back on Chemin de la Côte-Sainte-Catherine, take a moment to walk along Avenue Claude-Champagne. On the north side of the street are three residences whose architectural and patrimonial value is obvious: number 637, the country-style **Maison J.B. Aimbault**, built around 1820, is an extremely rare legacy of a bygone era in Outremont; number 645, the neighbouring house, which has a sharply pitched roof, the trademark of architect Beaugrand-Champagne and, finally, number 661, built at the very end of the last century, whose design, relatively unique for the neighbourhood, is inspired by the New England Georgian style.

Turn onto Avenue Claude-Champagne.

The **housing complex of the Sœurs des Saints-Noms-de-Jésus-et-de-Marie (10)** *(Édouard-Montpetit Métro)* is a string of big institutional buildings which extends along Avenue Claude-Champagne, and beyond, onto the mountain and along Boulevard Mont-Royal. It once belonged to a single community of nuns, the Sœurs des Saints-Noms-de-Jésus-et-de-Marie. These women came to Outremont in the last century with an essentially educational mission, which they managed to fulfil while this large area was developing. Walking along Avenue Claude-Champagne, visitors will first see the **Pensionnat du Saint-Nom-de-Marie** (boarding school), built in 1903, which stands out on Chemin de la Côte-Sainte-Catherine because of its architecture including a Renaissance style portico, silvery roof and dome crowned with a cupola, its massive size and its location on a heightened piece of ground. Farther up, immediately behind the boarding school, lies the much more modern **Pavillon Marie-Victorin**, which was originally used as a college by the nuns before being purchased by the Université de Montréal for its Faculty of Education. Even higher, this time right on the mountain, stands **Pavillon Vincent d'Indy**, which has also become part of the Université de Montréal and its Faculty of Music. The building's concert hall, **Salle Claude-Champagne**, has exceptionally good acoustics, and is used for recordings on a regular basis. The grounds offer a remarkable view of the municipality, as well as the entire northern part of the island of Montréal. Finally, east of this building, and a little below, on Boulevard Mont-Royal *(numbers 1360 to 1430)*, the nuns' mother house, built in the 1920's, completes the tableau.

Avenue Claude-Champagne, as part of "Outremont-en-haut," is also graced with residential buildings befitting the reputation of this section of the city. The imposing **"Villa" Préfontaine**, located at number 22, epitomizes the style many local residents wanted to give their property. Higher up, from number 36 to 76, visitors will notice a very well-executed series of twin houses, successfully differentiated from one another by certain ornamental and architectural details.

At the end of Avenue Claude-Champagne, turn left on Boulevard Mont-Royal and continue straight ahead to the traffic lights to reach Avenue Maplewood.

Also known as the "avenue of power," **Avenue Maplewood ★ (11)** *(Édouard Montpetit Métro)* forms the central axis of the area referred to as "Outremont-en-haut," where various opulent-looking houses with distinctive architecture lie perched in a very hilly landscape, occupied both now and in the past by numerous influential Quebecois.

The sober modern building at number 190 is in fact the home of Robert Bourassa, the former Premier of Québec. On Place Duchastel, numbers

161,159 and 6 are remarkable for their architecture, inspired by the Tudor and Elizabethan period. The massive structure at number 153, built by architect Randolph C. Betts, is impressive. The different coloured materials used for the facing and the roof, as well as the organized diversity of the architectural components used in the design, help tone down the building's impact on the landscape. The lovely residences at numbers 118 and 114, from a different period, hem in a lovely little stream, which adds to the beauty of the avenue. This stream once supplied a watering place for horses on Côte-Sainte-Catherine before forming the swamp where Parc Outremont is now located. Today, it disappears into the pipes located below the avenue, on the land of the *Religieuses de l'Imaculée-Conception* (Sisters of the Immaculate Conception).

Beyond Avenue McCulloch (where Pierre Elliott Trudeau, former Prime Minister of Canada, lived for a certain period of time, at number 84), Avenue Maplewood becomes even more picturesque. Its slight slope and gentle twists and turns, combined with the beauty of the residences and careful landscaping of the yards, sum up the appeal "Outremont-en-haut" has for the Quebecois intelligentsia. Many houses here are worth a quick look: number 77 is a fine example of the Colonial American style; numbers 71 and 69 resemble 1920's-style suburban houses; numbers 49 and 47, twin houses dating back to 1906 have a country look about them (they are the oldest homes on the street); and finally number 41, where the architectural style and large front yard bring to mind the great French manors of the Renaissance.

Take the footpath between numbers and 52, which leads to Bouleva Mont-Royal by way of the lane of t same name.

Boulevard Mont-Royal (12) is t second major artery of "Outremont-e haut." It was thus named because t first section of the road led to t Cimetière Mont-Royal. Although stric residential, the road now tends to quite busy with motorists en route the Université de Montréal. It is al used as a jogging path neighbourhood athletes.

The section of the boulevard includ in this tour serves as an example of t quality of the local architecture a landscaping. Lovely period residenc have been built here, some of whi were designed while bearing in mi their double access to the bouleva and Avenue Maplewood. This is t case, notably, with number 11E which has two well-balanced façade one facing each street. Number 113 meanwhile, is typically Art Deco style. The vast wooded area that h been preserved south of the bouleva adds to the beauty of t neighbourhood. Once threatened w over-development along the lines of t large residential high-rises found Chemin de la Côte-Sainte-Catherir the area is now part of Parc du Mo Royal.

From the end of the street (at the be in the road), there is a beautiful view the eastern end of Montréal (Plate Mont-Royal), which also reveals t radical difference between this part Outremont and the city at its fe After the turn, at the conclusion of tl tour, visitors will see the **Couvent d Sœurs de Marie-Réparatrice** on the le This convent, with its buff-colour brick, was considered very modern for its time (1911).

Mount Royal Cemetery ★★, see p108

Tour J:
Little Italy ★
(two hours)

Montréal has a large Italian community. By the beginning of the 19th century, many of the best hotels in town were already owned by Italians. At the end of the same century, the first group of immigrants from the poorer regions of southern Italy and Sicily settled in the area around Rue Sainte-Christophe, north of Rue Ontario. The largest wave, however, arrived at the end of World War II, when thousands of Italian peasants and workers disembarked at the port of Montréal. Many of these settled around Marché Jean-Talon and Église Madonna Della Difesa, and thereby created Little Italy, where visitors will now find cafés, trattorias, specialty food shops, etc. Since the 1960's, many of Montréal's Italians have moved to Saint-Léonard, a seperate municipality located in the northeast, but they still return to Little Italy to do their shopping.

From the Jean-Talon Métro station, head east to Rue Saint-Hubert, and turn right. The Jean-Talon station honours the memory of the man who served as administrator of New France from 1665 to 1668 and 1670 to 1672. During his two short mandates, he was responsible for reorganizing the colony's finances and diversifying its economy.

The numbers following the names of attractions refer to the map of Little Italy.

The **Casa d'Italia (1)** *(505 rue Jean-Talon Est, Jean-Talon Métro)* is the Italian community centre. It was built in 1936 in the Art Moderne style, a variation on Art Deco characterized by horizontal, rounded lines inspired by the streamlined designs of steamships and locomotives. A fascist group took up residence here before the Second World War.

Plaza Saint-Hubert (2) *(rue Saint-Hubert between rue de Bellechasse Est and Jean-Talon Est, Jean-Talon Métro or Beaubien Métro)* is one of Montréal's main shopping streets. Here, visitors will find a great many clothing and shoe stores, as well as restaurants serving North American cuisine. It was also on this street that the first Rôtisserie Saint-Hubert, now famous for its roast chicken, opened in 1951. The glass awnings were put up over the sidewalks in 1986.

Turn right on Rue Bélanger.

The former Rivoli and Château cinemas (3) *(6906 and 6956 rue Saint-Denis, Jean-Talon Métro)*, located on both sides of Rue Bélanger, are two examples of neighbourhood movie palaces that have been converted for other uses. The Cinéma Château was built in 1931 according to plans by architect René Charbonneau. The original decor, executed in an exotic Art Deco style by Emmanuel Briffa, has been preserved. The Cinéma Rivoli, however, was not so lucky—only the Adam façade dating back to 1926 remains; the interior was transformed into a pharmacy. This part of Rue Saint-Denis is lined with typical Montréal apartment buildings and their traditional exterior metal and wood staircases. Notice the many finely worked cornices and balconies, as well as the Art Nouveau style stained glass in the upper part of the windows and doors.

Continue heading west on Rue Bélanger, then turn left on Rue Drolet.

École Sainte-Julienne-Falconieri (4) *(6839 rue Drolet, Jean-Talon Métro)* was designed in 1924 by Ernest Cormier, architect of the Université of Montréal's main building. The school was clearly influenced by the buildings of American architect Frank Lloyd Wright, erected about ten years earlier.

Go back to Rue Bélanger and turn left. Take another left on Avenue Henri-Julien.

The design of **Église Madonna Della Difesa ★(5)** *(6810 avenue Henri-Julien, Jean-Talon Métro)*, or Our Lady of the Defense Church, is of Roman-Byzantine inspiration, characterized by small arched openings and varied treatment of the surfaces, arranged in horizontal bands. A basilica-style plan such as this is unusual in Montréal. The church was designed in 1910 by painter, master glass-worker and decorator Guido Nincheri who spent over 30 years working on it, finalizing himself every last detail of the decor. Nincheri was in the habit of depicting contemporary figures in his stained-glass windows and the vibrantly coloured frescoes, made with egg, a technique he had mastered. One of these, showing Mussolini on his horse, was a source of controversy for many years. To erase or not to erase? It may still be seen above the high altar.

At number 6841, visitors will find the Art Moderne style **École Madonna Della**

Difesa *(Jean-Talon Métro)*. The bas-reliefs depicting school children are particularly noteworthy. Parc Dante stretches west of the church, with the place of honour in its centre occupied by a modest bust of the Italian poet, sculpted by Carlo Balboni in 1924. Neighbourhood chess and checkers buffs meet here during the summer months.

Take Rue Dante west to Boulevard Saint-Laurent, turn right.

Boulevard Saint-Laurent (6) *(Jean-Talon Métro)* could be described as Montréal's "immigration corridor." Since 1880, immigrants to the city have been settling along different segments of the boulevard, depending on their ethnic background. After several decades, they leave the area, then scatter throughout the city or regroup in another neighbourhood. Some communities leave few traces of their passage on Boulevard Saint-Laurent, while others develop shopping areas where descendants of these first arrivals still come with their families. Between Rue de Bellechasse to the south and Rue Jean-Talon to the north, the boulevard is lined with numerous Italian restaurants and cafés, as well as food stores, swarmed by Montrealers of all origins on weekends. Some of the recently erected buildings along the street have interesting modern façades.

Turn right on Avenue Shamrock, whose name serves as a reminder that the neighbourhood was Irish before it was Italian.

The **Caserne de Pompiers no 31 (7)** *(7041 rue Saint-Dominique, Jean-Talon Métro)*, or Fire Station, was built as part of a job creation project initiated after the economic crisis of 1929. The building, which dates back to 1931,

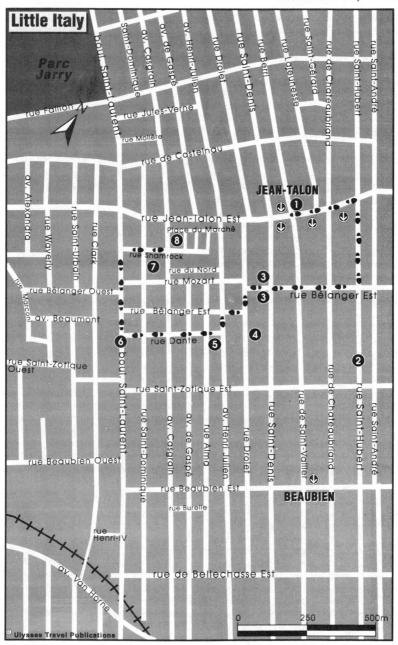

was designed by architect E.A. Doucet in the Art Deco style. At the intersection of Avenue Shamrock and Avenue Casgrain, a small, Art Moderne brick building with a rounded corner, once served as the Clinique Jean-Talon, where many new arrivals came for care and comfort.

Marché Jean-Talon ★ (8) *(avenue Casgrain, Jean-Talon Métro)* was built in 1934 on the site of the Irish lacrosse field known as Shamrock Stadium. The space was originally intended for a bus station, which explains the platforms with concrete shelters over them. Despite its less than attractive appearance, Marché Jean-Talon is a pleasant place to shop, because of the constant buzz of activity. The market is surrounded by specialty food shops, often set up right in the back yards of buildings facing the neighbouring streets. Passing through the neighbourhood, visitors will see vegetable gardens laid out in whatever meagre space is available, Madonnas in their niches and grape-laden vines climbing up trellises on balconies, all of which lend this part of Montréal a Mediterranean feel.

 Tour K:
Sault-au-Récollet ★
(three hours)

Around 1950, the Sault-au-Récollet neighbourhood was still a farming village isolated from the city on the banks of Rivière des Prairies. Today, it is easy to reach on the Métro, whose northernmost point is the Henri-Bourassa station. The history of the "Sault" dates back a long way. In 1610, Monsieur des Prairies headed into the river that now bears his name,

thinking it was the St-Laurent. Then, in 1625, Nicolas Viel, a Récollet, and his Native guide Ahuntsic drowned in the river's rapids, hence the name Sault (Rapids)... au-Récollet. In 1696, the Sulpicians established the Fort Lorette Huron mission here. In the 19th century, Sault-au-Récollet became a popular resort area among Montrealers looking for a spot close to the city during the summer months, which explains the existence of the handful of summer cottages that survived the recent development of the area.

From the exit of the Henri-Bourassa Métro station, head east on the boulevard of the same name. Turn left on Rue Saint-Hubert, then right on Boulevard Gouin Est.

The numbers following names of attractions refer to the map of Sault-au-Récollet.

Collège Sophie-Barat (1) *(1105 et 1239 boulevard Gouin Est)*. Monseigneur Ignace Bourget, Montréal's second bishop, courted a number of French religious communities during the 1840's, trying to get them to establish schools in the Montréal region. The *Dames du Sacré-Cœur* were among those who accepted to make the long voyage. In 1856, they settled on the banks of Rivière des Prairies, where they built a convent school for girls. The former day school (1858), at 1105 Boulevard Gouin Est, is all that remains of the original complex. After a fire, the convent was rebuilt in stages. The building resembling an austere English manor is the most interesting of the new facilities (1929). The school now bears the name of the founder of the *Dames du Sacré-Cœur* community, Sophie Barat.

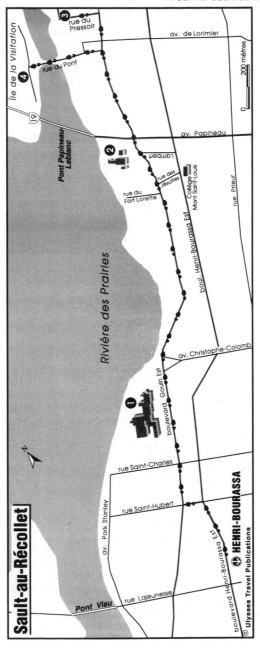

Before reaching Église de la Visitation, visitors will see a few ancestral homes, such as the **Maison David-Dumouchel**, at number 1737, built in 1839 for a carpenter from Sault-au-Récollet. It has high firebreak walls, even though there are no buildings adjoining it, showing that this architectural element, once strictly utilitarian, had become a decorative element, a symbol of prestige and urbanity.

Église de la Visitation ★★ (2) *(1847 boulevard Gouin Est)* is the oldest extant church on the island of Montréal. It was built between 1749 and 1752, but was considerably modified afterwards. Its beautiful Palladian façade, added in 1850, is the work of Englishman John Ostell, who designed the Vieille Douane (old customs house) on Place Royale and the Vieux Palais de Justice (old court house) on Rue Notre-Dame. The degree of refinement reached here is a tribute to the fierce competition between the parishioners of Sault-au-Récollet and those of Sainte-Geneviève, further west, who had just built themselves a church of the same style.

Viewed as a whole, the interior of Église de la Visitation is one of the most remarkable works of woodcarving in Québec. The decor, begun in 1764, was not completed until 1837. Philippe Liébert, born in Nemours, France, executed the first decorative elements, including the sculpted doors of the reredos, which are precious Louis XV style pieces. It was David-Fleury David, however, who completed the bulk of the work, namely the cornice, Louis XVI pilasters and finely chiselled vault. The church is adorned with beautiful paintings, such as *La Visitation de la Vierge* (The Visitation of the Virgin), purchased by Curé Chambon in 1756 and attributed to Mignard.

At the end of Rue Lambert, visitors will find the former Noviciat Saint-Joseph (1700 boulevard Henri-Bourassa Est), now **Collège du Mont-Saint-Louis**. The neoclassical building, erected in 1853, was enlarged by the addition of a Second Empire style pavilion in 1872. The heart of the village of Sault-au-Récollet lies along Boulevard Gouin Est, east of Avenue Papineau. There are some noteworthy buildings here, including number 1947, the Maison Boudreau, built around 1750; number 2010, the former general store, which is a small Second Empire building of urban design, transposed in a rural setting; and finally, number 2086, the proud Maison Persillier-Lachapelle, former residence of a prosperous miller and bridge-builder, erected around 1830.

Turn left on Rue du Pressoir.

La Maison du Pressoir ★ (3) *(free admission, Sep to Jun, Wed to Sun 12 p.m. to 5 p.m.; Jun to Sep Wed to Sun 1 p.m. to 8 p.m.; 10865 rue du Pressoir, ☎ 280-6783).* Around 1810, Didier Joubert built a cider press on his property in Sault-au-Récollet. As of now, research suggests that this is Montréal's only extant example of half-timbering architecture. Restored in 1982, it houses an exhibition on cidermaking and the historical background of the press and the Sulpician mission.

Backtrack along Boulevard Gouin, heading west. Turn right on Rue du Pont in order to reach Île de la Visitation.

The **Parc Régional de l'Île-de-la-Visitation (4)** regional park encompasses a vast area alongside Rivière des Prairies, as well as the island itself, a long strip of land hemmed in at each end by dykes used to control the level and flow of the river, thus eliminating the famous *sault* or rapids, for which the area was named. On the way to the island, visitors will cross over the Rue du Pont dyke. Under the French Regime, the Sulpicians built powerful mills alongside here; unfortunately, however, very little remains of these structures.

The dyke located at the east end of the island supports Rivière-des-Prairies's hydroelectric power station, built in 1928 by Montreal Island Power. The dam includes a fish trap, which makes it a favourite spot for shad fishing, since the river teems with this species.

Tour L: Île Sainte-Hélène and Île Notre-Dame ★★
(one day)

When Samuel de Champlain reached the island of Montréal in 1611, he found a small, rocky archipelago located in front of it. He named the largest of these islands in the channel after his wife, Hélène Boulé. Île Sainte-Hélène later became part of the seigneury of Longueuil. Around 1720, the Baroness of Longueuil chose the island as the site for a country house surrounded by a garden. It is also worth noting that in 1760, the island was the last foothold of French troops in New France, commanded by Chevalier François de Lévis. Recognizing Île Saint-Hélène's strategic importance, the British army built a fort on the eastern part of the island at the beginning of the 19th century. The threat of armed conflict with the Americans having diminished, the Canadian government rented Île Sainte-Hélène to the City of Montréal in 1874, at which time the island was turned into a park, linked to

Vieux-Montréal by ferry, and, from 1930 on, by the Pont Jacques-Cartier.

In the early 1960's, Montréal was chosen as the location of the 1967 World's Fair (Expo '67). The city wanted to set up the event on a large, attractive site near the downtown area; a site such as this, however, did not exist. It was thus necessary build one: using earth excavated during the construction of the Métro tunnel, Île Notre-Dame was created, doubling the area of Île Sainte-Hélène. From April to November 1967, 45 million visitors passed through Cité du Havre, the gateway to the fairground, and crisscrossed both islands. Expo, as Montrealers still refer to it familiarly, was more than a jumble of assorted objects; it was Montréal's awakening, during which the city opened itself to the world, and visitors from the world over discovered a new art of living, involving mini-skirts, colour television, hippies, flower power and protest rock.

It is not easy to reach Cité du Havre from downtown. The best way is to take Rue Mill, then Chemin des Moulins, which runs under Autoroute Bonaventure to Avenue Pierre-Dupuy. This last road leads to Pont de la Concorde and then over the St-Laurent to the islands. It is also possible to take bus number 168 from the McGill Métro station, or the taxi-boat from Quai Jacques-Cartier, in the Vieux-Port.

The numbers following names of attractions refer to the map of Île Sainte-Hélène and Île Notre-Dame.

The **Tropique Nord (1)**, **Habitat '67 (2)** and the **Parc de la Cité du Havre (3)** ★★ *(☎ 872-7678)* were all built on a spit of land created to protect the port of Montréal from ice and currents. This point of land also offers some lovely views of the city and the water. The administrative offices of the port are located at the entrance to the area, along with a group of buildings that once housed the Expo-Théâtre and Musée d'Art Contemporain (see p 79). A little further on, visitors will spot the large glass wall of the Tropique Nord, a residential complex composed of apartments with a view of the outdoors on one side, and an interior tropical garden on the other.

Next, visitors will see Habitat '67, an experimental housing development built for the Expo '67 in order to illustrate construction techniques using prefabricated concrete slabs and herald a new art of living. The architect, Moshe Safdie, was only 23 years old when he drew up the plans. Habitat '67 looks like a gigantic cluster of cubes, each containing one or two rooms. The apartments are as highly prized as ever, and are lived in by a number of notable Quebecois.

At the Parc de la Cité du Havre, visitors will find 12 panels containing a brief description of the history of the Fleuve St-Laurent. A section of the bicycle path leading to Île Notre-Dame and Île Sainte-Hélène passes through the park.

Cross Pont de la Concorde.

Parc Hélène-de-Champlain ★★ (4) lies on Île Sainte-Hélène, originally covering an area of 50 ha, but enlarged to over 120 ha for Expo '67. The original portion corresponds to the raised area studded with boulders made of breccia. Peculiar to the island, it is a very hard, ferrous stone that takes on an orange colour when exposed to air for a long time. In 1992, the western part of the island was transformed into a vast open-air amphitheatre, where large-cale shows are presented. On a lovely park

bordering the river, across from Montréal, visitors will find *L'Homme* (Man), an important metal sculpture by Alexandre Calder, created for Expo '67.

Follow the trails leading toward the heart of the island. The pool house, faced with breccia stone, and outdoor swimming pools, built during the crisis of the 1930's, lie at the edge of the original park. This island, with its varied contours, is dominated by the **Tour Lévis**, a simple water tower which looks like a dungeon, built in 1936, and by the blockhouse, a wooden observation post, erected in 1849.

Follow the signs for the Fort de l'Île Sainte-Hélène.

After the War of 1812 between the United States and Great Britain, the **Fort de l'Île Sainte-Hélène ★★ (5)** was built so that Montréal could be properly defended if ever a new conflict were to erupt. The construction, supervised by military engineer Elias Walker Durnford, was completed in 1825. Built of breccia stone, the fort is in the shape of a jagged "U," surrounding a drill ground, used today by the *Compagnie Franche de la Marine* and the 78th Regiment of the Fraser Highlanders as a parade ground. These two costumed mock regiments delight visitors by reviving Canada's French and Scottish military traditions. The drill ground also offers a lovely view of both the port and **Pont Jacques-Cartier**, inaugurated in 1930, which straddles the island, separating the park from La Ronde.

The arsenal is now occupied by the **Musée David M. Stewart ★★ (5)** *(adults $3; Mon to Sun 10 a.m. to 5 p.m., closed Tue; ☎ 861-6701)*, which exhibits a collection of objects from the 17th and 18th centuries, including interesting collections of maps,

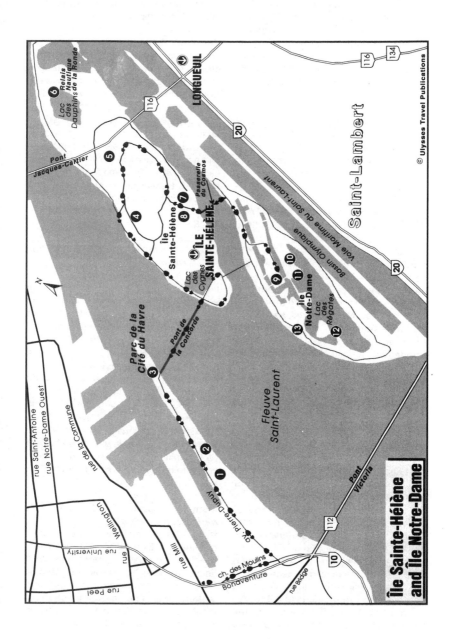

Île Sainte-Hélène
and Île Notre-Dame

firearms, and scientific and navigational instruments put together by Montréal industrialist David Stewart and his wife Liliane. The latter heads both the museum and the Macdonald-Stewart Foundation, which also manages the Château Ramezay and the Château Dufresne.

The vaults of the former barracks now house Le Festin des Gouverneurs, a restaurant geared mainly toward group reservations. Each evening, it recreates the atmosphere of a feast in the era of New France.

La Ronde ★ (6) *(adults $17.30, children 3 to 12 years old $8.55, families $40; Jun to Sep, open every day 11 a.m. to 11 p.m., Fri and Sat to 12 a.m.; ☎ 872-6222)*, an amusement park set up for Expo '67 on the former Île Ronde, opens its doors to both the young and the not so young every summer. For Montrealers, an annual trip to La Ronde has almost become a pilgrimage. An international fireworks competition is held here on Saturdays or Sundays during the months of June and July.

Head toward the Biosphere on the road that runs along the south shore of the island.

Built in 1938 as a sports pavilion, the **Restaurant Hélène-de-Champlain ★ (7)** was inspired by the architecture of New France, and is thus reminiscent of the summer house of the Baroness of Longueuil, once located in the area. Behind the restaurant, is a lovely rose garden, planted for Expo '67, which embellishes the view from the dining room. The **former military cemetery** of the British garrison stationed on Île Sainte-Hélène from 1828 to 1870 lies in front of the building. Most of the original tombstones have disappeared.

A commemorative monument, erected in 1937, stands in their place.

Very few of the pavilions built for Expo '67 have survived the destructive effects of the weather and the changes in the islands' roles. One that has is the former American pavilion, a veritable monument to modern architecture. The first complete geodesic dome to be taken beyond the stage of a model, it was created by the celebrated engineer Richard Buckminster Fuller (1895-1983). The **Biosphere ★★ (8)**, built of tubular aluminum measuring 80 m in diameter, unfortunately lost its translucent acrylic skin in a fire back in 1978.

Cross over to Île Notre-Dame on the Passerelle du Cosmos.

Île Notre-Dame emerged from the waters of the St-Laurent within the space of 10 months, with the help of 15 million tons of rocks and soil transported here from the Métro construction site. Because it is an artificial island, its creators were able to give it a fanciful shape by playing with both soil and water. The island, therefore, is traversed by pleasant **canals and gardens ★★ (9)**, laid out for the 1980 Floralies Internationales an international flower show. Boats are available for rent, enabling visitors to ply the canals and admire the flowers mirrored in their waters.

Montréal's **Casino ★ (10)** *(open every day from 11 a.m. to 3 a.m.; ☎ 392-2746)* occupies the French pavilion of Expo '67. The aluminum building, designed by architect Jean Faugeron, was renovated in 1993 in order to accommodate the casino. Visitors will find a combination of French and American gaming traditions. The upper galleries offer some lovely views of downtown Montréal and the Voie Maritime du St-Laurent (the Seaway). The strange structures to the south, were built as a new home for the swallows that used to nest in the nooks and crannies of the former French pavilion before it was taken over.

The **Pavillon du Québec ★ (11)** located beside the casino was erected in 1966, according to a design by Quebecois architects Papineau, Gérin-Lajoie, Leblanc and Durand. It was the first building in Canada to be given a reflective glass facing. Completely surrounded by water, it appears to be floating.

Nearby, visitors will find the entrance to the **Plage de l'Île Notre-Dame**, a beach enabling Montrealers to lounge on real sand right in the middle of the St-Laurent. A natural filtering system keeps the water in the small lake clean, with no need for chemical additives. The number of swimmers allowed on the beach is strictly regulated, however, so that the balance of the system will not be disrupted.

There are other recreational facilities here as well, namely the Olympic Basin created for the rowing competitions of the 1976 Olympics and the **Circuit Gilles-Villeneuve (13)**, where Formula One drivers compete every year in the Grand Prix Molson du Canada, part of the international racing circuit.

To return to downtown Montréal, take the Métro from the Île-Sainte-Hélène station.

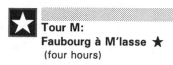

**Tour M:
Faubourg à M'lasse ★**
(four hours)

This neighbourhood, located on the edge of the downtown area, developed at the end of the 18th century when Vieux-Montréal extended eastward. Originally known as "Faubourg Québec," since it ran alongside the road leading to Québec City, it was renamed "Quartier Sainte-Marie" after becoming industrialized, then nicknamed "Faubourg à M'lasse" around 1880, when hundreds of barrels of sweet-smelling molasses started being unloaded every day onto the wharves of the nearby port (*mélasse* is the French word for molasses). In the mid 1960's, civil servants affixed the somewhat unromantic name "Centre-Sud" to the neighbourhood. This was before the homosexual community took it over in 1980 and made it the "Gay Village." Despite its many names, Faubourg à M'lasse is a place with a profound soul, that has always been marked by poverty and life on the fringe. Occasionally ugly and in poor taste, it is teeming with life and proves engaging if given a little time.

The Faubourg is divided into three zones of varying size from north to south: the port and industrial area, almost impassable on foot since Autoroute Ville-Marie was built between 1974 and 1977; the *Cité des Ondes* or on-air city, home to Radio-Canada, whose 1970 construction led to the demolition of a third of the neighbourhood, and finally Rue Sainte-Catherine, where visitors will find a large concentration of cafés, discothèques and bars.

From the Berri-UQAM métro station, head east on Rue Sainte-Catherine.

The numbers following the names of attractions refer to the map of Faubourg à M'lasse.

In 1979, the **Galeries Dupuis (1)** *(in front of Place du Quartier Latin, Berri-UQAM Métro)* replaced the Dupuis Frères department store, the French-Canadian counterpart of stores like Eaton and Ogilvy in the western end of Montréal. The section of Rue Sainte-Catherine around Rue Saint-Hubert was, moreover, considered the commercial hub of French-Canadian Montrealers up until the mid 20th century. The complex of shops at the Galeries Dupuis also includes Les Atriums, a multi-level shopping mall laid out around a hotel, an office building and classrooms belonging to UQAM.

A little farther east, visitors will find the former **Pilon Clothing Store** *(915 rue Sainte-Catherine Est)*. Its protorationalist, stone-frame structure dates back to 1878, making it the oldest commercial building in the neighbourhood. The lovely Art Deco façade at number 916 once belonged to the **Pharmacie Montréal** (1934), the first institution of its type in Québec to make home-deliveries and stay open both day and night.

Montréal's Gay Village starts east of Rue Amherst.

The **Gay Village (2)** *(rue Sainte-Catherine Est, between rue Amherst and avenue Papineau, Berri-UQAM Métro)*. Originally clustered in the "West," along Rue Stanley and Rue Drummond, the gay bars were considered too conspicuous by some local real-estate developers and town councillors. The continual badgering and periodic attempts to "clean house" led bar owners, then renters in the downtown area, to purchase inexpensive buildings in the Centre-Sud in hopes of running their businesses as they pleased. Thus was born the Gay Village, an entirely unique concentration of establishments catering to a homosexual clientele (saunas, bars, restaurants, clothing stores and hotels). Far from being hidden or mysterious, many of these establishments open onto the street with terraces and gardens, during the warm summer months.

The **Ouimetoscope (3)** *(1206 rue Sainte-Catherine Est, Beaudry Métro)*. Film-maker, distributor and theatre owner Ernest Ouimet (1877-1973) pioneered Montréal's film industry. In 1907, he built the Ouimetoscope, the first theatre designed for and devoted exclusively to film in all of Canada. Moved, modernized and recently closed, the Ouimetoscope is no more than a memory now. Immediately east lies the **former Théâtre National** *(1220 rue Sainte-Catherine Est)*, whose pretty little Renaissance Revival style theatre, inaugurated in 1900, is still intact. As indicated on a plaque outside the entrance, this theatre, which once specialized in burlesque and vaudeville, was run for many years by the hilarious Rose Ouellette, known as "La Poune." A few other old theatres dot Rue Saint-Catherine Est on its way to Pont Jacques-Cartier.

Turn right on Rue Beaudry, then left on Boulevard René-Lévesque Est.

From the end of small Rue Beaudry, an oversized structure set like an island in the middle of its parking lot is visible. This is the **Maison de Radio-Canada (4)** *1400 boulevard René-Lévesque Est, Beaudry Métro)*, built between 1970

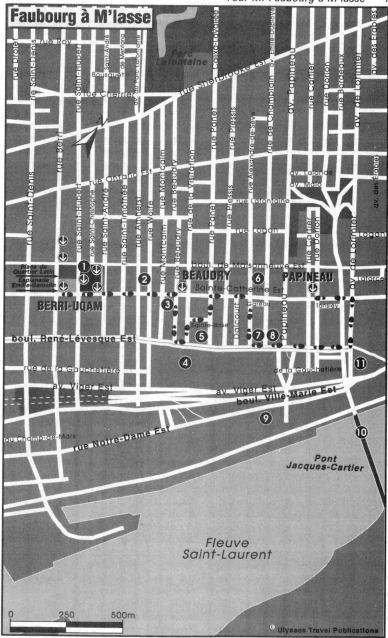

Faubourg à M'lasse

and 1973 according to a design by Scandinavian architect Tore Bjornstad in order to accommodate all of the French services of the CBC, or Canadian Broadcasting Corporation *(Société Radio-Canada* in French), the national radio and television network, as well as the local English-language services. When it was built, the traditional urban fabric of the neighbourhood was completely erased. Six hundred seventy-eight families, nearly 5,000 people, had to be relocated. Already, twenty years earlier, the width of Boulevard René-Lévesque (formerly Dorchester) had been tripled, separating the south part of the neighbourhood from the north.

Église Saint-Pierre-Apôtre ★★ (5) *(1323 boulevard René-Lévesque Est, Beaudry Métro)* is part of the monastery of the oblate fathers, who settled in Montréal in 1848, thanks to the assistance of Monseigneur Ignace Bourget. The building, completed in 1853, is a major work of Quebecois Gothic Revival architecture, as well as prolific architect Victor Bourgeau's first project in this style. Notable elements include the flying buttresses, exterior supports for the walls of the nave, rarely used in Montréal, and the spire, which measures 70 m at its tallest point, an exceptional height for the time. The finely decorated interior reveals a number of other uncommon elements, such as the limestone pillars separating the nave from the side aisles, here in a land where church structures were usually made entirely of wood. Some of the stained glass windows from the Maison Champigneule in Bar-le-Duc, France, merit careful examination, including the 9m tall St. Peter in the Choir.

Walk up Rue de la Visitation, then turn right on little Rue Sainte-Rose. On the way, visitors will pass alongside the neoclassical presbytery of Saint-Pierre-Apôtre and the former buildings of the Maîtrise Saint-Pierre, a choir school and priests' residence, which has been converted into a community centre. Rue Sainte-Rose is a picturesque street, lined to the north with a series of working-class homes with mansard roofs. It has preserved part of its appearance of days gone by. Since 1975, a number of neighbourhood houses have been restored by executives and artists working at nearby Radio-Canada.

Turn left on Rue Panet, then right on Rue Sainte-Catherine. Then cross small **Rue Dalcourt**, a secondary street between two main arteries patterned after London's mews. It is lined with cramped housing, intended in the past for the poorest workers. In 1982, Rue Dalcourt was redesigned by the City of Montréal as part of its *Place au Soleil* (Place in the Sun) program.

Télé-Métropole (6) *(at the corner of rue Alexandre-de-Sève, Papineau Métro)* occupies an entire block of the neighbourhood. Founded in 1961 by Alexandre-de-Sève, this private television network out-rated Radio Canada among working-class viewers for many years. Some of the network's studios are located inside the former Théâtre Arcade and the Pharmacie Gauvin (1911), a handsome four-story building made of glazed white terra cotta *(1425 rue Alexandre-de-Sève)*. Télé-Métropole, along with Sonolab, Radio-Canada, Radio-Québec, CJMS and Téléglobe, forms a veritable *Cité des Ondes* (on-air city) in eastern Montréal.

Turn right on Rue Alexandre-de-Sève. The red brick building on the left, preceded by a neighbourhood park, is the former École Sainte-Brigide (1125 rue Alexandre-de-Sève, Papineau Métro), opened by the Frères des Écoles Chrétiennes in 1895. It was converted into a retirement home in 1989.

Église Sainte-Brigide ★ (7) (1153 rue Alexandre-de-Sève, Papineau Métro). The high concentration of Catholic workers in Faubourg à M'lasse at the end of the 19th century, combined with the competition still being waged between the bishopric and the Sulpicians at that time, justified the 1878 construction of a second church only a few hundred metres from Église Saint-Pierre-Apôtre, described above. Église Sainte-Brigide was designed by architect Louis-Gustave Martin (Poitras et Martin) in the Romanesque Revival style then advocated by the Sulpicians. The interior of the church, which belongs to a now moribund parish, has undergone few changes since its construction, and contains lovely lamps dating back to the end of the 19th century, as well as a jumble of dingy plaster statues, serving as eloquent witnesses of better days.

Walk east on Boulevard René-Lévesque.

The Cathedral of St. Peter and St. Paul ★ (8) (1151 rue de Champlain, Papineau Métro) is Montréal's Russian Orthodox Cathedral. The building, a former Episcopal church, was erected in 1853. Those who attend the Sunday Mass can see a lovely collection of icons and a treasure from Russia, and listen to the spellbinding chants of the choir.

The Molson Brewery is visible from Boulevard René-Lévesque Est. Those wishing to visit it should be very careful crossing the busy streets of the area. The brewery's entrance hall contains

enlargements of photographs from the company archives, as well as a souvenir shop. Across the street, a monument commemorates the Accommodation, the first steamship launched on the St-Laurent by the Molson family (1815).

The Molson Brewery (9) (1650 rue Notre-Dame Est; organized tours available) was opened back in 1786 in the Faubourg Québec by an Englishman named John Molson (1763-1836). It would later become one of the most important businesses in Canada. This brewery, reconstructed and enlarged many times, still stands alongside the port. The Molsons, for their part, remain one of the pillars of Montréal's upper class. Involved in banking (see p 58), construction, rail transport and shipping, the family has never deviated from its first rule of conduct, which is to innovate constantly. At the beginning of the 19th century, a bourgeois neighbourhood with an Anglican church and market square (Avenue Papineau) all surrounded the brewery. The last signs of those years disappeared when Autoroute Ville-Marie was built in 1974.

Immediately to the east, are the former facilities of Canadian Rubber (1840 rue Notre-Dame Est), a firm specializing in rubber processing, in particular the manufacture of tires (Uniroyal). Its Second Empire style buildings on Rue Notre-Dame, erected in 1874, have been abandoned for many years.

Continue eastward on Boulevard René-Lévesque. Go under Pont Jacques-Cartier, then turn right onto Avenue de Lorimier. Cross at the corner of Avenue Viger in order to reach the head office of the Société des Alcools du Québec, located inside Montréal's former penitentiary, better known by its former name, Pied-du-Courant.

Pont Jacques-Cartier (10) was inaugurated in 1930. Up until then, the Pont Victoria, completed in 1860, was the only means of reaching the Rive-Sud (South Shore) apart from taking a ferry. Pont Jacques Cartier also made it possible to link Parc de l'Île Sainte-Hélène (see p 127) directly to the central neighbourhoods of Montréal. It was a true nuisance to build, because the city councillors couldn't agree on a plan that would make it possible to avoid demolishing all sorts of buildings. It was finally decided that the bridge should be curved on its way into Montréal, earning it the nickname *le pont croche* (the crooked bridge). Even today, this curve is the source of a great many headaches for the thousands of motorists who take the bridge every day to go to work.

Prison du Pied-du-Courant ★★ (11) *(2125 Place des Patriotes, Papineau Métro)* is thus named (literally, "Foot-of-the-Current") because it is located in front of the river, at the foot of the Sainte-Marie current, which used to offer a certain amount of resistance to ships entering the port. Built between 1830 and 1836 according to plans by George Blaiklock, it is a long, neoclassical cut stone building with a gate made of the same material. It is the oldest public building still standing in Montréal. In 1894, a house for the prison warden was added at the corner of Avenue de Lorimier. In 1912, the last prisoners left Pied-du-Courant, which became the head office of the *Commission des Liqueurs*, the liquor commission, in 1922. Over the years, annexes and warehouses were added to the old, forgotten prison. Between 1986 and 1990, however, the Québec government proceeded to demolish the

additions and restore the prison, rekindling old memories of tragic events that took place shortly after it was opened.

It was within these walls that 12 of the *Patriotes* who participated in the armed rebellion of 1837-38, an attempt to emancipate Québec, were executed. One of these was the Chevalier de Lorimier, after whom the neighbouring street was named. Five hundred others were imprisoned here before being deported to the penal colonies of Australia and Tasmania in the South Pacific. A handsome **Monument to the Patriotes** by Alfred Laliberté stands on the grounds of the former prison. The Gothic Revival style warden's residence now houses the S.A.Q.'s reception rooms.

To return to Rue Sainte-Catherine, head north on Avenue de Lorimier, then turn left toward the Papineau Métro station.

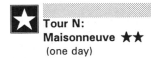

Tour N:
Maisonneuve ★★
(one day)

In 1883, the city of Maisonneuve was founded in the east part of Montréal, installations expanded into the area, promoting its development. Then, in 1918, the formerly autonomous city was annexed to Montréal, becoming one of its major working-class neighbourhoods, with a 90% Francophone population. In the course of its history, Maisonneuve has been profoundly influenced by men with grand ideas, who wanted to make this part of the country a place where people could thrive together. Upon taking office at the Maisonneuve town hall in 1910, brothers Marius and Oscar Dufresne

instituted a rather ambitious policy of building prestigious Beaux-Arts style public buildings, intended to make "their" city a model of development for French Québec. Then, in 1931, Frère Marie-Victorin founded Montréal's Jardin Botanique (botanical garden) in Maisonneuve; today, it is the second largest in the world. The last major episode in the area's history was in 1971, when Mayor Jean Drapeau initiated construction on the immense sports complex used for the 1976 Olympic Games.

From the Pie-IX Métro station, climb the hill leading to the corner of Rue Sherbrooke Est.

The numbers following names of attractions refer to the map of Maisonneuve.

The **Jardin Botanique** and **Insectarium** ★★★ (1) *(admission to the greenhouses and Insectarium, adults $7; mid-Jun to beginning of Sep, open every day 8:30 a.m. to 7 p.m.; mid-May to mid-June and beginning of Sep to mid-Oct, Mon to Fri 9 a.m. to 5 p.m., Sat and Sun to 6 p.m.; mid-Oct. to mid-May 9 a.m. to 4:30 p.m.; 4101 rue Sherbrooke Est, ☎ 872-1400).* The Jardin Botanique, covering an area of 73 ha, was begun during the economic crisis of the 1930's on the site of Mont-de-La-Salle, home base of the brothers of the Écoles Chrétiennes. Behind the Art Deco building occupied by the Université de Montréal's institute of biology, visitors will find a stretch of 10 connected greenhouses, which shelter, notably, a precious collection of orchids and the largest grouping of bonsais and *penjings* outside of Asia. The latter includes the famous Wu collection, given to the garden by master Wu Yee-Sun of Hong Kong in 1984.

Thirty outdoor gardens, open from spring through autumn, and designed to inform and amaze visitors, stretch to the north and west of the greenhouses. Particularly noteworthy are the symmetrical display gardens around the restaurant, the Japanese garden and its *sukiya* style tea pavilion, as well as the very beautiful Chinese *Lac de Rêve* garden, whose pavilions were designed by artisans who came here from China specifically for that purpose. Since Montréal is twinned with Shanghai, it was deemed appropriate that it should have the largest garden of this type outside of Asia.

The complementary **Insectarium** *(☎ 872-8753)* is located to the east of the greenhouses. This innovative, living museum invites visitors to discover the fascinating world of insects.

Return to Boulevard Pie-IX. The Musée des Arts Décoratifs stands on the west side of the street, immediately south of Rue Sherbrooke Est.

The **Musée des Arts Décoratifs** ★★ (2) *(adults $3; Wed to Sun 11 a.m. to 5 p.m.; 2929 rue Jeanne-d'Arc, ☎ 259-2575)* has been housed since 1979 in the Château Dufresne, which is in fact two, 22-room bourgeois residences behind the same façade. The château was built in 1916 for brothers Marius and Oscar Dufresne, shoe-manufacturers and authors of a grandiose plan to develop Maisonneuve. The plan was abandonned after the onset of World War I, causing the municipality to go bankrupt. Their home, designed by Marius Dufresne and Parisian architect Jules Renard, was supposed to be the nucleus of a residential upper-class neighbourhood, which never materialized. It is one of the best examples of Beaux-Arts architecture in Montréal.

The museum's entrance is located at the back of the building, and leads into the basement. This floor serves as an exhibition space, where visitors can see International style (1935 to the present day) furniture and decorative objects from the Liliane and David Stewart collection, as well as travelling exhibitions on glass, textiles, etc. The main floor still appears as it did in the time of the Dufresnes. The atmosphere of a comfortable residence owned by affluent industrialists is tangible in these rooms, with their varied styles, ranging from a Moorish smoking room to a Louis XVI-Ritz drawing room. A number of them are adorned with murals by artist Guido Nincheri, author of several church and cinema decors in Montréal. These unusual works depict scenes from contemporary life (people dressed in 1918 fashions, a Christmas celebration around the tree), rather than the standard mythological scenes and overfed cherubs.

Go back downhill on Boulevard Pie-IX, then turn left on Avenue Pierre-de--Coubertin.

The **Stade Olympique** ★★★ **(3)** *(adults $7; guided tours in French at 11 a.m. and 2 p.m., and in English at 12:40 p.m. and 3:40 p.m.; closed Jan to mid-Feb; 4141 avenue Pierre-de--Coubertin, ☎ 252-8687)* is also known as the Olympic Stadium and the "Big O". Jean Drapeau was mayor of Montréal from 1954 to 1957, and from 1960 to 1986. He dreamt of great things for "his" city. Endowed with exceptional powers of persuasion and unfailing determination, he saw a number of important projects through to a successful conclusion, including the construction of Place des Arts and the Métro, Montréal's hosting of the World's Fair in 1967 and, of course, the 1976 Summer Olympics. For this

last international event, however, it was necessary to equip the city with the appropriate facilities. In spite of the controversy this caused, the city sought out a Parisian visionary to design something completely original. A billion dollars later, the major work of architect Roger Taillibert, who also designed the stadium of the Parc des Princes in Paris, stunned everyone with his curving, organic concrete shapes. The 60,000-seat oval stadium is covered with a retractable kevlar roof supported by cables stretching from the 190 m leaning tower. Because of the canvas's expensive upkeep and short life span, the *Régie des Installations Olympiques* (R.I.O. Olympic Installations Board) wants to build a permanent roof, to be installed by the end of 1995. In the distance, visitors will see the two pyramid shaped towers of the Olympic Village, where the athletes were housed in 1976. Every year, the stadium hosts different events, such as the Salon de l'Auto (Car Show) and the Salon National de l'Habitation (National Home Show). From April to September, Montréal's baseball team, the Expos, plays its home games here. A **funicular** *($7; Sep to mid-Jun, 10 a.m. to 6 p.m.; mid-Jun to Aug, Mon to Thu 10 a.m. to 9 p.m., Fri to Sun 10 a.m. to 11 p.m.)* takes visitors to the top of the tower, which commands a full panoramic view of the eastern part of Montréal.

The foot of the tower houses the swimming pools of the Olympic Complex, while the former cycling track, known as the Vélodrome, located nearby, has been converted into an artificial habitat for plants and animals called the **Biodôme** ★★★ **(4)** *(adults $8.50; open every day 9 a.m. to 6 p.m.; mid-Jun to beginning of Sep, to 8 p.m.; 4777 avenue Pierre de Coubertin;*

☎ 868-3000). This new type of museum, associated with the Jardin Botanique, contains four very different ecosystems—the Tropical Rainforest, the Laurentian Forest, the St-Laurent Marine Ecosystem and the Polar World—within a space of 10,000 m². These are complete microcosms, including vegetation, mammals and free-flying birds, and close to real climatic conditions. Be careful not to catch a cold!

Return to Boulevard Pie-IX, and head south.

ÉgliseSaint-Jean-Baptiste-de-LaSalle(5) *(at the corner of Rue Hochelaga)* was built in 1964 within the context of the Vatican II liturgical revival. In an effort to maintain its following, members of the Catholic clergy cast aside traditions and introduced an audacious style of architecture, that still, however, did not enable them to accomplish their goal. The evocative mitre-like exterior conceals a depressing interior made of bare concrete, which seems to be falling onto the congregation.

Continue south on Boulevard Pie-IX, then turn left on Rue Ontario.

The **Ancien Hôtel de Ville ★ (6)** *(4120 rue Ontario Est)*. In 1911, the Dufresne administration kicked off its policy of grandeur by building a city hall, designed by architect Cajetan Dufort. From 1926 to 1967, the building was occupied by the *Institut du Radium*, which specialized in cancer research. Since 1981, the edifice has served as the Maison de la Culture Maisonneuve, one of the City of Montréal's neighbourhood cultural centres. On the second floor, a 1915 bird's-eye view drawing of Maisonneuve shows the prestigious buildings

completed at the time, as well as those that remained only on paper.

Built directly in line with Avenue Morgan in 1914, the **Marché Maisonneuve ★ (7)** *(Place du Marché)* is in keeping with a concept of urban design inherited from the teachings of the École des Beaux-Arts in Paris, known as the City Beautiful movement in North America. It is a mixture of parks, classical perspectives and civic and sanitary facilities. Designed by Cajetan Dufort, the market was the most ambitious of Dufresne's projects to be completed. The centre of Place du Marché is adorned with an important work of sculptor Alfred Laliberté, entitled *La Fermière* (The Woman Farmer). The market closed in 1962, then partially reopened in 1980.

Follow Avenue Morgan.

Although it is small, the **Bain Morgan ★ (8)** *(1875 avenue Morgan)*, a bath house, has an imposing appearance, due to its Beaux-Arts elements—a monumental staircase, twin columns, a balustrade on the top and sculptures by Maurice Dubert from France. There is also another bronze by Alfred Laliberté, entitled *Les Petits Baigneurs* (The Little Swimmers). Originally, people came to the public baths not only to relax and enjoy the water, but also to wash, since not all houses in working-class neighbourhoods such as this were equipped with bathrooms.

In 1977, the former *Cinéma Granada* was converted into a theatre, and renamed **Théâtre Denise Pelletier (9)** *(4353 rue Sainte-Catherine Est)* after one of the great actresses of the Quiet Revolution, who died prematurely. The terra cotta façade is decorated in the Italian Renaissance style. The original interior (1928), designed by Emmanuel

Briffa, is of the "atmospheric" type, and has been partially preserved. Above the colonnade of the mythical palace encircling the room, is a black vault that used to be studded with thousands of stars, making the audience feel as if they were attending an outdoor presentation. A projector was used to create images of moving clouds and even airplanes flying through the night.

Parc Morgan (10) *(at the southernmost end of avenue Morgan)* was laid out in 1933 on the site of a Henry Morgan's country house, owner of the stores of the same name. From the cottage in the centre there is an interesting perspective on the Marché Maisonneuve silhouetted by the enormous Olympic Stadium.

Follow Rue Sainte-Catherine Est west to Avenue Létourneux, and turn left.

Maisonneuve boasted two firehouses, one of which had an altogether original design by Marius Dufresne. He was trained as an engineer and businessman, but also took a great interest in architecture. Impressed by the work of Frank Lloyd Wright, he designed the **Caserne de Pompiers no 1 ★ (11)** *(on the south side of Rue Notre-Dame)*, or fire station, as an adaptation of the Unity Temple in Oak Park, on the outskirts of Chicago (1906). The building was therefore one of the first works of modern architecture erected in Canada.

Turn right on Avenue Desjardins. Due to the unstable ground in this part of the city, some of the houses tilt to an alarming degree.

Behind the somewhat drab Romanesque Revival façade of the **Église du Très-Saint-Nom-de-Jésus ★ (12)** *(at the corner of rue Adam)*, built

in 1906, visitors will discover a rich, polychromatic decor, created in part by artist Guido Nincheri, whose studio was located in Maisonneuve. Particularly noteworthy are the large organs built by the Casavant brothers, divided up between the rear jube and the chancel, very unusual in a Catholic church. Since this building stands on the same shifting ground as the neighbouring houses, its vault is supported by metal shafts.

 Tour O: Little Burgundy and Saint-Henri ★
(four hours)

These two working-class sections of Montréal were both autonomous municipalities in the past. The city of Saint-Henri-des-Tanneries and Little Burgundy, then officially known as the City of Sainte-Cunégonde, were however annexed by Montréal in 1905. Saint-Henri was founded at the end of the 18th century around the Rolland family's tannery, which no longer exists (it was located at the corner of Chemin Glen and Rue Saint-Antoine). After the opening of the Canal de Lachine in 1825, the little town grew significantly, with industries clustering in its southern portion, around the canal. Little Burgundy's prosperity was also ensured by the industries along the canal, as well as by rail transport, since the town was crossed by a series of railroad tracks leading up to the Gare Bonaventure on Rue Peel (destroyed in 1952). The tracks were dismantled during the 1970's to make way for housing, the suburban appearance of which does not fit in with the rest of the neighbourhood at all.

From the Georges-Vanier Métro station, head to the boulevard of the same name. Both honour the memory of General Georges-Philias Vanier (1888-1971), governor general of Canada from 1959 to 1967. His son Jean founded L'Arche, an organization providing assistance to the mentally challenged in Trosly-Breuil, in northern France. *Turn right onto little Rue Coursol.*

The numbers following the names of attractions refer to the map of Little Burgundy and Saint-Henri.

Rue Coursol (1) is lined with charming single-family row houses, built around 1875 for foremen and semi-skilled workers at the factories in Sainte-Cunégonde. The Second Empire style stone residences on Rue Saint-Antoine Ouest, farther north, were occupied by the local noteworthy residents and certain shop owners. Since Sainte-Cunégonde was located near the downtown train stations (Bonaventure and Windsor), a number of houses on these two streets later became boarding houses for railway employees, mainly those who worked on the trains (waiters, packers, cooks, etc.). Before 1960, most of these employees were Black. Little Burgundy was thus identified with this community from the late 19th century on, although there was never a Black majority in the neighbourhood. These individuals, who came here from the United States between 1880 and 1900 in hopes of a better future, contributed greatly to the history of music in Montréal. In fact, Little Burgundy was the birthplace of celebrated jazz pianist Oscar Peterson, as well as the location of a famous cabaret, Rockhead's Paradise, which opened in 1928 at the corner of Rue Saint-Antoine and Rue de la Montagne, and where Louis Armstrong and Cab Calloway played and sang regularly (closed in 1984).

Turn left on Rue Vinet. On the corner lies the former **St. Jude's Church** *(2390 rue Coursol),* now the Bible-Way Pentecostal Church (1878, Goodwin and Mann, architects).

Église Sainte-Cunégonde ★ (2) *(2641 rue Saint-Jacques),* at the corner of Rue Saint-Jacques, is a large Catholic Beaux-Arts style church, designed by architect Jean-Omer Marchand in 1906. The building has a remarkable rounded chevet, as well as an ingenious roof with a single-span steel framework, that makes it possible to open up the spacious interior, which is completely free of columns and pillars. Decorated with lovely woodwork and vibrantly coloured remounted paintings, shown off to advantage by the natural light coming through the large windows, the interior was damaged when the church was closed in 1971. The building was scheduled to be demolished, but was fortunately saved at the last moment, and is now used, notably, for traditional Catholic services, given in Latin.

Take Rue Vinet to Rue Notre-Dame Ouest.

The **former Hôtel de Ville of Sainte-Cunégonde (3)** *(in front of Parc Vinet),* erected at the end of the 19th century, also served as a post office, a firehouse and a police station. Famous strong man Louis Cyr was a member of the local police force for several years.

Turn right on Rue Notre-Dame Ouest. The part of the street between Rue Guy to the east and Rue Atwater to the west is nicknamed the *rue des antiquaires* (antique street), due to the presence of about thirty shops dealing

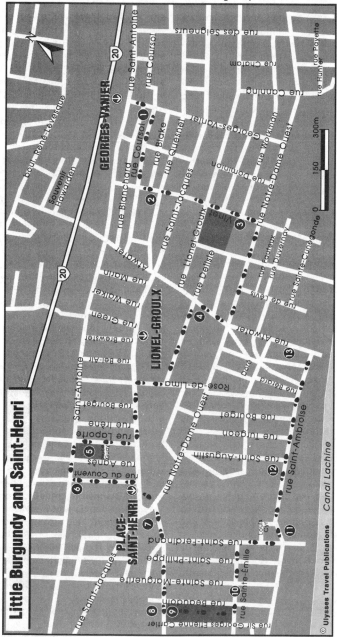

Little Burgundy and Saint-Henri

in secondhand goods and, in some cases, local antiques (especially Victorian and Art Deco style furniture). These shops, where all sorts of treasures lay hidden, are set up inside handsome 19th century commercial buildings, all located on the south side of the street. Behind these sprawl the dilapidated factories along the Canal de Lachine. Some of these were converted into housing complexes during the 1980's. At number 2490 Rue Notre-Dame Ouest, visitors can see the façade of the **former Cinéma Corona** (1912), whose interior is still intact (closed to the public).

Turn right on Avenue Atwater.

Église Saint-Irénée (4) *(3030 rue Delisle)* is one of those churches whose copper bell towers, coated with verdigris, pierce through the low skyline of Montréal's working-class neighbourhoods. It was built in 1912, incorporating a portion of the walls of an earlier church, built in 1904 and burned in 1911. Its cramped interior is the work of architects MacDuff and Lemieux. Particularly noteworthy are the exaggerated curves of the arches and the typical Belle Époque motifs used in the decoration.

Saint-Henri starts on the west side of Avenue Atwater. Head west on Rue Delisle. The Union United Church, dating back to 1899, stands on the corner. Turn right on Rue Rose-de-Lima, left on Rue Saint-Jacques and, finally, right on Avenue Laporte.

Square Saint-Henri ★ (5) *(between avenue Laporte, Place Guay, rue Agnès and rue Saint-Antoine)*. As in Sainte-Cunégonde, Saint-Henri's upper-class neighbourhood lies along Rue Saint-Antoine. The beautiful Square Saint-Henri, adorned with a cast iron fountain topped with a statue of Jacques Cartier (1896), served as a gathering point for the municipality's affluent residents. Mayor Eugène Guay, who was responsible for laying out these areas, also had a residence built for himself in front of the square, at number 846 Rue Agnès, in 1902. The house was recently converted into a pleasant bed and breakfast.

Turn left on Rue Saint-Antoine, then left again on Rue du Couvent.

Église Saint-Henri (6) *(872 rue du Couvent)*. When the venerable Église Saint-Henri was demolished in 1969, the French-Canadian Catholic parish of Saint-Henri was relocated to this little church on Rue du Couvent, originally used by the St. Thomas Aquinas English Catholic community. Erected in 1923, it is an Italianized Baroque Revival style building by architect Joseph-Albert Karch. The stained glass inside is particularly lovely.

Continue southward on Rue du Couvent, then turn right on Rue Saint-Jacques to reach Place Saint-Henri, which is centred around the Métro station of the same name.

The once remarkable **Place Saint-Henri (7)** has been altered beyond recognition. In an unbridled attempt at modernization, the college, school, convent and church, whose Renaissance Revival style façade fronted on the north side of the square, were torn down in 1969-70 and replaced by a high school and a public pool, concealed behind a blind brick wall. This grouping faces away from the square, which grew up naturally at the railroad crossing of Rue Saint-Jacques and Rue Notre-Dame (the train station was located nearby), which, at the end of the 18th century, was the main route to the west part of the island of Montréal.

Only a few buildings have survived the wave of changes that took place in 1960's. These include the Art Deco **fire station**, built in 1931 on the site of the former town hall of Saint-Henri; the **Caisse Populaire** *(4038 rue Saint-Jacques Ouest)*, or credit union, which occupies the former post office and the **Banque Laurentienne** *(4080 rue Saint-Jacques Ouest)*. The latter building used to belong to the Banque d'Épargne de la Cité et du District de Montréal, whose branches across Montréal display a quality of architecture worthy of special mention.

Cross the square to return to Rue Notre-Dame-Ouest. Turn right on this street and continue walking to Église Saint-Zotique.

Église Saint-Zotique (8) *(4565 rue Notre-Dame Ouest)* was erected in stages between 1910 and 1927 for the least affluent parish in Saint-Henri. This explains the brick facing on the church, a less expensive material than stone. The Baroque Revival style steeples rises up from a structure not unlike the industrial buildings along the nearby Canal de Lachine. The neighbouring *caisse populaire* oddly resembles some sort of futuristic spaceship.

Square Sir-Georges-Étienne-Cartier ★ (9) *(rue Notre-Dame Ouest, in front of Église Saint-Zotique)* honours the memory of one of the Fathers of Canadian Confederation. It was among the improvements approved by the city of Montréal, to clean up the neighbourhood and improve the city's bad reputation, as we shall see a little further on. In 1912, this green space surrounded by typical Montréal triplexes replaced the Saint-Henri

slaughterhouses, whose putrid stench had permeated the entire area. The pretty cast iron fountain in the middle of the square is particularly interesting.

Cross the square and head east on Rue Sainte-Émilie. Turn right on Rue Saint-Ferdinand.

Rue Sainte-Émilie (10) is lined with typical 19th century working-class houses. Saint-Henri, like Sainte-Cunégonde and Pointe-Saint-Charles, corresponds to the lower town of Montréal, which, before 1910, was among the poorest areas in North America. Infant mortality was four times higher here than elsewhere on the continent. The workers lived in poverty, enveloped in pollution and at the mercy of destructive fires and infectious diseases. In 1897, local reformist Herbert Browne Ames published *The City Below the Hill*, a work that stands out in the history of urban renewal movements. It revealed to the world at large the decrepit state of Montréal's working-class neighbourhoods at the end of the 19th century. Today, renovation and social assistance programs have put some order back into the local streets, but Saint-Henri's future nevertheless remains uncertain, since its aging industrial facilities have led to the closing down of a number of the factories that provided local families with a living. As if to exaggerate the contrast between the upper and lower city, the hill of Westmount, surrounded by large, luxurious residences shrouded in greenery, is visible to the north if you look straight down most of the streets intersecting with Rue Sainte-Émilie.

Turn left on Rue Saint-Ambroise, which runs alongside the Canal de Lachine.

For many years, the **factory of the Merchants Manufacturing Company (11)** *(4000 rue Saint-Ambroise)* was the main employer in Saint-Henri. Purchased by Dominion Textile in the early 20th century, it was used for the manufacture of fabric, blankets, sheets and clothing. A great many women worked in the factory, which, in 1891, was the scene of the first textile strike in Montréal. The long, low building, erected in 1880, is a good example of late 19th century industrial architecture, characterized by large glass windows and staircase towers crowned with brick cornices.

On **Rue Saint-Augustin (12)** *(immediately east of the railroad tracks serving the factories along the Canal de Lachine)*, visitors will find some of Saint-Henri's oldest houses, lived in for many years by the poorest local families. Of modest size, they are made of wood (some recently covered with aluminum siding). The Maison Clermont *(110 rue Saint-Augustin)*, dating back to 1870, was admirably restored in 1982, and provides a good idea of what this type of working-class dwelling looked like when it was new. It was from these houses with their backs against the railroad tracks that Canadian novelist Gabrielle Roy drew her inspiration for her famous novel *Bonheur d'Occasion (The Tin Flute*, 1945).

Take Rue Saint-Ambroise to Marché Atwater.

Marché Atwater ★ (13) *(110 avenue Atwater, Lionel-Groulx Métro)* is one of the only two public markets in Montréal still open all year round, the other being Marché Jean-Talon (see p 124). Farm-fresh fruits and vegetables are sold outside during summer and fall, while the interior specialty shops selling meat, cheese and fish are open all year long. The market was built in 1932 as part of the job creation programs initiated during the economic crisis of 1929. Designed by architect Ludger Lemieux, it is an elegant Art Deco style building.

Head north on Avenue Atwater in order to reach the Lionel-Groulx métro station, erected on the Sainte-Cunégonde railroad tracks.

 Tour P: Pointe-Saint-Charles and Verdun ★
(four hours)

The actual point of Pointe-Saint-Charles was named by fur traders Charles LeMoyne and Jacques LeBer, to whom the piece of land was first granted. They sold it to Marguerite Bourgeoys, who built the Ferme Saint-Gabriel for the Sœurs de la Congrégation de Notre-Dame here in 1668. The location's pastoral nature was greatly disrupted by the construction of the Canal de Lachine between 1821 and 1825, which attracted various types of mills to the area, turning it into the cradle of the Canadian Industrial Revolution. The village of Saint-Gabriel grew up on Saint-Charles point, south of the factories. With the construction of Pont Victoria, between 1854 and 1860, and the laying-out of various railroad installations near the St-Laurent, Saint-Gabriel developed into a veritable little city.

The Irish, omnipresent on the construction sites of these two major projects, settled in large numbers in Saint-Gabriel and other villages farther east (Griffintown, Sainte-Anne and Victoriatown), of which, unfortunately,

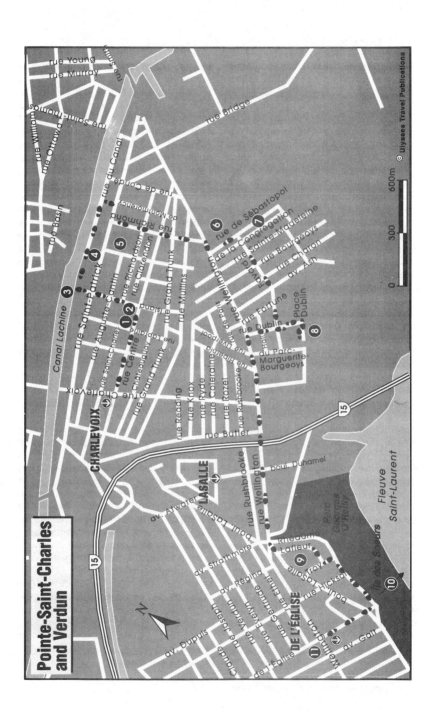

Pointe-Saint-Charles and Verdun

rue Young
rue Murray
rue Saint-Thomas
rue Ottawa
rue William
rue Basin
rue Bridge
Canal Lachine
rue de Condé
rue du Canal
de Montmorency
rue Richmond
rue de Sébastopol
③
④
⑤
rue Saint-Patrick
rue Auguste-Cantin
rue Richardson
rue Clarendon
rue Grand Trunk
rue Mullins
⑥
rue de la Congrégation
⑦
rue Sainte-Madeleine
rue Bourgeoys
Favard
rue Charon
av. Ash
① ②
rue Centre
rue de l'Église
rue Sainte-Charles
rue Châteauguay
rue Grand Trunk
rue Fortune
rue Dublin
Place Dublin
⑧
CHARLEVOIX ↺
rue Charlevoix
rue Reading
rue Knox
rue Ryde
rue Coleraine
rue Rozel
rue Liverpool
rue Wellington
rue Sébastopol
rue Butler
du Parc-
Marguerite-
Bourgeoys
rue Rushbrooke
15
LASALLE ↺
av. Atwater
rue LaSalle
rue Rushbrooke
rue Wellington
boul Duhamel
Fleuve
Saint-Laurent
15
av. Strathmore
av. Regina
av. Dupuis
Claude
rue Joseph
rue Verdun
rue Evelyn
rue Ethel
rue Galt
rue Rielle
rue Gertrude
rue de l'Église
boul LaSalle
rue Hickson
rue Willibrord
⑨
Rhéaume
Lafleur
Troy
Elliot
Parc
Georges-O'Reilly
Île des Sœurs
⑩
DE L'ÉGLISE ↺
⑪
av. Galt
N

© Ulysses Travel Publications

0   300   600m

only a few traces remain. The village of Saint-Gabriel was annexed by Montréal in 1887 and renamed Pointe-Saint-Charles. Though it is located near the downtown area, it is separated from it by the canal and a number of highways, and bisected by railroad tracks. It boasts a rich heritage from the Industrial Revolution. Today, Pointe-Saint-Charles resembles a working-class area whose aging production facilities can barely generate any more jobs. A few factories have been converted into housing complexes, while the area along the Canal de Lachine, closed in 1959, has been transformed into a linear park with a pleasant bicycle path. Verdun, located to the west, has a more recent history. Many descendants of Irish Catholic immigrants, mixed with French Canadians, took up residence there in the period between the two World Wars.

Head east on Rue Centre from the Charlevoix Métro station. This tour can also easily be completed by bicycle, starting from the bike path alongside the Canal de Lachine.

The numbers following the names of attractions refer to the map of Pointe-Saint-Charles and Verdun.

Saint-Gabriel Church(1) *(2157 rue Centre, Charlevoix Métro).* Victims of a dreadful famine caused by potato blight, the Irish fled their island in large numbers to seek refuge in Canada. The sick and very weak, however, did not make it past Grosse Île, downriver from Québec City. Those able to overcome illness went to work on the colonial building sites, forming an inexpensive, unskilled workforce. These people lived in poverty for many years. Their first medieval-looking wooden houses, built in Victoriatown (also known as Village aux Oies), have been torn down and replaced in the name of progress.

Église Saint-Gabriel was built in 1893 by the Irish Catholic community of Pointe-Saint-Charles. At the same time, a French-Canadian Catholic church was being constructed on the neighbouring piece of land. In fact, the two imposing buildings were built side by side according to designs by the same architects (Perrault and Mesnard), thus creating an unusual sight that makes Montréal truly worthy of the nickname "city of a hundred steeples." The original interior decoration of Église Saint-Gabriel was destroyed by fire in 1959. It was replaced by a minimalist decor, that highlights the building's thick rubble stone walls. Next to the church, is a lovely Romanesque Revival style presbytery with Queen Anne details.

Église Saint-Charles ★ (2) *(2125 rue Centre, Charlevoix Métro),* by architects Perrault and Mesnard, was consumed by flames in 1913. The following year, it was rebuilt according to the plans of architects MacDuff and Lemieux, who preserved its Romanesque Revival style appearance. The interior, with its columns painted with imitation marble patterns, is worth a short visit. The presbytery of the parish of Saint-Charles is, unlike that of Église Saint-Gabriel, a symmetrical building whose design was influenced by the École des Beaux-Arts.

Turn left on Rue Island. Cross Rue Saint-Patrick to reach the Parc du Canal de Lachine. Be very careful crossing the bike path, where cycling enthusiasts sometimes ride at high speeds; do not stop here thinking it is a pedestrian trail.

The **Canal de Lachine** ★ *(3) (on the southwest part of the island of Montréal, between Vieux-Montréal and Lachine, Charlevoix Métro).* In the 17th century, a farm owned by the Messieurs de Saint-Sulpice, then seigneurs of the island of Montréal, occupied the entire northern part of Pointe-Saint-Charles. In 1689, the Sulpicians, anxious to develop their island, began digging a canal next to Rivière Saint-Pierre, which bordered their property. Their goal was to bypass the famous Rapides de Lachine, a hindrance to navigation on the St-Laurent upriver from Montréal. These visionary priests, perhaps too ambitious for their time, launched the project before even asking permission from their order or obtaining funds from the king, both of which they were later denied. The enterprise was thus suspended until 1821, when work was begun on the present canal. Enlarged twice afterward, it was used until the opening of the seaway in 1959. The Canadian Parks Service purchased the canal and its banks in 1979.

Walk eastward along the canal in order to enjoy the view of the industrial buildings and the skyscrapers in the business centre.

The water in the canal was used not only for navigation, but also as a source of power. The machines in the **former Belding-Corticelli silk mill** ★ *(4) (1790 rue du Canal, Charlevoix Métro)* was one of the establishments that ran on hydraulic energy. The red brick building has a cast iron structure. It was erected in 1884, and has since been renovated to make room for appartment lofts. The abandoned former buildings of the Redpath sugar refinery, founded by John Redpath in 1854, stand a little farther along. Redpath, a native of Berwickshire,

Scotland, had 17 children and was one of McGill University's principal donors.

Head back to Rue Saint-Patrick by walking through the residential complex at the former Belding-Corticelli mill, and cross over one of the few arms of the canal that have not been filled in. Turn left on Rue Saint-Patrick, then right on Rue Richmond, which runs alongside the former Northern Electric factory.

The **former Northern Electric factory (5)** *(rue Richmond and rue Richardson, Charlevoix Métro)* houses the Nordelec business "incubator." Dozens of little clothing and contemporary furniture manufacturers share the same secretarial services, as well as the advice of marketing specialists, thereby reducing the start-up expenses and making it possible to avoid costly errors while manufacturing the goods or placing them on the market. The huge, monolithic edifice was built between 1913 and 1926 for the Northern Electric Company which manufactured everyday electrical appliances here The company is now known as Northern Telecom. Across the street is the *Société des Alcools du Québec*'s (Québec liquor commission), distribution centre for restaurants and bars, as well as the old **Caserne de Pompiers no 15**, fire station, erected in 1903 in a vaguely Romanesque Revival style *(72 rue Richardson).*

Continue heading south on Rue Richmond. In the area around Rue Mullins, there are some good examples of the residential working-class architecture of Pointe-Saint-Charles. Some houses have even retained their original fenestration. Turn right on Rue Wellington, which passes under the viaduct for the railroad tracks leading up to the Canadian National workshops. Turn left on small Rue de

Sébastopol and continue alongside the marshalling yard. The street was built in 1855, when the Crimean War, marked by the siege of Sebastopol (Ukraine), was raging in Europe.

The Canadian National workshops (6) *(east of rue de Sébastopol, Charlevoix Métro)* used to belong to the Grand Trunk Railway *(Grand-Tronc* in French), a company founded in London in 1852 with the aim of developing railroads in Canada. It merged with Canadian Northern Railway in 1923 to form Canadian National. The Grand Trunk Railway was behind the construction of the Pont Victoria, and built its repair shops near the exit of the bridge in 1856.

The Grand Trunk houses (7) *(422 to 444 rue de Sébastopol, Charlevoix Métro)* are among the earliest examples of North American housing specially designed by a company for its workers. These "company houses," inspired by British models, were built in 1857 according to plans by Robert Stephenson (1803-1859), engineer and designer of Pont Victoria and son of the inventor of the steam engine. Of the seven houses designed by Stephenson, each containing four apartments, only about half remain, while the others are in a sad state of disrepair.

From Rue de Sébastopol, take Rue Favard. Like the neighbouring streets, Rue Favard is lined with diverse examples of residential working-class architecture. Particularly interesting are the patterns of the brick, the woodwork and the terra cotta inlays. The names of the streets indicate that this is an area once owned by the Sœurs de la Congrégation de Notre Dame. The nuns' lands were gradually sold off in lots, which explains why the neighbourhood seems newer as you approach the Saint-Gabriel farmhouse. Turn left at Place Dublin.

Ferme Saint-Gabriel ★★ (8) *(2146 Place Dublin, Charlevoix or LaSalle Métro)* offers precious evidence of what daily life was like in New France. The farmhouse and nearby barn, now surrounded by the city, were built between 1662 and 1698. Marguerite Bourgeoys purchased the entire property from the Le Ber family in 1668 as a place of residence for the Dames de la Congrégation de Notre-Dame, a religious community founded by her in 1653. The house later served as a school for young Amerindian girls and as accommodations for the *Filles du Roy.* These were young women with no families, whom Louis XIV sent from Paris to Montréal to find husbands amongst the men here. In 1964, the house was restored and opened to the public. Since then, it has housed displays of 17th and 18th century objects belonging to the community. The building itself is of great interest, as it has, notably, one of the only authentic 17th century roof frames in North America, as well as rare sinks made of black stone.

Head north on Place Dublin, and then along the street of the same name. Turn left onto Rue Wellington. Here, visitors will find two Gothic Revival style brick churches dating back to the end of the 19th century *(625 rue Fortune and 2183 rue Wellington)*, Art Deco style public baths, built during the economic crisis of the 1930's *(2188 rue Wellington)* and a row of Victorian houses designed around 1875 by the architect of Montréal's City Hall, Henri-Maurice Perrault.

It takes about ten minutes to reach Verdun on foot. Walk along Rue Wellington to Boulevard La Salle. Take a left on Avenue Lafleur, where there are some rare examples of exterior staircases that wind all the way up to the third floor of several triplexes and quadruplexes.

Vieux-Verdun (9) *(east of avenue Willibrord, De l'Église Métro).* Verdun is an autonomous municipality with about 60,000 inhabitants. Its history began in 1665, when eight militiamen settled alongside the river, west of the Ferme Saint-Gabriel. These armed colonists, nicknamed *"les Argoulets,"* were nevertheless massacred by the Iroquois. In 1671, the territory was granted to Zacharie Dupuys, a native of Saverdun, near Carcassone, who named it Verdun in memory of his former village. Between 1852 and 1865, the channel of the aqueduct of Montréal was dug in the northern portion of Verdun. A village emerged south of the aqueduct, but its development was slowed by frequent spring floods. Once a dyke was built alongside the river (1895), its growth accelerated. Today, 97% of Verdun is urbanized. The city contains a large number of buildings typical of Montréal, as well as an astonishing variety of charming loggias.

Avenue Lafleur runs into Avenue Troy. In the thirties and forties, many families from the Îles de la Madeleine were attracted to this area by the jobs offered at the nearby Hôpital du Christ-Roi. In those years, nurses were required to be fully bilingual, since the hospital served a population that was half anglophone and half francophone. At the time, the *Madelinots*, as natives of the Îles de la Madeleine are known, were among the only people in Québec capable of expressing themselves easily in both of Canada's official languages. One of the entrances to Parc Therrien, which runs alongside the St-Laurent, is located at the end of Rue Troy. From inside the park, visitors can enjoy a lovely view of the skyscrapers of downtown Montréal to the east and the residential high-rises of Île des Sœurs to the south. Île des Sœurs proves extremely interesting for contemporary architecture buffs. Anyone wishing to go there should, however, make a separate trip, as the island is difficult to reach from Verdun, even though it is part of the municipality. (To go there by car, head east on Rue Wellington, then take Highway 20 toward Pont Champlain until the Île des Sœurs Exit).

Île des Sœurs ★ (10) *(in the Fleuve St-Laurent),* literally Nun's Island, was purchased by the Dames de la Congrégation de Notre-Dame in 1676. They named it Île Saint-Paul. Around 1720, a large stone manor and various farm buildings were erected on the northern part of the island. After the nuns left in 1956, the buildings were destroyed by fire. The island passed into the hands of an important developer, who laid out the first streets and built three residential high-rises (on Boulevard de l'Île des Sœurs, southwest of Rue Corot), designed in 1967 by the celebrated German architect Ludwig Mies van der Rohe, who also drew up the plans for the elegant service station near Rue Berlioz (1968). The more recent projects carried out on Île des Sœurs have been more or less worthy of interest. The best include the yellow brick houses on Rue Corot, designed in 1982 by architect Dan Hanganu, and the housing in the L'Isle development (Chemin du Golf and Chemin Marie-LeBer), the work of architect and professor Aurèle Cardinal.

Walk westward along Parc Therrien to the Auditorium de Verdun, then take Avenue de l'Église to Rue Wellington.

Église Notre-Dame-des-Sept-Douleurs ★ (11) *(4155 rue Wellington, De l'Église Métro)* is one of the largest parish churches on the island of Montréal. It was built between 1907 and 1914 according to plans by Joseph Venne. The Baroque Revival style interior is particularly interesting. A handsome Art Deco style bank (1931) stands across the street.

The nearby De L'Église Métro station, is on the same line as the Charlevoix station.

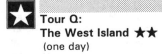

**Tour Q:
The West Island ★★**
(one day)

The only real riverside tour on the island of Montréal, this visit to the West Island will allow visitors to discover old villages and the loveliest panoramic views of the St-Laurent, Lac Saint-Louis and Lac des Deux-Montagnes. Although a number of the towns that make up the West Island were founded by French colonists, many now have an anglophone majority. Therefore, do not be surprised to hear the language of Shakespeare more often than that of Molière in the shops and along the residential streets, not unlike those found in affluent American suburbs.

This is not considered an urban walking tour, since it covers nearly 12 km. It can, however, be enjoyed on bicycle, because a good part of the excursion runs along either a well laid-out bike path or streets with low speed limits. It

is possible to reach the starting point of the tour by following the Canal de Lachine bike path from Vieux-Montréal. Visitors should then take Rue Charlevoix to Rue Wellington and continue until Rue Marguerite-Bourgeoys, which leads to Place Dublin. By car, take Highway 20 west, to the Lasalle Exit and follow the signs for Avenue Lafleur. Turn right on Avenue Lafleur, then left on Boulevard Lasalle, which follows the river all the way to Lachine.

■ Lachine ★★
(pop. 35,266)

In 1667, the Messieurs de Saint-Sulpice granted some land in the west part of the island of Montréal to explorer Robert Cavelier de La Salle, who, obsessed with the idea of finding a passage to China, finally discovered Louisiana at the mouth of the Mississippi. Montrealers mockingly referred to his land as *La Chine* (China), a name that later became official. In 1689, the inhabitants of Lachine were victims of the worst Iroquois massacre of the French Regime. However, instead of leaving the area, the population grew. Two forts were built to protect Lachine, strategically located upriver from the rapids of the same name, which at the time still hindered shipping on the St-Laurent. Consequently, the precious furs from the hinterland destined for the European market had to be unloaded at Lachine and transported by land to Montréal, located down river from the rapids. In the years following the opening of the Canal de Lachine in 1825, many industries set up shop in Lachine, leading to an important period of urbanization. Today, its aging industry is fortunately counterbalanced by an enchanting location that still

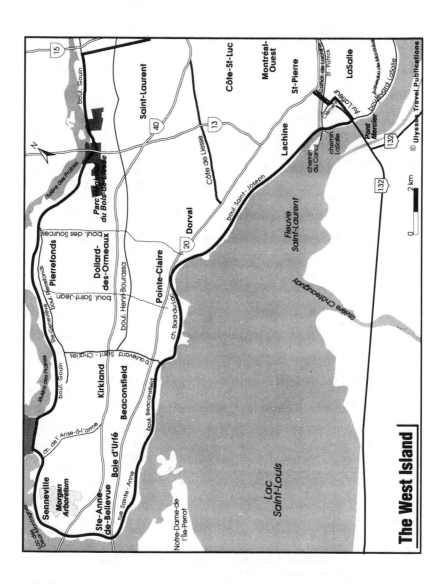

The West Island

charms and attracts enthusiastic residents.

The **Moulin Fleming** *(free admission; May, Jun and Sep, Thu to Mon 1 p.m. to 6 p.m.; Jul and Aug, Wed to Mon 12 p.m. to 8 p.m.; in Parc Stinson,* ☎ 367-1000). Although located within the limits of the city of LaSalle, this mill is closely linked to the development of Lachine, to which it used to belong. Built in 1816 for a Scottish merchant, it is cone-shaped like American mills. An exhibition tells its history.

Fort Rémy, one of the two fortified enclosures in Lachine, stood nearby. The former factory of the Burrows-Wellcome pharmaceutical company, visible to the west, now serves as the Hôtel de Ville of La Salle.

Take Boulevard LaSalle to Chemin du Musée. Turn left to reach the parking lot of the Musée de Lachine, which faces Chemin LaSalle.

Musée de Lachine ★ *(free admission; Apr to end of Nov, Wed to Sun 11:30 a.m. to 4:30 p.m.: 110 chemin LaSalle,* ☎ *634-3471 ext. 346).* Erected in 1670, this former trading post and its fur warehouse, perforated with loopholes for its defence, are the oldest extant structures in the entire Montréal region. At the time of their construction, Lachine was the last inhabited area in the valley of the St-Laurent before the wild regions to the west. It was also the final destination of cargos of fur, for many years, Canada's main natural resource and the true reason for being of the French colonies in North America. The building was erected for Jacques LeBer and Charles LeMoyne, two wealthy Montréal merchants. Since 1948, it has served as a historical museum, as well as an art gallery, where contemporary works by local artists are exhibited.

Take Chemin LaSalle, in front of the museum. Turn right on Chemin du Canal, then left on Chemin du Musée, which turns into Boulevard Saint-Joseph.

Three narrow, man-made spits of land make up the **mouth of the Canal de Lachine** ★★ *(Parc Monk)*, which resembles a sprawling estuary widening at the end. Majestic Lac Saint-Louis extends beyond **Parc René-Lévesque**, accessible from Chemin du Canal. The park is scattered with a number of contemporary sculptures, including *Les Forces Vives* by Georges Dyens, in homage to the former premier of Québec after whom the park is named. The Lachine Yacht Club occupies the second strip of land, while the **Promenade du Père Marquette** and **Parc Monk** lie between the original entrance of the canal, opened in 1825, and the 1848 widening. It is on this last spit of land that visitors will find the **Centre d'Accueil et d'Interprétation du Canal de Lachine**, information centre *(free admission; mid May to beginning of Sep, Tue to Sun 10 a.m. to 12 p.m. and 1 p.m. to 6 p.m.)*.

The centre recounts the history of the canal, which enabled ships to bypass the Rapides de Lachine on their way to the Great Lakes and the middle of the continent (see p 154). The canal, now replaced by the Voie Maritime du Saint-Laurent (the seaway), on the south shore of the river, is closed to ships. The other end of this artificial waterway is found in the Vieux-Port, opposite Vieux-Montréal.

By following the Promenade du Père Marquette, visitors can reach the Lieu

Historique National du Commerce-de-la-Fourrure-à-Lachine.

The **Lieu Historique National du Commerce-de-la-Fourrure-à-Lachine** ★ *(free admission; end of Mar to mid Oct, Tue to Sun 10 a.m. to 12 p.m. and 12:30 p.m. to 6 p.m., closed Mon mornings; mid Oct to mid Dec, Tue to Sun 10 a.m. to 12 p.m. and 1 p.m. to 5 p.m.; closed mid Dec to end of Mar; 1255 boulevard Saint-Joseph, ☎ 637-433).* For nearly two centuries, the fur trade was the main economic activity in the Montréal region. Lachine played a crucial role in the transport of pelts to the European market—so much so that the Hudson's Bay Company made it the centre of its operations. The National Historic Site occupies the company's former warehouse, erected in 1803. Various objects and examples of furs and clothing made with these pelts are on display. Temporary exhibits also explore the lives of the trappers or *voyageurs*, the Amerindian tribes who, in the 17th century, caught most of the animals, as well as the heads of powerful French and English companies, who were engaged in a bitter struggle for a monopoly on this lucrative trade.

Continue heading west on Boulevard Saint-Joseph.

The **Couvent de Lachine** ★ *(1250 boulevard Saint-Joseph).* In 1861, the sisters of Sainte-Anne purchased a house built in 1833 for Sir George Simpson, then head of the Hudson's Bay Company. They built their mother house, and then a convent school for young girls, around the original building. This building was later demolished and replaced in 1889, with an imposing, Russian-style chapel topped with a silvery dome, designed by architects Maurice Perrault and

Albert Mesnard. The interior of the chapel, reminiscent of a Victorian concert hall, is worth a short visit.

Behind the convent, visitors will find St. Stephen's Anglican Church *(25 12e Avenue)*, built in 1831 to serve the executive personnel of the Hudson's Bay Company. The humble, vaguely Gothic Revival style building, made of rubble stone, contrasts with the immense Catholic church located nearby.

Up until 1865, the Catholic church of Lachine was located farther east, in the enclosure at Fort Rémy. That year, a French Gothic Revival style church was inaugurated on the present site, in the centre of the town. Unfortunately, a violent fire destroyed the church in 1915. The present **Église des Saints-Anges Gardiens** *(1400 boulevard Saint-Joseph)* was erected on the ruins of the former one in 1919, according to plans by architects Dalbé Viau and Alphonse Venne. The Romanesque Revival style edifice is one of the largest parish churches located outside the city of Montréal.

St. Andrew's United Church, once Presbyterian, is located near the Catholic church, west of 15e Avenue. It was built in the Gothic Revival style in 1832, according to a design by John Wells. Its bell tower was damaged by fire a few years ago. At 1560 Boulevard Saint-Joseph, visitors will see the lovely residence of the church's pastor, the Reverend Doctor, whose openings are framed by small, neoclassical columns (1845). The municipal library nearby was recently renamed Saul Bellow Library in honour of this famous writer who is a Lachine native.

The **Vieille Brasserie Dawes** ★ *(2801 boulevard Saint-Joseph)* (not to be confused with the Dow Brewery) opened in Lachine in 1811 to provide beer for trappers and traders passing through. The company closed in 1922 after the merger of several small regional breweries. The facilities, among the oldest of their kind in North America, can nevertheless still be found on either side of Boulevard Saint-Joseph. On the lake side, visitors will see the brewery (two rubble stone buildings erected around 1850), as well as the home of Thomas Amos Dawes, son of the company founder, built in 1862 *(2901 boulevard Saint-Joseph)*. This lovely Victorian residence now serves as Lachine's cultural centre. The great ice house, converted into apartments (1878), and the old warehouse, located at the end of 21e Avenue (circa 1820), lie on the city side. The remains of the working-class neighbourhood centred around the brewery completes this grouping, which is of exceptional anthropological value.

Continue westward on Boulevard Saint-Joseph.

A monument reminds visitors that **Fort Rolland** *(west of 34e Avenue)*, the main trading post in Lachine in the 17th century, was once located on this site. Military troops were stationed here to ensure the protection of local inhabitants and supervise the transshipment of precious cargos of fur. On their way past, visitors can see some lovely houses dating back to the French Regime, including the Maison Quesnel *(5010 boulevard Saint-Joseph)*, built around 1750, and the Maison Picard *(5430 boulevard Saint-Joseph)*, erected in 1719.

Once in the city of Dorval, Boulevard Saint-Joseph is known as Lakeshore Drive, sometimes awkwardly translated as Chemin du Bord-du-Lac, but it remains essentially the same road.

■ **Dorval**
(pop. 17,249)

In 1691, Sieur d'Orval purchased La Présentation, a fort established by the Sulpicians in 1667, from the estate of Pierre Le Gardeur of Repentigny, and named it after himself. Later, from 1790 to 1821, small Dorval island, located opposite the city, became the point of departure of the Northwest Company's *coureurs des bois* and *voyageurs*, who travelled to the Outaouais and Great Lakes regions in search of beaver pelts each year. Nowadays, Dorval is a comfortable suburb of Montréal, known mainly for its airport. It is still possible to find old farmhouses here, carefully restored by Anglo-Saxon families who know how to appreciate the decorative elements of Québec's French heritage.

The stone walls at the base of the **Maison Frederick Barlow** *(900 chemin du Bord-du-Lac)*, are supposedly those of the Sulpicians' Fort de La Présentation, erected in the 17th century. At number 940, visitors can see the **Maison André Legault, dit Deslauriers**, with its decorative firebreak walls (1817). Before being carefully restored by architect Galt Durnford in 1934, it was the summer home of Lord Strathcona, one of Canadian Pacific's principal shareholders.

The **Maison Minnie Louise Davis** *(1240 chemin du Bord-du-Lac)*, built in 1922, reveals the interest certain architects of British descent and their clients took in traditional Québec architecture between the two World Wars. These individuals even went so far as to build new homes in the style of the 18th century. Percy Nobbs, a professor of architecture at McGill University, drew up the plans for the Davis house, which its owner called "Le Canayen" (*Le Canadien*, or The Canadian, as pronounced with a heavy Quebecois accent).

The **Maison Brown** *(1800 chemin du Bord-du-Lac)*. A number of sporting clubs once favoured by Montréal's Anglo-Saxon bourgeoisie are located in Dorval, including the Royal Montreal Golf Club, the oldest golf club in North America (it was founded in 1873), and the Royal St. Lawrence Yacht Club, founded in 1888, whose facilities may still be seen alongside Lac Saint-Louis. The strangest of these clubs, however, is without question the Forest and Stream Club, which occupies the former villa of Alfred Brown, erected in 1872. Though still in existence, the organization has seen better days. Back in the 1920's, tea was served to dozens of people in its gardens on Saturday and Sunday summer afternoons.

Continue to Pointe-Claire.

■ **Pointe-Claire** ★
(pop. 27,640)

One of the first missions established by the Sulpicians along the periphery of the island of Montréal, Pointe-Claire has become a comfortable suburb, that has nevertheless preserved the core of its original village. Up until 1940, Chemin du Bord-du-Lac, which leads through the municipalities on the West Island, from Lachine to Sainte-Anne-de-Bellevue, passing through Pointe-Claire on the way, was the only route for motorists travelling from Montréal to Toronto.

Stewart Hall *(open every day 2 p.m. to 5 p.m., Mon and Wed 2 p.m. to 5 p.m. and 7 p.m. to 9 p.m.; 176 chemin du Bord-du-lac, ☎ 630-1220)* is a rather long house, built in 1915 for industrialist Charles Wesley MacLean, according to a design by Robert Findlay. Since 1963, it has served as Pointe-Claire's cultural centre, and is therefore open to the public, offering visitors a chance to see its interior and enjoy unobstructed views of Lac Saint-Louis from its back porch, a pleasure previously reserved for its owner alone.

Built back in 1710, the small **Maison Antoine-Pilon** *(258 chemin du Bord-du-Lac)* is the oldest house in Pointe-Claire. A recent restoration has given it back its former appearance.

Turn left on Rue Sainte-Anne to reach Pointe Claire (the actual point), extending into Lac Saint-Louis. The institutional buildings of the traditional village are clustered here.

Église Saint-Joachim, the mill and the convent ★ *(1 rue Saint-Joachim)*. The Gothic Revival style church (1882) has an extremely original steeple that dominates the entire institutional grouping. It is one of the last buildings designed by Victor Bourgeau, architect of dozens of churches in the Montréal area. Its flamboyant, polychrome wooden interior, decorated with numerous statues, is worth a short visit. The convent of the Sœurs de la Congrégation de Notre-Dame was built in 1867 on the southern portion of the windswept point. The mill, which could not have been built in a better spot, was erected in 1709 by the Messieurs de Saint-Sulpice.

Return to Chemin du Bord-du-Lac and head toward Beaconsfield and Baie d'Urfé. These two municipalities form the heart of anglophone West Island. They also, however, include a number

of old properties once owned by great French-Canadian families.

Jean-Baptiste de Valois, a direct descendant of the French royal family, settled in Canada in 1723. His son, Paul Urgèle Gabriel, built **Le Bocage** ★ *(26 Lakeshore Drive, Beaconsfield)* in 1810. Houses with cut stone façades were extremely rare in rural areas in the early 19th century, and this one thus indicated the special status of the owner of the residence. In 1874, Le Bocage was sold to Henri Menzies, who converted the property into a vineyard. The experiment was a pitiful failure, due to the unproductive soil and, above all, the location's exposure to warm and cold winds alike. Menzies was more successful naming the estate Beaconsfield, in honour of British prime minister Disraeli, made Lord Beaconsfield by Queen Victoria. Then, from 1888 to 1966, the house was used by a private club, before becoming the lodge of the Beaconsfield Yacht Club.

■ **Sainte-Anne-de-Bellevue** ★
(pop. 4,030)

Just like Lachine, Sainte-Anne-de-Bellevue has a more or less compact centre, compressed along the panoramic road that now takes on the name Rue Sainte-Anne. Here, visitors will find numerous boutiques and a number of restaurants, most of which have pleasant terraces looking out on the water behind the buildings. The houses on Île Perrot are visible across the water. The village owes its

existence to the lock, today used by pleasure crafts to pass from Lac Saint-Louis to the very beautiful Lac des Deux-Montagnes, into which the Rivière des Outaouais (Ottawa River) flows. Just east of the old village, visitors will find a comfortable suburb and institutions such as the military hospital, Macdonald College and John Abbot College, an anglophone *cégep*.

Macdonald College ★ *(21111 chemin du Bord-du-Lac)*. Arriving in Sainte-Anne-de-Bellevue, visitors will be surprised to see a whole series of English Baroque Revival style buildings faced with orange-coloured brick, surrounding a vast, closely trimmed lawn. Erected between 1905 and 1908, they are part of the Macdonald Campus of McGill University's Department of Agriculture. Some of the buildings belong to the John Abbott College *CÉGEP*, the only educational institution of this level west of Collège de Saint-Laurent. At the **Experimental Farm** *(free admission, guided tours $2.75; open every day 2 p.m. to 5 p.m.; from Montréal, take Highway 40 West, Exit 41, and follow the signs for Chemin Sainte-Marie, turn left at the first stop, then left again at the second stop; ☎ 398-7701)*, visitors can see a number of animals bred on the farm. The gardens and Morgan Arboretum (see p 166, 168, 169), complete the facilities and are open to the public.

The mission of the **Ecomuseum** *(adults $4; open every day 9 a.m. to 5 p.m., arrive before 4 p.m.; from Montréal, take Highway 40 West, Exit 41, and follow Chemin Sainte-Marie; 21125 chemin Sainte-Marie; ☎ 457-9449)* is to familiarize the public with the flora and fauna of the St-Laurent. In a large, well-laid out park, visitors can see several different animal species, including the fox and the black bear. There is also an aviary for aquatic birds.

Around 1960, the **Maison Simon Fraser** *(153 rue Sainte-Anne)* was scheduled for demolition in order to make way for the ramp of the bridge on Highway 20. It was saved by a historical society, but the bridge, built a few years later, passes less than 5 m from the house, occupied sporadically by Simon Fraser in the early 19th century. This Montréal merchant was one of the heads of the Northwest Company, which specialized in fur trading.

It was here that Irish poet Thomas Moore (1779-1852) stayed during his trip to North America in 1804, and composed his famous *Canadian Boat Song*, in memory of the *voyageurs* who passed through Sainte-Anne-de-Bellevue on their way to the forests of the Canadian shield. The house now serves as a non-profit café run by the Victorian Order of Nurses, a charitable organization founded in the 19th century to provide assistance to the sick in their homes.

This is the western tip of the island of Montréal, 32 km from the eastern extremity at Pointe-aux-Trembles, and about 16 km from downtown Montréal. Running alongside the **lock** *(mid May to mid Oct; 170 rue Sainte-Anne* ☎ *457-5546)*, is a pleasant promenade where the doors of the lock can be observed opening and closing as well as the chambers filling with water and crowded with the boats of *marins d'eau douce* (literally, fresh-water sailors, a term for amateurs) and their Sunday afternoon captains. A tiny beach and a picnic area lie nearby. Église Sainte-Anne (1853-1875) and the convent face the lock north of the bridges.

Follow the curve of Rue Sainte-Anne, then turn left on Chemin Senneville. This road passes through Senneville, the most rural of all the municipalities on the island of Montréal. As a matter of fact, it is here that visitors will find the last farms on the island, as well as a number of large properties on the shores of Lac des Deux-Montagnes. The country setting lends itself marvellously well to cycling excursions. The road then leads through Pierrefonds, where two important regional parks are located.

Parc Régional de L'Anse-à-l'Orme see "Outdoor Activities" section, p 166, 169.

Parc Régional du Cap-Saint-Jacques see "Outdoor Activities" section, p 166, 167, 168, 169.

At Pierrefonds, Chemin Senneville becomes Boulevard Gouin, from here it keeps this name across the entire Montréal territory.

■ **Sainte-Geneviève** ★
(pop. 3,197)

The old village of Sainte-Geneviève is a francophone enclave in the city of Pierrefonds. Its origins date back to 1730, when a small fort was built here to defend the portage of the Rapides du Cheval-Blanc on Rivière des Prairies, which ran alongside the village. In the 19th century, the *cajeux*, robust fellows who floated logs down the river toward Québec, where the largest shipyards were then located, used to stop in Sainte-Geneviève. They then made rafts (called *cages*, hence their name) with the logs, in order to pass through the many rapids along Rivière des Prairies. Starting in 1880, this method of floating logs was gradually replaced by rail transport.

Église Sainte-Geneviève ★★ *(16037 boulevard Gouin Ouest)* is the only building designed by the Baillargé family in the Montréal region. Thomas Baillargé designed the church in 1836, giving it an imposing neoclassical façade with two bell towers, and thereby influencing the architecture of Catholic churches across the entire region during the 1840's and 1850's. The interior was inspired by a since vanished church in Rotterdam, by the architect Guidichi. Of particular interest are the tabernacle and the tomb of Ambroise Fournier, as well as the painting in the choir, entitled *Sainte-Geneviève*, by Ozias Leduc. The church is flanked by the convent of Sainte-Anne and the presbytery, and has outdoor Stations of the Cross made of bronzed cast iron, executed by the *Union Artistique de Vaucouleurs* in France.

Just like the church, the **Maison d'Ailleboust-de-Manthet** *(15886 boulevard Gouin Ouest)* is neoclassical in style. It was built in 1845 and occupied by the d'Ailleboust de Manthet family, one of the great French-Canadian families of the 18th and 19th centuries, whose members won renown in both military and civilian spheres on a number of occasions. *(Closed to the public)*.

At the bend in the road, visitors will see the Lombard style **former Monastère Sainte-Croix ★** *(15693 boulevard Gouin Ouest)*, which looks as if it came straight out of the Middle Ages. It was in fact built for the fathers of Sainte-Croix in 1932, according to plans by talented architect Lucien Parent. The cloister, in the centre, is a haven of peace and serenity. Since it was sold in 1968, the building has been used as an alcohol rehabilitation centre, known as the Centre Dom-Rémy.

Continue on Boulevard Gouin. After crossing the eastern portion of Pierrefonds, the road leads through Roxboro and then on to Montréal. At the meeting point of these two municipalities, there are two regional parks, Parc Régional du Bois-de-Liesse and Parc Régional du Bois-de-Sanaguay.

Parc Régional du Bois-de-Liesse see "Outdoor Activities" section, p 166, 167.

Turn right on Boulevard O'Brien, then take the fork in the road leading to Boulevard Sainte-Croix, the last leg on this tour.

■ **Saint-Laurent ★**
(pop. 72,402)

The residential part of Saint-Laurent is concentrated on a fifth of the municipality's territory. All the rest is monopolized by a huge industrial park, making it the second largest city in Québec from that standpoint. Saint-Laurent developed inland after the signing of the peace treaty with the Iroquois tribes in 1701. The arrival of the Fathers, Brothers and Sisters of Sainte-Croix in 1847, encouraged by Monseigneur Ignace Bourget, the second bishop of Montréal, made it possible for the village to grow, dominated by the institutions of this community from Le Mans, France.

The former convent school of the Sisters of Sainte-Croix, the **Pensionnat Notre-Dame-des-Anges** *(821 boulevard Sainte-Croix)*, was founded in 1862, while the modern chapel by architect Gaston Brault, was added in 1953. A wing of the building was once occupied by Collège Basile-Moreau, one of the only institutions in Québec to offer higher education in French to young women before the Quiet Revolution. In 1970, the convent became Vanier College, an anglophone *CÉGEP*.

The design of **Église Saint-Laurent ★** *(805 boulevard Sainte-Croix)*, built in 1835, was inspired by Montréal's Église Notre-Dame, inaugurated six years earlier. Unfortunately, both the pinnacles and the decorative battlements of the façade and aisles were removed in 1868. What was the oldest extant Gothic Revival style interior decor in a Catholic church, executed by François Dugal and Janvier Archambault between 1836 and 1845, was spoiled during the frenzied wave of religious revival of Vatican II in the early 1960's.

South of the church, visitors will find the **Chapelle Mariale Notre-Dame-de-l'Assomption**, the presbytery and the former grain warehouse (1810), where parishioners could pay their tithe in the form of grain or other foodstuffs. It now serves as the church hall. In front of it, is a monument commemorating the visit of Monseigneur de Forbin-Janson, the apostle of temperance, to Saint-Laurent in 1841.

When the Fathers and Brothers of Sainte-Croix arrived in Canada in 1847, they were lodged in the house located at number 696 Boulevard Sainte-Croix. In 1852, they moved across the street to their college. The building has been modified and enlarged on several occasions. Over the course of its history, **Collège de Saint-Laurent ★** *(625 boulevard Sainte-Croix, Du Collège Métro station)* has stood out for its avant-garde policies. Accordingly, it did not hesitate to train businessmen at a time when greater importance was

given to the priesthood, law, medicine and the notarial profession. During the 1880's, a biology museum was created here. It was later set up inside an octagonal tower in 1896. That same year, the college built a 300-seat auditorium for the students' theatrical productions. In 1968, as part of the wave of changes of the Quiet Revolution, the college became a *cégep*, and the priests who had founded the institution and directed it for over a century had only a few days to pack their bags.

The **Musée d'Art** and the **Salle Émile-Legault ★★** *(free admission, donations appreciated; Tue to Fri and Sun 12:30 p.m. to 5 p.m., closed Mon and Sat; 615 boulevard Sainte-Croix, Du Collège Métro station, ☎ 747-7367)*. In 1928, the administration of Collège de Saint-Laurent decided to build a new chapel, since the old one was overflowing with students. In the meantime, a graduate of the institution, then president of the executive committee of the City of Montréal, suggested purchasing the Presbyterian Church of St. Andrew and St. Paul (then located on Boulevard René-Lévesque where the Hôtel Reine-Elizabeth now stands) and reconstructing it in Saint-Laurent. The building, expropriated by the Canadian National railway company in 1926, had to be destroyed to make way for the railroad tracks of the Gare Centrale. The project was approved, despite its unusual character.

In 1930-31, the Protestant church, erected in 1866 according to a design by architect Frederick Lawford, was dismantled stone by stone and reconstructed in Saint-Laurent. Lucien Parent made a few modifications to the structure. For example, the basement was raised to make space for a modern auditorium. During the thirties and forties, this room played a large role in the evolution of the arts in Québec, thanks, notably, to the *Compagnons de Saint-Laurent*, a theatre company founded by Père Paul-Émile Legault in 1937, which enabled a number of the province's actors to learn their trade. The chapel, meanwhile, was the scene of numerous concerts. In 1968, however, when the college was transformed into a *CÉGEP*, the building lost its purpose. The Musée d'Art de Saint-Laurent, founded a few years earlier by Gérard Lavallée, was set up there in 1979. It displays collections of tools, traditional fabrics and Québec furniture, as well as a number of 18th and 19th century religious *objets d'art*.

To get back on the highway, take Boulevard Sainte-Croix south to the Highway 40 junction. To return to the centre of Montréal, head south on Chemin Lucerne, turn left on Rue Jean-Talon and then right on Chemin de la Côte-des-Neiges.

The Top Montréal Attractions for Children

■ **Vieux-Montréal**

At the **Vieux-Port**, there is a whole range of activities for children, including SOS Labyrinthe, Expotec, quadricycles and shows where the performers make sure everyone is entertained (see p 64).

At the **Château Ramezay**, children can participate in thematic tours specially designed for them. They learn about various facets of daily life in the time of New France, such as weaving. These educational tours are offered to groups. Reservations required (see p 67).

The **Musée d'Archéologie et d'Histoire de la Pointe-à-Callière** *(adults $7, children free)* offers guided tours adapted for a young audience, and available only to groups. Furthermore, families visiting the museum on Sundays *(from 1 p.m. to 5 p.m.)* can participate in an activity known as *Jeune Découvreur* (Young Discoverer), intended to introduce the public to an archeologist's work (see p 62).

■ **Downtown**

During summer, the **Musée des Beaux-Arts** organizes day camps *(5 days, $140)*, aiming to awaken children's creativity. Accompanied by counsellors, the children visit the temporary summer exhibition on comic strips and then participate in a workshop, where they can create their own artwork, inspired by the tour (see p 70).

During Sunday workshops *(from 1 p.m. to 5 p.m.)* at the **Musée d'Art Contemporain** *(adults $4.75, children free)*, children have the opportunity to learn various techniques used in painting and the plastic arts (see p 79).

In spring and autumn, children are invited to the **Centre Canadien d'Architecture** *(free admission; Sat and Sun 1:30 p.m. to 2:45 p.m.)*, to participate in game sessions in a workshop, where participants can tinker about and build models, among other activities (see p 91).

In order to introduce the very young to the marvellous world of astronomy, the **Planétarium Dow** *(adults $4.50, children $2.50)* has organized a visual presentation entitled *Le Royaume du Soleil* (The Kingdom of the Sun), which deals with subjects such as the solar system and the seasons. This presentation is offered to groups, and reservations are required; when there are extra seats available, the public is also welcome to attend (see p 75).

■ **Maisonneuve**

The **Biodôme** *(adults $8.50, children $4.25)*, with its reconstructed natural habitats (the Fleuve Saint-Laurent, the Amazon forest, the Laurentian forest and the polar world), populated by diverse species of animals, is always a hit with children (see p 139).

The mission of the **Insectarium** is to promote a greater understanding of insects and present a whole assortment of these fascinating and mysterious little beings. Young people also have the opportunity to test their knowledge of entomology by means of interactive games (see p 138).

■ **Ile Sainte-Hélène and Ile Notre-Dame**

The ultimate playground of today's youth, **La Ronde** *(families $40)* amusement park, with its thousand and one incredible games and rides, is sure to please young people with a taste for thrills (see p 130).

■ **The West Island**

The **Lieu Historique National du Commerce-de-la-Fourrure-à-Lachine** presents an exhibition on the lucrative fur trade, which promoted the development of the colony. Everything to capture children's interest and unveil new aspects of a piece of history to them is included, like furs they can touch and interactive games (see p 155).

At Macdonald College's **Ecomuseum**, children can see several specimens of Québec's animal life in their natural environment (see p 158).

OUTDOOR ACTIVITIES

T he island of Montréal is strewn with parks where visitors can enjoy all sorts of activities. Year round, Montrealers take advantage of these small islands of greenery to unwind far from the urban tumult, while remaining right in the heart of the city.

A Few Parks

All year round, Montrealers flock to **Parc du Mont-Royal**, a huge green expanse in the middle of the city, to enjoy a wide range of athletic activities. During summer, footpaths and mountain bike trails are maintained. Bird feeders have been set up along one trail for the benefit of bird-watchers. During winter, the paths serve as cross-country ski trails, leading across the snowy slopes of the mountain, and Lac aux Castors (Beaver Lake) becomes a big, beautiful skating rink, where people of all ages come to enjoy themselves.

Parc des Îles (☎ 872-4537) encompasses both Île Sainte-Hélène and Île Notre-Dame. In summer, Montrealers flock here on sunny days to enjoy the beach and the swimming pools. Footpaths and bicycle trails crisscross the park. In wintertime, a whole host of activities are organized here, including cross-country skiing (14 km), tobogganing, ice fishing and skating on the 2 km long Olympic rowing basin.

Parc Angrignon *(3400 boulevard des Trinitaires)*, **Parc Lafontaine** (see p 103), **Parc Jeanne-Mance** *(avenue de l'Esplanade, between avenue du Mont-Royal and rue Duluth)* and **Parc René-Lévesque** *(at the west end of the Canal de Lachine)* are all very pleasant places to relax in a peaceful atmosphere away from the bustle of the city.

Ecological trails winding through forests of various species of trees traverse the **Morgan Arboretum** *(autoroute 40 Ouest, Exit 41, corner chemin Sainte-Marie and chemin des Pins,* ☎ *398-7811)*. The beautiful diversity of nature is the main attraction, as is the opportunity to discover and learn to identify the different species.

Parc Régional du Cap Saint-Jacques *(20099 boulevard Gouin Ouest,* ☎ *280-6784)* is located on the north shore of the island of Montréal on a point measuring 375 ha, which extends out into Lac des Deux-Montagnes. Its shores are lined with relaxing beaches. Trails and an interpretation centre have been organized to highlight the diversity of the plant and wildlife. An outdoor centre, open year round, offers accommodation and various ecological activities.

Parc Régional du Bois-de-Liesse *(9432 boulevard Gouin Ouest,* ☎ *280-6806)* offers an exceptional variety of wildlife for visitors to admire. It is ideally located amidst hardwood forests and fields of wildflowers. Hiking trails, bike paths and cross-country ski trails help visitors discover the winged and aquatic wildlife that call this park home.

Parc de l'Anse-à-l'Orme *(autoroute 40 Ouest, Exit chemin Sainte-Marie Nord, then follow chemin de l'Anse-à-l'Orme to boulevard Gouin Ouest)* is intended exclusively for windsurfers, as it is swept by exceptional westerly winds. There is also a picnic area.

Covering 188 ha, the **Parc Régional du Bois-de-l'île-Bizard** *(187 chemin du Cap-Saint-Jacques, Pierrefonds,* ☎ *280-6784)* occupies the western extremity of the island of Montréal, and offers mostly ecological activities.

Parc de l'Île-de-la-Visitation *(2425 boulevard Gouin Est,* ☎ *280-6733)* attracts crowds of city-dwellers yearning for nature, who come here to enjoy picnics and walks along the short trails. Washed by the waters of Rivière des Prairies, the park has magnificent scenery. There are also two historic houses here, the **Maison du Pressoir** *(*☎ *280-6783)* and the **Maison du Meunier** *(*☎ *872-5913)*, both of which are open to the public. During winter, people come here to go cross-country skiing and tobogganing.

With an area of 288 ha, the **Parc Régional de la Pointe-aux-Prairies** *(12300 boulevard Gouin Est,* ☎ *280-6767)* offers 10 km of hiking trails, 12 km of bicycle trails and 13 km of cross-country skiing trails. All of these traverse wooded areas and open fields bordering marshlands; observation points are set up beside the latter to observe the many species of birds.

 Bicycle Paths

Cyclists will be thrilled to discover the interesting bicycle paths that traverse the island of Montréal. A map of the paths is available at tourist information offices, or visitors can purchase the *Great Montreal Bike Path-Guide* map in travel bookstores. Below are some of the more picturesque excursions available.

■ The Canal de Lachine

The area around the **Canal de Lachine** has been redesigned in an effort to highlight this communication route, so important during the 19th and early 20th centuries (see p 154). A pleasant bike path was laid out alongside the canal. Very popular with Montrealers, especially on Sundays, the path leads out to **Parc René-Lévesque**, a narrow strip of land jutting out into Lac Saint-Louis, and offering splendid views of the lake and surroundings. There are benches and picnic tables in the park and plenty of seagulls to keep you company. The path leads around the park, returning beside the river and the Rapides de Lachine. Many birds frequent this side of the park, and if you are lucky you might see some great herons.

■ Boulevard Gouin

To the north of the island (accessible via the bicycle path that crosses the island north-south, or by Métro to the Henri-Bourassa station), a bicycle path follows Boulevard Gouin and Rivière des Prairies. It leads to **Parc de l'Île-de-la-Visitation**. Continuing alongside the river, the trail then leads to a very peaceful part of Montréal. It is possible to ride all the way to **Parc Régional de la Pointe-aux-Prairies**, and from there follow the path to Vieux-Montréal, through the southeast part of the city (expect a good half-day).

■ The Islands

Île Notre-Dame and Île Sainte-Hélène are accessible from Vieux-Montréal. The path runs through an industrial area, then through the Cité du Havre before reaching the islands (cyclists cross the river on the Pont de la Concorde). It is easy to ride from one island to the other. The islands are well maintained and are a great place to relax, stroll and enjoy and admire Montréal's skyline.

■ Parc Régional du Bois-de-Liesse

This park is criss-crossed by 8 km of bicycle paths through a hardwood forest.

 Hiking

Parc Régional du Bois-de-Liesse has 12 km of walking trails, some of which are nature interpretaion trails.

Parc Régional du Cap Saint-Jacques offers 27 km of hiking trails through mature maple forests (beech and *caryers*), transitional zones (birch and poplar), as well as vast expanses of varied aquatic and riverside plant life.

Parc Régional de l'Île-de-la-Visitation has 10 km of ecological walking paths.

Right next to downtown, **Parc du Mont-Royal** is an oasis of greenery ideal for hiking and walking.

Parc Régional de la Pointe-aux-Prairies covers a variety of different ecosystems crisscrossed by 12.5 km of hiking trails.

 Birdwatching

Bird feeders have been set up along a special trail in **Parc du Mont-Royal** to attract birds, including cardinals and sometimes pheasants, for the benefit of birdwatchers.

Once a year between the months of October and November, an owl-watching visit to the **Morgan Arboretum**, promising a unique show, is organized. Migrating birds are also commonly seen during this period.

Countless species of birds can be observed along the shores of Lac des Deux-Montagnes in the **Parc Régional du Bois-de-l'Île-Bizard**, particularly American coots and several species of ducks.

More than a hundred species of winged creatures can be observed at the **Parc Régional du Cap Saint-Jacques**, mostly wading birds, birds of prey, and other types of aquatic birds. Wood ducks, eagle owls and red-tailed hawks, among others, take advantage of these natural surroundings.

A good number of birds from over 125 species nest in **Parc Régional de la Pointe-aux-Prairies**.

 Swimming

Neighbourhood swimming pools abound in Montréal. Prices and schedules are subject to change, so it is best to check with the administrative offices before.

Interior pool at the **Cégep du Vieux-Montréal** (free admission; 255 rue Ontario Est, ☎ 872-2644).

Interior pool at the **Centre Claude-Robillard** (free admission; 1000 rue Émile-Journault, ☎ 872-6911).

Interior pool at the **Université de Montréal** (adults $4; 2900 boulevard Édouard-Montpetit, ☎ 343-6150).

Interior pool at **John-Abbott College** (adults $2; 21275 Bord du Lac, Sainte-Anne-de-Bellevue, ☎ 457-2737).

Weston interior pool at **McGill University** (admission $4; 555 B rue Sherbrooke Ouest, ☎ 398-7018).

Currie interior pool at **McGill University** (adults $5; May to Aug; 475 avenue des Pins, ☎ 398-7000).

Interior pool at the **Parc Olympique** (adults $3; 4141 avenue Pierre-de-Coubertin, ☎ 252-4622).

Exterior pool on **Île Sainte-Hélène** (Île Sainte-Hélène, ☎ 872-6093).

The fine sandy beaches bordering Lac des Deux-Montagnes in the **Parc Régional du Cap Saint-Jacques** are a beautiful place to relax and take a dip.

All sorts a water activities can be practised at the beautiful beach of the **Parc Régional du Bois-de-l'Île-Bizard**.

The water at **Île Notre-Dame** beach is naturally filtered, allowing beachgoers to swim in clean, chemical-free water.

 Rafting

Les Descentes sur le Saint-Laurent (beginning of May to end of Oct; 8912 boulevard LaSalle, LaSalle, ☎ 983-3707, ⇄ 466-3933) offer various types of river rides in inflatable boats down the Rapides de Lachine, and are located only minutes from downtown. Along with the river ride, there is a presentation on the history and ecology of the rapids and the bird reserve on Île aux Hérons. A shuttle service is offered free of charge from the Centre Infotouriste and the major hotels in the downtown area.

Expéditions Dans les Rapides de Lachine Ltée *(105 rue de la Commune Ouest,* ☎ *284-9607)* organizes various different excursions on the Rapides de Lachine.

 Sailing

Parc Régional de l'Anse-à-l'Orme is dedicated exclusively to windsurfing.

The **École de Voile de Lachine** *(2105 boulevard Saint-Joseph, Lachine,* ☎ *634-4326)* rents out windsurfers and small sailboats as well as offering private and group lessons.

 Skating

During the winter, a number of public skating rinks are set up to everyone's delight. Among the nicest ones are **Lac aux Castors** (at Parc du Mont-Royal), the rink at **Parc Lafontaine** (between Sherbrooke and Rachel), the rink at the **Vieux-Port** *(333 rue de la Commune Ouest,* ☎ *496-PORT)*, the one at **Parc**

Maisonneuve *(4601 rue Sherbrooke Ouest,* ☎ *872-5558)* and the one at **Parc des Îles** (set up on the Olympic rowing basin on Île Notre-Dame).

 Cross-Country Skiing

Cross-country ski trails leading alongside several species of trees are maintained in the **Morgan Arboretum**. On weekends, during the months of January and February, only members have access.

In winter the 27 km of hiking trails that traverse the **Parc Régional du Cap Saint-Jacques** are transformed into cross-country ski trails and are open to everyone.

The **Parc Régional de la Pointe-aux-Prairies** has 13 km of cross-country ski trails, laid out attractively through the area's abundant vegetation.

Cross-country skiing is possible through the winter plantlife of the **Jardin Botanique**.

Parc du Mont-Royal maintains several well laid-out cross-country trails offering great views of the city.

ACCOMMODATION

Montréal is one of those cities where it is difficult to see everything in one day. We have thus included a number of different kinds of accommodation in this guide, in order to enable visitors to make the most of several days here. The following establishments are listed in the same order as the tours and according to price, starting with the least expensive.

There are hotels and inns in all price ranges in Montréal. Rates vary greatly from one season to the next. Accordingly, during the busy summer season, rooms are more expensive. Furthermore, prices are generally lower on weekends. The weeks of the Formula One Grand Prix and the Festival de Jazz are among the busiest of the year; anyone intending to visit Montréal during this period is therefore advised to reserve far in advance.

The *Fédération des Agricotours* produces an annual publication entitled **Best Bed & Breakfasts in Québec**, which lists the names and telephone numbers of all of its members, who provide rooms for travellers. The rooms offered have been selected according to the federation's standards of quality. They are also fairly economical. The guide is sold in travel bookstores.

Gîte Montréal *(3458 avenue Laval, H2X 3C8,* ☎ *514-289-9749)* is an association of nearly 100 bed & breakfasts (*gîtes*). In order to make sure that all rooms offered are comfortable, the organization visits each one. Reservations required.

About thirty bed & breakfasts are also registered with the **Relais Montréal Hospitalité** *(3977 avenue Laval, H2W 2H9, ☎ 514-287-9635, ⇄ 287-1007)*. All have been carefully inspected, and the rooms are clean and comfortable.

The **Male Accommodation Network** *(☎ 514-933-7571 or 1-800-363-1626)* is an accommodation reservation service for gay visitors to Montréal, which takes each traveller's special needs and budget into consideration.

Vieux-Montréal

Even though Vieux-Montréal is visited by thousands of tourists, it has little to offer in the way of accommodation. There is however, set in the heart of Vieux-Montréal, the **Passants du Sans-Soucy** *($85; 171 rue Saint-Paul Ouest, ☎ 514-842-2634, ⇄ 842-2912)* an extremely pleasant inn, whose charming rooms are furnished with antiques. Reservations required.

Except for one of its wings, the **Hôtel Inter-Continental** *($170; ≈, ⊗, △, ℜ; 360 rue Saint-Antoine Ouest, H2Y 3X4, ☎ 514-987-9900 or 1-800-327-0200, ⇄ 847-8550)*, located on the edge of Vieux-Montréal, is a recent structure. It has an original appearance, due to its turret with multiple windows, where the living rooms of the suites are located. The rooms are tastefully decorated with simple furniture. Each one is equipped with a spacious bathroom, among other nice touches. Guests are courteously and attentively welcomed.

Downtown and the Golden Square Mile

The **Auberge de Jeunesse** *($15 per person; 3541 rue Aylmer, H2X 2B9, ☎ 514-843-3317)*, or youth hostel, located a stone's throw from the downtown area, is one of the least expensive places to sleep in Montréal. It has a number of rooms, including a few doubles, for a total of about 100 beds.

During summer, it is possible to rent a room in one of the student residences of the city's universities. Comfort here is basic; the rooms are equipped with a single bed and a small chest of drawers, and all bathrooms are communal. Nevertheless, this is an economical way to stay in the city. Reservations are recommended. The student residences at the **Université de Montréal** *($21 and $31 per person; 2350 boulevard Édouard-Montpetit, H3C 1J4, ☎ 514-343-6531)* stand at the foot of Mont Royal, in a quiet neighbourhood. They are located a few kilometres from downtown, which is easily accessible. It is also possible to rent rooms in the residence halls of **Concordia University** *(students $19 and $20 per person, for a room for two; 7141 rue Sherbrooke Ouest, H4B 1R6, ☎ 514-848-4756)*. These are located west of downtown. Lastly, in the heart of the downtown area, are the residence halls of **McGill University** *(students $26.50, non-students $36.50 per person; 3935 rue University, H3A 2B4, ☎ 514-398-6367)*.

Located on Rue Sherbrooke, near Place des Arts, beside an abandoned lot, the **Casa Bella** *($50 with shared bathroom, $65 with pb; 264 rue Sherbrooke*

Ouest, H2X 1X9, ☎ *514-849-2777,* ⇄ *849-3650)* is a charming hotel. The rooms are pretty, and reflect the care that has gone into decorating them. The friendly welcome makes guests feel quickly at ease. This hotel offers good value for the money.

Manoir Ambrose *($55 with shared bathroom, $65 with pb, including breakfast; 3422 rue Stanley, H3A 1R8,* ☎ *514-288-6922)* is a big, beautiful house made of hewn stone, located on a peaceful street. It has several little rooms, scattered all over the house. The outdated decor will amuse some guests, but the rooms are well-kept and the service is friendly.

Guests of the **Hôtel Appartement Montréal** *($75; ≈, △, K; 455 rue Sherbrooke Ouest,* ☎ *514-284-3634 or 1-800-363-3010,* ⇄ *287-1431)* enjoy pretty, well-kept rooms equipped with a kitchenette. This is a reasonable way to stay in the heart of the downtown area.

Located in a quiet section of Rue Crescent, the **Comfort Suites** *($79; ℜ; 1214 rue Crescent, H3G 2A9,* ☎ *514-878-2711,* ⤴ *878-0030)* hotel is just a few steps from a busy area full of restaurants and boutiques. Each of the rooms is simply, yet comfortably decorated and has a small balcony.

The **Radisson Gouverneurs** *($99; ~, ℜ, △, ☯; 777 rue University,* ☎ *514-879-1370)* is visible when arriving in Montréal via the Autoroute Bonaventure. The rooms are attractive, but small. On the top floor, there is a revolving restaurant, from which diners enjoy a spectacular view of the city.

The **Château Versailles** *($115; 1659 rue Sherbrooke Ouest, H3H 1E3,* ☎ *514-933-3611,* ⤴ *933-7102)* is

composed of four handsome buildings dating back to the Edwardian era. All things considered, however, the rooms are disappointing. The furnishings in most of them are too modern, entirely inappropriate for a château. Furthermore, the insufficient amount of furniture leaves the rooms looking bare. The larger rooms are nevertheless adorned with very pretty mouldings.

Novotel *($118; ☯, ℜ; 1180 rue de la Montagne, H3G 1Z1,* ☎ *514-861-6000,* ⤴ *861-0992)* is a French hotel chain. The pleasant rooms in its downtown Montréal hotel are equipped with numerous extras, including a large desk and outlets for computers. Special packages are available for guests travelling with children.

A step away from downtown, the **Hôtel Shangrila** *($119; ℜ; 3407 rue Peel, H3A 1W7,* ☎ *514-288-4141,* ⤴ *288-3021)* offers plainly decorated but comfortable rooms, some of which are equipped with fitness machines. The lobby, however, with its assortment of little shops, is not very inviting.

Howard Johnson *($125; ☯, ℜ; 475 rue Sherbrooke Ouest, H3A 2L9,* ☎ *514-842-3961,* ⤴ *842-0945)* offers simple, but very comfortable rooms.

Guests of the **Bonaventure Hilton** *($125; 1 Place Bonaventure, H5A 1E4,* ☎ *514-878-2332,* ⤴ *878-3881 and 878-1442),* located on the boundary between downtown and Vieux-Montréal, enjoy a number of little extras that make this hotel a perfect place to relax. The rooms are decorated in a simple manner, without a hint of extravagance, and the bathrooms are small. The hotel has a heated outdoor swimming pool, where guests can swim all year round.

La Citadelle *($139; ≈, △, ◎, ℜ; 410 Sherbrooke Ouest, H3A 1B3, ☎ 514-844-8851, or 1-800-465-6654, ⇌ 844-0912)* stands at the edge of the downtown area. There are 180 rooms, yet no more than 9 per floor, which gives this hotel the feeling of a small inn. Renovations were recently finished. The attractively decorated rooms offer views of either the mountain or the river. Some rooms, the *suites juniors (expect to pay $25 more than a standard room)*, are equipped with kitchenettes. The hotel also has conference rooms and a fitness centre.

The **Château Champlain** *($140; ≈, ◎, △, ℜ; 1 Place du Canada, H3B 4C9, ☎ 514-878-9000, ⤣ 878-6761)* is a very original-looking white building with semicircular windows, much resembling a cheese-grater. Unfortunately, this renowned hotel has small rooms, which are less attractive than one might expect from an establishment in this class (see also p 182).

The **Hôtel Europa** *($150; ≈, ◎, ℜ; 1240 rue Drummond, H3G 1V7, ☎ 514-866-6492, ☎ 861-4089)* is a plain modern building. The rooms are small, and quite expensive for what they offer. The lobby is surrounded by uninteresting boutiques, and is too noisy.

The **Reine-Elizabeth** *($150; ℜ, △; 900 boulevard René-Lévesque Ouest, H3B 4A5, ☎ 514-861-3511, ⤣ 954-2256)*, or Queen-Elizabeth, is one Montréal hotel that has set itself apart over the years. Its lobby, decorated with woodwork, is magnificent. The hotel has the advantage of being located in the heart of downtown. Visitors will find a

number of shops on the main floor. The building's underground corridors, furthermore, provide easy access to the train station.

The **Ritz Carlton** *($160; ℜ; 1228 rue Sherbrooke Ouest, H3G 1H6, ☎ 514-842-4212, ⤣ 842-4907)* was inaugurated in 1912. Renovated over the years in order to continue offering its clientele exceptional comfort, it has managed to preserve its original elegance. The rooms are decorated with superb antique furniture. The marble bathrooms, moreover, add to the charm of this outstanding establishment (see also p 182).

The **Hôtel Méridien** *($170, less expensive packages available on weekends; ≈, △, ◎, ℜ; 4 Complexe Desjardins, H5B 1E5, ☎ 514-285-1450 or 1-800-361-8234, ⇌ 514-285-1243)* is part of Complexe Desjardins. Consequently, on the main floor, there is a series of shops, movie theatres and restaurants. Located a step away from Place des Arts, the hotel has a prime downtown location. The large, comfortable rooms correspond with what one would expect from a hotel in this category.

Standing over 30 stories high, the **Centre Sheraton** *($175; ≈, ◎, △, ℜ; 1201 boulevard René-Lévesque, H3B 2L7, ☎ 514-878-2000, ⤣ 878-3958)* has 824 rooms. A number of little extras (coffee machine, hair-drier, non-smoking floors) are evidence of the meticulous service provided here. The rooms are pretty without being luxurious. Take some time to enjoy the beautiful lobby, decorated with picture windows and tropical plants.

At first sight, the **Hôtel Vogue** *($195; ≈, ◉, ℜ; 1425 rue de la Montagne,*

H3G 1Z3, ☎ 514-285-5555, ⇆ 849-8903), a glass and concrete building with no ornamentation, looks bare. The lobby, embellished with warm-coloured woodwork, gives a more accurate idea of the luxuriousness and elegance of this establishment. The large rooms, with their elegant furniture, reveal how comfortable this hotel is (see also p 182).

The **Delta Montréal** ($200; ≈, ⊘, ℜ; 450 rue Sherbrooke Ouest, H3A 2T4, ☎ 514-286-1986 or 1-800-463-1133, ⇆ 284-4342 and 284-4306) is a recently built hotel with two entrances, one on Rue Sherbrooke and the other on Avenue du Président-Kennedy. It has pleasant rooms, which are attractively decorated with wooden furniture made to look like mahogany.

One of the most renowned hotels in Montréal, the **Quatre Saisons** ($220; ≈, ⊘, ℜ; 1050 rue Sherbrooke Ouest, H3A 2R6, ☎ 514-284-1110, ⇆ 845-3025) offers comfortable, spacious accommodations. Nevertheless, the standard rooms are decorated in an unoriginal fashion and the bathrooms are small for such a prestigious establishment. The lobby, however, is large and elegant, and the hotel is famous for its restaurants (see p 182).

Village Shaughnessy

Le Richebourg ($65; K; 2170 avenue Lincoln, H3H 2N5, ☎ 514-935-9224, ⇆ 935-5049) has spacious rooms, each one equipped with a kitchenette. The hotel is somewhat modest-looking, but its location, on a quiet street on the western edge of the downtown area, makes it an excellent place to stay.

Manoir Le Moyne ($72; ⊘, △, ℜ, K; 2100 boulevard de Maisonneuve Ouest, H3H 1K6, ☎ 514-931-8861, ⇆ 931-7726) is located on a busy street near downtown. A cold atmosphere pervades the lobby, which is decorated with mirrors and gilded chandeliers. The rooms, equipped with a kitchenette, are nevertheless decent.

Quartier latin

On Rue Saint-Hubert, between Rue Ontario and Rue Sherbrooke, visitors will find a fair number of little hotels, which are lacking in charm and offer a very ordinary level of comfort, but have the advantage of being inexpensive. **Le Breton** ($40 with shared bathroom, $65 with pb; 1609 rue Saint-Hubert, H2L 3Z1, ☎ 514-524-7273) is a good example. The lobby is run-down and the rooms are unremarkable. The **Louisbourg**, next door, has similar rooms.

Bed & Breakfast Turquoise ($50; 1576, rue Alexandre de Sève, H2L 2V7, ☎ 523-9943). This B&B, located in the heart of the gay village, has been open since November 1993. Everything feels new here, even though the Victorian house (the interior alone bears witness to that era) is over a century old. The owners, Luc and Gilles, hope to finish renovating the terrace by summer 1994, so that they can serve breakfast outside when the weather permits.

The very simple façade of the **Château de l'Argoat** ($65 breakfast and parking included; 524 rue Sherbrooke Est, H2L 1K1, ☎ 514-842-2046, ⇄ 286-2791) is not at all luxurious, and the entrance is not very inviting. The rooms are decorated with old-fashioned furniture, which looks as if it came from another era. Nevertheless, the room where breakfast is served is adorable.

The **Manoir Sherbrooke** *($65; 157 rue Sherbrooke Est, H2X 1C7,* ☎ *514-285-0895,* ⇄ *284-1126)* is established in an old stone house. The rooms are modest, and the reception could be more friendly.

The hotel **Émérillon** *($69; 1600 rue Saint-Hubert, H2L 3Z3,* ☎ *514-849-3214,* ⇄ *849-9812)* is advantageously located next door to the bus terminal, and provides visitors with a convenient place to stay.

Located on bustling Rue Saint-Denis, **Jardin d'Antoine** *($70 with shower, $80 with pb, breakfast included; 2024 rue Saint-Denis, H2X 3K7,* ☎ *514-843-4506,* ⇄ *281-1491)* has a few rooms that look out on the garden behind the building, and are thus very peaceful. These rooms have been carefully renovated and have a certain style about them.

The façade of the **Lord Berri** *($85; 1199 rue Berri, H2L 4C6,* ☎ *514-845-9236,* ⇄ *849-9855)* conceals a bare lobby. The rooms are large, with ordinary, slightly drab decorations.

Plateau Mont-Royal

The **Auberge de Jeunesse Lafontaine** *($16 shared rooms, $60 double rooms; 1250 rue Sherbrooke Est, H2L 1M1,* ☎ *514-522-3910)*, or youth hostel, accepts students during the school year and then in the summer transforms into a charming hostel for young travellers.

Guests have access to furnished rooms, a kitchen, a living room and a small laundry room. The hostel is ideally located next to Parc Lafontaine and close to Rue Saint-Denis.

The **Gîte Sympathique** *($40; 3728 rue Saint-Hubert, H2L 4A2,* ☎ *514-843-9740)* has three charming rooms, a large sitting room and a dining room where breakfast is served. The calm and well-kept nature of this bed and breakfast make it a good address to remember.

Le Palois *($55 with shared bathroom, $70 with pb; 3950 avenue Laval, H2W 2J2,* ☎ *514-844-5897)* is a bed & breakfast with charming rooms. A peaceful atmosphere pervades the nicely maintained house, making it an ideal place to relax. Shared bathroom.

The **Auberge de la Fontaine** *($105 breakfast and parking included; 1301 rue Rachel Est, H2J 2K1,* ☎ *514-597-0166,* ⇄ *597-0496)* lies opposite lovely Parc Lafontaine. Designed with a great deal of care, it has a lot of style. A feeling of calm and relaxation emanates from the rooms, all of which are nicely decorated. All these attractive features have made this a popular place - so much so that it is best to make reservations.

Near the Airports

■ **Mirabel Airport**

Directly accessible from Mirabel Airport, the **Château de l'Aéroport-Mirabel** *($87; ≈, △, ℜ; Mirabel Airport, C.P. 60, J7N 1A2,* ☎ *514-476-1611 or 1-800-268-9420,* ⇄ *476-0873)* was built to accommodate travellers with early morning flights. The rooms are very functional and comfortable.

■ **Dorval Airport**

The rooms in the **Best Western Hôtel International** *($85; ≈, ℜ; 13000 chemin Côte-de-Liesse,* ☎ *514-631-4811 or 1-800-361-2254,* ⇄ *631-7305)* are pleasant and affordable. The location, in an industrial area next to the airport, is unfortunate.

The **Hilton International** *($167; ≈, △, ℜ; 12505 chemin Côte-de-Liesse, H9P 1B7,* ☎ *514-631-2411 or 1-800-268-9275,* ⇄ *631-0198)* has pleasant rooms. Its main advantage is its proximity to the airport.

RESTAURANTS

A s far as food is concerned, Montréal's reputation is enviable, to say the least; it is also well-deserved. The culinary traditions of countries around the world are represented here by restaurants of all different sizes. The best thing is that no matter what your budget, a memorable meal is always possible! The following listings are grouped according to location, in the same order as the tours in the "Exploring" section (see p 55), to make it easier for visitors to find those hidden treasures while they are exploring a particular area!

 Vieux-Montréal

Ambiance *($; 1874 rue Notre-Dame Ouest, ☎ 939-2609)* is both a tea-room and an antique shop, the combination makes the decor particularly charming.

For health food, **Bio Train** *($; 410 rue Saint-Jacques, ☎ 842-9184)* is a favourite self-serve restaurant. At lunchtime, things move very quickly.

The menu at **Chez Better** *($; 160 Notre-Dame Est, ☎ 861-2617)*, a chain of restaurants, consists mainly of German sausages, French fries and sauerkraut. While the lay-out varies from one location to the next, the atmosphere is always relaxed (see also p 184, 185).

Business people crowd into **Steak Frites** *($; 12 rue Saint-Paul Est,* ☎ *842-0972)* at noon, perfectly comfortable in the relatively small, noisy dining room. They come here for well presented steaks and French fries drenched in a variety of sauces.

The building that houses the restaurant **Il Était une Fois** *($; 600 Place d'Youville,* ☎ *842-6783)* served as a train station during the first half of this century. The decor consists of wood floors and walls, an old stove in the middle of the room and a profusion of advertisements from days gone by. People come here to feast on hamburgers this big, and French fries this long.

The sumptuous modern northern-Italian decor of the wine bistro **L'Altro** *($$; 205 avenue Viger Ouest,* ☎ *393-3456)* welcomes a clientele composed mainly of business people and congress-goers. Wine has the place of honour, and there is a large variety of good vintages to choose from, by the glass or bottle. The food Italian is delicious.

The varied menu of the French restaurant **Bonaparte** *($$; 443 rue Saint-François-Xavier,* ☎ *844-4368)* always includes some delicious surprises. The tables on the mezzanine offer a lovely view of Vieux-Montréal.

The specialty of **Chez Delmo** *($$; 211 rue Notre-Dame Ouest,* ☎ *849-4061)* is seafood and fish. The outstanding bouillabaisse is not to be missed. The first room, with its two long oyster bars, is the most pleasant one.

Located on bustling Place Jacques-Cartier, **La Marée** *($$$; 404 Place Jacques-Cartier,* ☎ *861-9794)* has managed to maintain an excellent reputation over the years. The chef prepares fish and seafood to perfection. The dining room is spacious, so everyone is comfortable.

Every evening, the **Festin des Gouverneurs** *($$$; 1000 rue Saint-Antoine Ouest,* ☎ *879-1141)* recreates a colonial feast from the early days of New France. Servers in period costume lead guests back in time to these festive evenings. The menu features traditional Québec dishes. The restaurant only serves groups, and reservations are required.

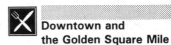

Downtown and the Golden Square Mile

Besides a great selection of draft beers and Viennese breads, **Van Houtte** *($; 1255 avenue McGill College,* ☎ *861-5260),* offers a beautiful, comfortable decor.

The **Van Houtte** *($; Place des Arts)* at Place des Arts has a modern decor that is well adapted to its surroundings. It is the ideal spot to grab a bite to eat before the show. Croissants, coffees and muffins make up the menu.

At lunchtime, the place to be is the **Grand Comptoir** *($; 1225 Place Phillips,* ☎ *393-3295),* not for its decor, which is rather nondescript, but for the bistro menu at unbeatable prices.

Jazz musician Charlie Biddle's haunt, **Biddle Jazz & Ribs** *($; 2060 rue Aylmer,* ☎ *842-8656)* presents live music on a regular basis. Business people and hungry jazz fans come here to savour the delicious ribs and chicken wings, while enjoying music at just the right volume, so as not to preclude conversation.

The **Bar-B-Barn** *($; 1201 rue Guy,* ☎ *931-3811)* serves sweet, delicious pork ribs cooked just right. The food is hardly refined, especially seeing as you have to eat it with your hands, but it appeals to many Montrealers. Those planning to come here on the weekend should prepare to be patient, since there is often a long wait.

At the beginning of the century, a Lithuanian immigrant modified a recipe from his native country to suit the needs of workers, and thus introduced the smoked meat sandwich to Montréal, and in the process created **Ben's Delicatessen** *($; 900 boulevard de Maisonneuve Ouest,* ☎ *844-1000).* Over the years, the restaurant has become a Montréal institution, attracting a motley crowd from 7 a.m. to 4 a.m. This is where people come when the discotheques close! The worn, formica tables and photographs yellowed by time give the restaurant an austere appearance.

Chez Better *($; 1430 rue Stanley,* ☎ *848-9859)* see description p179.

Le Commensal *($; 1204 McGill College,* ☎ *871-1480)* is a buffet-style restaurant. The food, all vegetarian, is sold by weight. Le Commensal is open every day until 11 p.m. The inviting modern decor and big windows looking out on the downtown streets make it a pleasant place to be.

Dunn's *($; 892 rue Sainte-Catherine Ouest,* ☎ *866-4377)* has acquired a solid reputation thanks to its delicious smoked meat sandwiches. Don't base your impression on the questionable display in the window. At lunchtime the restaurant is overrun with downtown business people. It is open 24 hours a day.

The menu of **L'Entrecôte Saint-Jean** *($; 2022 rue Peel,* ☎ *281-6492)* is very simple, and therefore inexpensive; it consists of rib-steak *(entrecôte)* prepared in a variety of different ways.

The **Tulipe Noire** *($; Maison Alcan, 2100 rue Stanley,* ☎ *285-1225)* (meaning black tulip) is located in the superb *Maison Alcan* complex. Everything is excellent at this café-restaurant, from the salads to the sandwiches and hamburgers. The *table d'hôte* is always good, in the afternoon as well as the evening. The Tulipe Noire also has an impressive selection of pastries.

L'Actuel *($$; 1194 rue Peel,* ☎ *866-1537),* the most typically Belgian restaurant in Montréal, is always full for both lunch and dinner. It has a large, fairly noisy and very lively dining room, where affable waiters hurry about among the clientele of business people. The restaurant serves mussels, of course, as well as a number of other specialties.

The superb dining room at **Eaton, le 9** *($$; 677 rue Sainte-Catherine,* ☎ *284-8421)* is worth a brief visit, if only to experience the sensation of stepping back into another era. The restaurant is open for lunch and dinner and is located on the ninth floor.

With a name like **Jardin Sakura** *($$; 2114 rue de la Montagne,* ☎ *288-9122),* diners might expect a more refined decor. "Sakura" is the beautiful flower on Japanese cherry trees. The menu offers respectable Japanese cuisine, considering sushi is not always a success. The service is very attentive.

Chez Gauthier (*$$; 3487 avenue du Parc*, ☎ 845-2992) is located in a long room decorated with wood panelling. In true bistro fashion, the menu is displayed on a chalkboard. Everything is delicious, particularly the desserts, which come from the Pâtisserie Belge next door.

The Élysée Mandarin (*$$, 1221 rue Mackay*, ☎ 866-5975) is definitely one of the most beautiful Chinese restaurants in Montréal, tastefully decorated in a style suited to the old Victorian residence it occupies. The *menu dégustation* enables guests to taste a number of house specialties, including Peking duck, shrimp with basil and frogs' legs, and also lists a wide range of appetizers. This is a good place to keep in mind for fine exotic cuisine.

Made up of several large dining rooms, the restaurant **La Mère Tucker** (*$$; 1175 Place du Frère André*, ☎ 866-5525) is ideal for families and large groups. The all-you-can-eat roast beef has developed a solid reputation with gourmet eaters. The atmosphere is relaxed.

La Troïka (*$$$; 2171 rue Crescent*, ☎ 849-9333) epitomizes a typical Russian restaurant. Hanging tapestries, souvenirs, hidden nooks and crannies, and live accordion music conjure up images of the old country. The food is authentic and excellent.

Le Caveau (*$$$; 2063 rue Victoria*, ☎ 844-1624) occupies a charming white house, nestled against the downtown skyscrapers. The restaurant serves skilfully prepared, refined French cuisine.

The Café de Paris (*$$$; 1228 Sherbrooke Ouest*, ☎ 842-4212) is the renowned restaurant of the magnificent Ritz-Carlton Hotel (see p 174). Its sumptuous blue and ochre decor is refined and beautiful. The carefully thought-out menu offers delicious dishes.

Located on the 32nd floor of the elegant, gigantic cheese-grater known as the Hôtel Château Champlain(see p 174), **L'Escapade** (*$$$; Hôtel Château Champlain, 1 Place du Canada*, ☎ 878-9000) offers an exceptional panoramic view. The polynesian elements of the decor leave a bit to be desired, but the view makes up for it. The smorgasbord of a supper buffet features such delicacies as lobster and roast beef. There is an orchestra and dancing. The restaurant is open Friday, Saturday and Sunday morning.

The stylishly decorated restaurant **Le Cercle** (*$$$; Hôtel Quatre Saisons, 1050 rue Sherbrooke Ouest*, ☎ 284-1110), in the Four Seasons Hotel (see p 175), serves succulent, skilfully cooked dishes. The place is particularly pleasant at breakfast.

At **Katsura** (*$$$; 2170 rue de la Montagne*, ☎ 849-1172), located in the heart of downtown, visitors can savour refined Japanese cuisine. The main dining room is furnished with long tables, making this a perfect place for groups. Smaller, more intimate rooms are also available.

The restaurant and bar of **Café Société** (*$$$; 1415 rue de la Montagne*, ☎ 987-8168), located inside the very stylish Hôtel Vogue (see p 174), both have a remarkable, 1960's-style decor. The menu is composed of exquisite Eurasian dishes.

In the former rectory of the Christ Church Cathedral, the **Parchemin** *($$$; 1333 rue University,* ☎ *844-1619)* is distinguished by its stylish decor and velvety atmosphere. Guests enjoy carefully prepared French cuisine, suitable for the finest of palates. For those with a well-lined purse, the six-course *ménu dégustation* is a real feast ($43 per person), while the four-course *table d'hôte*, with its wide range of choices, is also a treat.

Cafés

Café Toman *($;* 1421 rue Mackay, ☎ 844-1605) is popular among students from the neighbouring universities. The menu features delicious Czech specialties, including cakes, soups and salads. Unfortunately, the restaurant closes early (5 p.m.) and is open on neither Sunday nor Monday.

 Village Shaughnessy

The Pique Assiette *($; 2051 rue Sainte-Catherine Ouest,* ☎ *932-7141)* has an Indian-style decor and a quiet atmosphere. The lunchtime Indian buffet is well worth the trip. The menu lists excellent curries and Tandoori specialties. Guests can have as much *nan* bread as they please. Anyone with a weak stomach should stay away, because the food is very spicy. English beer washes these dishes down nicely.

The **Rôtisserie Italienne** *($; 1933 rue Sainte-Catherine Ouest,* ☎ *935-4436)* is a self-serve restaurant, where visitors can enjoy a quick, delicious plate of pasta. The place is pleasant, but the rustic decor lacks charm.

Le **Bistro Gourmet** *($$; 2100 rue Saint-Mathieu,* ☎ *846-1553)* is a pleasant little French restaurant, where visitors can savour delicious dishes, always prepared with fresh ingredients and carefully served.

A small Thai restaurant, **Pattaya** *($$; 1235 rue Guy,* ☎ *933-9949)* has a simple, tasteful lay-out and serves good, exotic-tasting cuisine.

Cafés

Calories *($; 4114 rue Sainte-Catherine Ouest,* ☎ *933-8186),* which welcomes a noisy clientele late into the night, features delicious cakes, served in generous portions.

 Around the Hôtel-Dieu

Beauty's *($; 93 avenue du Mont-Royal Ouest,* ☎ *849-8883)* is known for its hearty, delicious brunches. The place is often crowded in the mornings during the weekend.

The **Café Ciné-Lumière** *($; 5163 boulevard Saint-Laurent,* ☎ *495-1796)* is decorated with the set of a Paris bistro leftover from the Cité Ciné exposition. Old movies are shown on a giant screen. The comfortable atmosphere is a little trendy, but not too much! For $2 you can rent earphones and listen to the movies. This is the ideal spot to enjoy a meal alone.

A small sign announces the **Café Côte Ouest** *($; 4563 boulevard Saint-Laurent,* ☎ *284-3468),* which has a simple decor, but an out of the ordinary menu. Fish and seafood are prepared in an original manner with a British Columbian flare.

Popular with groovy diners of all ages, the **Café Santropol** *($; 3990 rue Saint-Urbain,* ☎ *842-3110)* serves enormous sandwiches, quiches and salads. It is also known for its wide variety of herbal teas and coffees, great decor and fantastic terrasse.

Cafétéria *($; 3581 boulevard Saint-Laurent,* ☎ *849-3855)* attracts young professionals, who come here for hamburgers and people-watching through the big picture window that looks out on Boulevard Saint-Laurent. The tasty, healthy vegetarian burger is definitely worth a try. The fifties decor is the epitome of kitsch.

Chez Better *($; 4382 boulevard Saint-Laurent,* ☎ *845-4554)*, see description p 179).

The two-level, modern-decor **City Pub** *($; 3820 boulevard Saint-Laurent,* ☎ *499-8519)* draws a young crowd. The main attractions are the *steak frites*, steak and fries, the inexpensive beer and the great view of Saint-Laurent.

A beacon in the Montréal night, "open even during the day," **Lux** *($; 5220 boulevard Saint-Laurent,* ☎ *271-9272)* energizes an entire population with its industrial, multi-floor architecture, international magazines and original T-shirts. The atmosphere is at its peak at around 3:30 in the morning. Avoid the hamburgers.

The third location of the restaurant **Pizzaïolle** *($; 3616 boulevard Saint-Laurent,* ☎ *842-6383; see also p 191)* will amaze design freaks with its obvious attention to harmony and detail.

The restaurant **Pizzédélic** *($; 3509 boulevard Saint-Laurent,* ☎ *282-6784)* has a modern decor, but is unfortunately too narrow, so that customers seem to be sitting on top of each other. This is a good place to eat *nouvelle* pizza made with quality ingredients and a thin crust.

The **Shed Café** *($; 3515 boulevard Saint-Laurent,* ☎ *842-0220)* serves salads, hamburgers and desserts. The interior, which definitely plays a role in attracting the restaurant's clientele, is wacky and avant-garde. The café is open until 3 a.m. every day.

According to most Montrealers, **Schwartz's Montréal Hebrew Delicatessen** *($; 3895 boulevard Saint-Laurent,* ☎ *842-4813)* serves the best smoked meat in the city. The main attraction is definitely the smoked meat, since the decor is far from inviting.

The beautiful wood panelling interior of the **Bistro la Folie** *($$; 4806 avenue du Parc,* ☎ *273-4088)* is reminiscent of Belgian *brasseries*. The dining room can seem large and dull at times, nevertheless, the attentive service and superior quality of the food make up for it.

It is impossible to walk down Boulevard Saint-Laurent without noticing **Buona Notte** *($$; 3518 boulevard Saint-Laurent,* ☎ *848-0644)*, a restaurant similar to those in Soho. And once up close, it is nearly impossible resist the temptation of going inside. Buona Notte is Italy rediscovered, a combination of Little Italy and Soho, a piece of New York in Montréal.

Chao Phraya *($$; 50 rue Laurier O.,* ☎ *272-5339)* see p 188.

For a break from the urbanity of Montréal, try the exotic and friendly Caribbean restaurant **Chez Flora** *($$; 3615 boulevard Saint-Laurent,* ☎ *849-7270).* The food is deliciously different.

A pioneer in the no-man's-land along Boulevard Saint-Laurent, between Avenue Mont-Royal and Avenue Laurier, **La Loggia** *($$; 4833 boulevard Saint-Laurent,* ☎ *985-5366)* is Montréal's latest trendy restaurant. Artists and intellectuals come here to savour fine Italian cuisine, which is both innovative and reasonably priced.

The **Palais de l'Inde** *($-$$; 5125 boulevard Saint-Laurent,* ☎ *270-7402)* is one of the many great Indian restaurants along Saint-Laurent near Rue Laurier. The menu includes a good selection of main dishes, which though prepared with quality ingredients, lack originality. The service is a bit aloof.

Moishe's *($$$; 3961 boulevard Saint-Laurent,* ☎ *845-3509)* has an ugly, garish exterior. Appearances can be deceiving, however; this restaurant serves what are without a doubt the best steaks in town. The secret of this deliciously tender meat lies in the aging process. Reservations are recommended.

Cafés

La Desserte *($; 5258 boulevard Saint-Laurent,* ☎ *272-5797)* features heavenly cakes made with quality natural ingredients. The decor lacks charm, however.

The brick and wood decor of the **Café El Dorado** *($; 5226 boulevard Saint-Laurent,* ☎ *278-3333)* creates a warm atmosphere. Guests are offered a wide choice of coffee from many different countries. The desserts are delicious, and light meals are served as well.

Kilo *($; 5206 boulevard Saint-Laurent,* ☎ *277-5039)* looks like a fairy-tale house from the year 2000, with its aesthetically placed profusion of candies, grey-coloured walls, metal furnishings and high ceiling. A young, dynamic clientele crowds in here at all hours to nibble and chat. People don't come here to relax, but to mingle with the *beau monde,* the beautiful people!

Café Meliès *($; 3682 boulevard Saint-Laurent,* ☎ *281-0525),* which adjoins Cinéma Parallèle, was named after the French film-maker. It serves simple food, such as quiches, sandwiches and cakes. People are attracted by the pleasant, intellectual atmosphere (see p 95).

 Quartier Latin

Chez Better *($; 1310 boulevard de Maisonneuve Est,* ☎ *525-9832),* see description p 179.

Le Commensal *($; 2115 Saint-Denis,* ☎ *845-2627),* see description p 181.

Tiny **La Paryse** *($; 302 rue Ontario Est,* ☎ *842-2040)* is often crowded with students, for a very simple reason: it serves delicious hamburgers and homemade French fries in generous portions.

Steak Frites *($; 2070 rue Saint-Denis,* ☎ *842-6626)* see description p 180.

At the charming restaurant **Azuma** *($$; 901 rue Sherbrooke Est,* ☎ *525-5262),* visitors can sample Japanese cuisine. Reservations are recommended, as this restaurant is too small to seat all its customers. The service is polite and attentive.

Modigliani *($$; 1874 rue Plessis, ☎ 522-2267)*, see description p 189.

All true lovers of Italian cuisine know and adore **Le Piémontais** *($$; 1145-A rue de Bullion, ☎ 861-8122)*. The dining room is narrow and the tables are close together, making this place very noisy, but the soft, primarily pink decor, the kind, good humoured and efficient staff, and the works of culinary art on the menu make dining here an unforgettable experience. Reservations are recommended.

A restaurant with a warm, sophisticated, modern wooden decor, the **Quartier Latin** *($$, 318 Ontario E. ☎ 845-3301)* serves French bistro-style cuisine, presented in an innovative fashion. One particularly noteworthy dish is the pralines with orange purée, an unusual iced dessert. The restaurant's motto is *"Bonum vidum loetificat cor hominis,"* which means "good wine warms the heart of man," and guests are indeed offered a wide selection of wine sold by the glass.

At the restaurant **Les Mignardises** *($$$; 2037 rue Saint-Denis, ☎ 842-1151)*, visitors can savour gourmet French cuisine. The skilfully prepared dishes are a heavenly treat for the taste buds. The building looks modest from the outside, but the interior is pleasant.

Cafés

The **Brioche Lyonnaise** *($; 1593 rue Saint-Denis, ☎ 842-7017)* is a pastry shop and café offering an extremely wide selection of pastries, cakes and sweetmeats, all the more appealing because everything really is as delicious as it looks!

Located near Rue Saint-Denis, **Le Pèlerin** *($; 330 rue Ontario Est, ☎ 845-0909)* is a pleasant, unpretentious café. The wooden furniture, made to look like mahogany, and the works of modern art on exhibit create a friendly atmosphere, which attracts a diverse clientele. This is a perfect place to grab a bite and chat with a friend. The service is attentive and friendly.

Second Cup *($; 1551 rue Saint-Denis, ☎ 285-4468)* is a charming café, which serves sandwiches and coffee all day long. It is often full of students from the neighbouring university, who come to enjoy the relaxed and friendly atmosphere.

 Plateau Mont-Royal

L'Anecdote *($; 801 rue Rachel Est, ☎ 526-7967)* serves hamburgers and vegetarian club sandwiches made with quality ingredients. The place has a 1950's-style decor, with movie posters and old Coke ads on the walls.

Diners who seek something out of the ordinary on their menus should head to **Anubis** *($; 11:30 a.m. to 2 p.m. and from 5 p.m. on; 35 avenue du Mont-Royal Est, ☎ 843-3911)*. The atmosphere is warm, and on some evenings there is a singer.

The cozy decor of the **Bistro Méditerranéen** *($; 3857 rue Saint-Denis, ☎ 843-5028)* conjures up images of Maghreb. The menu consists of North African specialties, such as couscous and kebabs. The food is good and the prices, unbeatable.

With its decor made up of four tables and a counter, the **Binerie Mont-Royal** *($; 367 ave Mont-Royal Est, ☎ 285-9078)* looks like a modest little neighbourhood restaurant. It is known for its specialty, baked beans *(fèves au lard* or *"binnes")* and also as the backdrop of Yves Beauchemin's novel, *Le Matou* (The Alley Cat).

A small, very modest-looking restaurant whose walls are decorated with Persian handicrafts, **Byblos** *($; 1499 rue Laurier est, ☎ 523-9396)* appears both simple and exotic. The light, refined dishes are marvels of Middle Eastern cuisine. The service is attentive and guests are always greeted with a smile.

Cap-Pelé *($; 4593 rue Saint-Denis, ☎ 849-3522)* offers visitors an introduction to Acadian cuisine. The scattering of posters on the walls and the unmatched chairs give the place a modest look and a relaxed atmosphere. The food, though it is not refined, is good.

Chez Claudette *($; 351 avenue Laurier Est, ☎ 279-5173)*, is a comfortable family bistro is decorated with posters on the walls, a long counter and an open kitchen. Typical North-American fare makes up the menu.

A large bare room, a few posters and an atmosphere conducive to conversation awaits diners at **Aux Entretiens** *($; 1577 avenue Laurier Est, ☎ 521-2934)*. This neighbourhood café serves all sorts of sandwiches and salads.

Frite Alors *($; 1562 avenue Laurier Est, ☎ 524-6336)*, see description p 190.

An aluminum structure decorated with neon lights, the **Galaxie Diner** *($; 4801 rue Saint-Denis, ☎ 499-9711)* can seem somewhat surprising in this quiet neighbourhood. Admittedly, however, it does have a certain charm. People come to this 1950's-style diner for quick, simple food. Breakfast served.

In search of good Thai food? Try **Le Goût de la Thaïlande** *($; wine; 2229 avenue du Mont-Royal Est, ☎ 527-5035)* where exotic flavours and savoury dishes make up the menu.

A Greek *brochetterie*, the **Jardin de Panos** *($ wine; 521 rue Duluth Est, ☎ 521-4206)* serves simple cuisine made with quality ingredients. The restaurant is set up inside a house with a large terrace, which is extremely pleasant in the summer. The decorations are unfortunately somewhat inelegant.

The **Lélé da Cuca** *($; wine; 70 rue Marie-Anne Est, ☎ 849-6649)* restaurant serves Mexican and Brazilian dishes. The cramped dining room can only accommodate about 30 people, but exudes a relaxed and laid-back ambience.

At **Madame Kim** *($; 4157 rue Saint-Denis, ☎ 842-0708)*, the owner's goal is to introduce her guests to authentic Vietnamese cuisine. Each skillfully prepared dish is as good as the last, and the service is polite and attentive.

Ouzeri *($; 4690 rue Saint-Denis, ☎ 845-1336)* set out on a mission to offer its clientele refined Mediterranean cuisine, and succeeded. The food is excellent, and the menu includes several surprises, such as vegetarian moussaka and scallops with melted cheese. With its high ceilings and long windows, this is a pleasant place, where you'll be tempted to linger on and on, especially when the Greek music sets your mind wandering.

Newly opened in Montréal, **Piazzetta** *($; 4097 rue Saint-Denis,* ☎ *847-0184)* serves pizza made in the true Italian style, with a thin, crisp crust.

At **Pied de Poule** *($; 3945 rue Saint-Denis,* ☎ *288-1000)*, eating barbecue becomes a trendy dining experience. The decor is extremely appealing—sober furniture strewn with hound's-tooth (called *pied de poule* or "chicken's-foot" in French) fabric, richly coloured walls, discreet halogen lighting, a bar with draft beer, and to top it off a warm friendly staff. Due to its affordable prices, this restaurant has quickly been adopted by neighbourhood residents.

With its menu of sandwiches and quiches, **Le Tartruffe** *($; 3945-A rue Saint-Denis,* ☎ *847-5233)* is a perfect place to stop for a healthy bite to eat.

The cozy atmosphere in this attractively decorated restaurant always guarantees a good time.
Inexpensive and good Peruvian food is served at the simple restaurant, **La Selva** *($; wine; 862 rue Marie-Anne Est,* ☎ *525-1798)*. The place is often filled with regulars, and reservations are recommended.

The **Bistro Latin** *($$; 775 avenue du Mont-Royal Est,* ☎ *521-8432)* serves Latin American cuisine in a cheerful atmosphere. The works of art adorning the walls give the place a real Peruvian flavour, made even more authentic by the music. The food is refined and carefully prepared.

The meeting place of an entire contingent of thirty-something yuppies, as well as a singles spot, the terrace at the **Café Cherrier** *($$; 3635 rue Saint-Denis,* ☎ *843-4308)* is full all summer long, starting in spring as patrons excitedly celebrate the arrival of the warm weather. The tables, which are practically on top of one another, the crush of people and the indifferent employees, who can't cope with all the customers, make a visit to this shrine a somewhat uncomfortable experience. The menu lists light meals and bistro-style dishes.

Cactus *($$; 4461 rue Saint-Denis,* ☎ *849-0349)* offers refined Mexican food in a warm atmosphere. Service is available in Spanish, to give guests the exotic sensation of being in a foreign land. The restaurant's little terrace is very popular during summer.

The decor of **Chao Phraya** *($$; 50 rue Laurier O.,* ☎ *272-5339; 4088 rue Saint-Denis,* ☎ *843-4194)* lacks character, but that does not seem to bother the restaurant's many customers, who come here to savour delicious Thai cuisine (see also p 184).

The staging is very subtle at the **Continental** *($$; 4169 Saint-Denis,* ☎ *845-6842)*. Some evenings, the restaurant is positively charming, with its attentive, courteous staff, stylish clientele and updated 1950's-style decor. The varied menu includes a few surprises, such as veal kidneys with thyme and *linguine carbonara*, which ranks among the best in Montréal.

Éduardo *($$; wine; 404 avenue Duluth Est,* ☎ *843-3330)* is popular with locals thanks to its generous portions and great food. This is a "bring your own wine" establishment, which explains the great prices (see also p 190)

The yuppie gathering place during the mid-eighties, **L'Express** *($$; 3927 rue St-Denis,* ☎ *845-5333)* is still highly rated for its dining car decor; lively Parisian bistro atmosphere, which few restaurants have managed to recreate, and consistently appealing menu. Over the years, this restaurant has developed a solid reputation.

A pleasant bistro decorated with woodwork and mirrors, **Le Flambard** *($$; 5064 avenue Papineau,* ☎ *596-1280)* excels in the preparation of quality French cuisine. Though the place is charming, the narrow dining room and closely-set tables offer little room for intimacy.

Fondue Mentale *($$; 4325 rue Saint-Denis* ☎ *499-1446)* occupies an old house, which, with its superb woodwork, is typical of Plateau Mont-Royal. As the restaurant's name suggests, fondue is the specialty here—and what a choice, each one more appetizing than the last! The Swiss fondue with pink pepper is particularly delicious.

Set up inside a superb residence, **Laloux** *($$; 250 avenue des Pins Est,* ☎ *287-9127)* is a chic, tastefully designed Parisian-style bistro. People come here to enjoy nouvelle cuisine of consistently high quality.

Located off the beaten track, the Italian restaurant **Modigliani** *($$; 1251 rue Gilford,* ☎ *522-0422)*, with its abundance of plants, has an inviting atmosphere and decor. The food is original and consistently good.

A small restaurant with a trendy decor, **Le Parigot** *($$; 330 avenue du Mont-Royal Est,* ☎ *845-6557)* will remind diners of France. The peach-coloured decor is well-suited to the sophisticated

somewhat cold atmosphere of the place. The clientele seems to be made up of regulars, who appreciate the classic cuisine, and the polished staff.

The blue and white decor and warm, island spirit of the service at **La Psarotaverna du Symposium** *($$; 4293 rue Saint-Denis,* ☎ *842-0867; 5334 A avenue du Parc,* ☎ *274-7022)* transports guests instantly to the Aegean Sea. Fish (sea bream) and seafood are the specialties here. Try the delicious moussaka and *saganaki*. For dessert, make sure to sample the delicious, milk-based *galatoboureco*.

L'Exotic *($$$; 3788 avenue Laval,* ☎ *843-4741)* has an appropriate name, seeing as it is the only Madagascar restaurant in North America. To say that guests would almost think they were in the middle of the Indian Ocean, on the island of Madagascar, would be a slight exaggeration; the decor does, however, have a certain authenticity about it. The friendly service complements the cuisine nicely.

Cafés

La Brûlerie *($; 3967 rue Saint-Denis,* ☎ *286-9158)* imports its coffees from all over the world and offers the widest selection in Montréal. The coffee is roasted on the premises, filling the place with a very distinctive aroma. The menu offers light meals and desserts.

The most romantic of café settings, **La Chartreuse** *($; 3439 rue Saint-Denis,* ☎ *842-0793)* is the ideal spot to enjoy delicious cakes and goodies.

At the charming **Le Daphnée** tea room *($; 3803 rue Saint-Denis,* ☎ *849-3042)*, visitors can enjoy dainty little treats of the sweet or salty variety. During summer, the balcony offers a choice view of Rue Saint-Denis. The staff is sometimes a bit pretentious.

 Mont Royal and Westmount

Café Lale *($; 5175-A rue Sherbrooke Ouest, ☎ 481-7137)* is decorated with posters of tulips (*lale* is Turkish for tulip). This little restaurant offers its guests a reasonably priced daily *table d'hôte*. The dishes are good, though there is nothing extravagant about the menu. Both breakfast and lunch are served.

The **Commensal** *($; 3715 chemin Queen Mary, ☎ 733-9755)* see description p 181.

Encore une Fois *($; 351 Prince-Albert, ☎ 488-3390)* is a small, neighbourhood health-food restaurant, where customers enjoy simple fare like sandwiches and salads, usually with alfalfa in the starring role. The place is attractively decorated in the style of days gone by, and has a warm, relaxed atmosphere.

The crazy red and yellow decor of **Pasta Casa Reccia** *($; 5849 rue Sherbrooke O., ☎ 483-1588)* attracts a clientele of all different ages. The house specialty is fresh pasta. The service, provided by the family that owns the place, is courteous and attentive.

Upon entering **Pizzafiore** *($; 3518 Lacombe, ☎ 735-1555)*, visitors will see the cook standing beside the wood-burning oven in which the pizzas are baked. He makes pizza for every taste, with every different kind of sauce, topped with the widest range of

ingredients imaginable. This pleasant restaurant is often filled with locals and people from the university.

For those partial to Indian food, **Le Sitar** *($$; 4961-D chemin Queen Mary, ☎ 735-9801)* serves delicate, refined cuisine at moderate prices. The decor is simple, without an ounce of extravagance, and soft Indian music envelops the dining room, adding a touch of exoticism.

Café

Franni *($; 5528 rue Monkland, ☎ 486-2033)*, a café decorated with woodwork, ceramic tiles and plants, is unfortunately too small for its many customers who flock here for the delicious cakes in particular the excellent cheesecake.

 Outremont

The second **Éduardo** *($$; 1014 avenue Laurier Ouest, ☎ 948-1826)* location on Avenue Laurier (see p 188), offers the same quality meals as on Duluth. There is, however, one small difference: you cannot bring your own wine on Laurier.

Frite Alors *($; 5235 A avenue du Parc, ☎ 948-2219)*, began as a re-creation of a typical *friterie belge*, Belgian fry-stand, where patrons could stop by at any time of the day for fries and a sausage. Unfortunately it lacks the exoticism of Europe, and feels more like a Montréal snack-bar. Nevertheless, these are the best fries in town (see also p 190).

Laurier B.B.Q. *($; 381 avenue Laurier Ouest, ☎ 273-3671)* has been a favourite of Montréal families for years.

barbecued chicken. Meals are a bit expensive, however.

Lester's *($; 1057 avenue Bernard Ouest,* ☎ *276-6095),* serves good smoked meat sandwiches. There is not much decor to speak of, creating a sterile and cold atmosphere, but no matter - it doesn't take long to eat a smoked meat sandwich!

Pizzaïolle *($; 5100 rue Hutchison,* ☎ *274-9349; 1446 A rue Crescent,* ☎ *845-4158)* was one of the first restaurants in Montréal to serve pizza cooked in a wood-burning stove. They also do the best job. The tables are a little close together, but the atmosphere is still very pleasant.

The stark modern decor of the Vietnamese restaurant **L'Escale à Saïgon** *($$; 107 avenue Laurier Ouest,* ☎ *272-3456)* defies the stereotype, with a beautiful bar, stylized fans and exotic flowers. The cuisine is exquisite.

The bistro **La Lucarne** *($$; 1030 avenue Laurier Ouest,* ☎ *279-7355)* underwent a few changes; first the owners opted for a modern decor typical of present-day bistros, and second a new name, it is now known as the **Chez Lévesque**). Luckily, the excellent food remained the same.

Fans of mussels should check out **La Moulerie** *($$; 1249 avenue Bernard Ouest,* ☎ *273-8132) (moules* is French for mussels) to experience the elaborate menu and distinguished atmosphere. The menu includes mussels served in a variety of sauces, and also a section entitled *j'haïs les moules,* or "I hate mussels."

La Spaghettata *($$; 399 avenue Laurier Ouest,* ☎ *273-9509)* is a large restaurant with a modern yet classic decor. Tables are set up on various different levels, creating the sensation that each table has its own private corner. The extensive menu includes pasta and veal dishes.

From the outside, **Le Passiflore** *($$$; 872 avenue Querbes,* ☎ *272-0540)* looks a bit questionable, but the spell is cast as soon as you cross the threshold into this bar-restaurant: pointillist murals that create an atmosphere of impressionism, Asian furniture, pseudo painted-silk drapes that could have come from Thailand... Le Passiflore is another world, one of peace and serenity, with its glasswork and garden in the inner court, where a concrete wall has been cleverly dressed-up to form an important part of the decor. The nouvelle cuisine is California style, with unique blends of flavours, like basil and citrus sauce.

Cafés

Ice-cream lovers of all ages flock to **Bilboquet** *($; 1311 avenue Bernard Ouest,* ☎ *276-0414)* for the countless different flavours. This little café is located in the heart of Outremont. It has a cute little terrace which is always full on summer evenings.

La Croissanterie *($; 5200 rue Hutchison,* ☎ *278-6567)* is one of those neighbourhood treasures so delightful to discover. Small marble tables, old-fashioned chandeliers and beautiful wood panelling make up a decor perfectly suited to leisurely breakfasts and intimate conversations when you wish time could stand still. The bright morning sun streams through large windows. This café almost seems like it came from a bygone era! Regulars include struggling artists and distracted intellectuals.

Le Paltoquet *($; 1464 avenue Van Horne, ☎ 271-4229)* is both a pastry shop and a café. Run by a friendly French couple, it serves delicious sweets worthy of the pickiest of sweettooths.

Maps of large European cities like Paris decorate the walls of the **Café Souvenir** *($; 1261 avenue Bernard Ouest, ☎ 948-5259)* (literally Memory Café). The ambiance of a French café pervades this comfortable little restaurant. Rainy Sundays bring out the locals in droves, for a quick coffee and chat. The menu is not extraordinary, but the meals are well prepared.

 Little Italy

People don't go to the **Café Italia** *($; 6840 boulevard Saint-Laurent, ☎ 495-0059)* for the decor, consisting of mismatched chairs and dominated by a large television, but for the comfortable atmosphere, the excellent sandwiches and most of all the cappuccino, considered by many to be the best in the city.

Pizzeria Napoletana *($-$$; wine; 189 rue Dante, ☎ 276-8226)* is small and nondescript but usually overrun with a large, lively crowd. These regulars keep coming back for the consistently delicious pastas and pizzas, not to mention that guests can bring their own wine and thus choose from an inexpensive menu.

 Sault-au-Récollet

For fondue and grilled food connoisseurs, **À la Fondue** *($; 335 rue Fleury Ouest, ☎ 381-7548)* is a good name to remember.

If simple traditional food is more your speed, try the **Café Burger** *($; 1826 rue Fleury Est, ☎ 389-7229)*.

L'Estaminet *($; 1340 rue Fleury Est, ☎ 389-0596)* is a comfortable little café serving salads, soups and desserts.

La Fonderie *($; 10145 rue Lajeunesse, ☎ 382-8234)* enjoys a solid reputation for its many delicious fondues.

The Chinese restaurant **Hanchow** *($; 10236 rue Lajeunesse, ☎ 388-9291)* occupies an immense red and gold pagoda. The decor is quite extraordinary and also quite attractive. The menu lists traditional Chinese dishes, adapted to suit North American tastes. In the large dining rooms, a pleasant family-oriented, festive atmosphere reigns.

Generous portions of Tunisian food are served at the neighbourhood restaurant **Le Kerkennah** *($; 1021 rue Fleury Est, ☎ 387-1089)*.

Lesage J.B. *($; 669 rue Millen, ☎ 383-9217)* is an excellent place to grab a quick meal, no frills: hot dogs, hamburgers and delicious fries make up the menu.

The chinese restaurant **Au Parasol Chinois** *($; 325 boulevard Henri-Bourassa Est, ☎ 384-1070)* is located near the Henri-Bourassa Métro station. It opens everyday at 11 a.m. and offers a buffet and a complete menu.

The little restaurant **Pasta Express** *($; 1501 rue Fleury Est,* ☎ *384-3174)*, which serves unpretentious Italian cuisine, is frequented by neighbourhood residents. The pasta dishes are inexpensive and always delicious.

Besides traditional pizza, the **Pizzeria Granada** *($; 1034 boulevard Henri-Bourassa Est,* ☎ *384-0050* or *389-6834)* offers a varied menu including brochettes, submarines and pasta.

On the way back from Sault-au-Récollet, visitors can stop in Villeray, at the restaurant **Si On Mangeait** *($; 694 rue Jarry Est,* ☎ *279-1903)*, a nice little bistro frequented mainly by locals, yet without a doubt the best in the area. Here, the customer is treated with care; the chef sometimes even comes out of the kitchen at the end of the evening to ask guests if they enjoyed their meal. The dishes are innovative and the ingredients fresh; the *rognons* (kidneys), for example, melt in your mouth, and the *ris de veau* (sweetbreads) with thin slices of pear, are exquisite.

Le Wok de Szechuan *($; 1950 rue Fleury Est,* ☎ *382-2060)*, as you may have guessed, serves good Szechuan food to a clientele of Chinese and locals.

Le Balada *($$; 1386 rue Fleury Est,* ☎ *858-5689)* is a large Russian, Romanian and Hungarian restaurant. Excellent folklore shows, gypsy music and classic dancing provide the entertainment.

Il Cicerone *($$; 679 boulevard Henri-Bourassa Est,* ☎ *388-3161)* attracts mainly a business crowd, and a few locals in search of good Italian cuisine.

The Italian restaurant **La Molisana** *($$$; 1014 rue Fleury Est,* ☎ *382-7100)* has a quiet atmosphere. The menu is not terribly original, consisting mainly of pasta dishes and pizza cooked in a wood-burning oven, but the food is good and the portions are generous. On weekends, live musicians liven up the evening with a few songs.

Il Mondo *($$$; 10724 rue Millen,* ☎ *389-8446)* is rather nondescript from the outside, but don't let first impressions fool you, because the menu includes some delicious dishes. Many say that this restaurant serves the best sauces in Montréal, and after just a few tastes, you'll be convinced.The service is attentive.

Île Sainte-Hélène and Île Notre-Dame

On Île Sainte-Hélène, the restaurant **Hélène de Champlain** *($$$;* ☎ *395-2424)* lies in an enchanting setting, without question one of the loveliest in Montréal. The large dining room, with its fireplace and view of the city and the river, is extremely pleasant. Each corner has its own unique charm, looking over the ever-changing surrounding landscape. Though the restaurant does not serve the fanciest of gastronomic cuisine the food is excellent. The service is courteous and attentive.

Faubourg à M'lasse

Pizzédélic *($; 1329 rue Sainte-Catherine Est,* ☎ *526-6011)*, see description p 184.

Located in the heart of the gay village, the **Saloon** *($; 1333 Sainte-Catherine Est,* ☎ *522-1333)* has the same menu as the Shed Café (see p 184), in a setting less like a warehouse and more like a saloon.

Located in a simple house **Chez la Mère Berteau** *($$; 1237 rue Champlain,* ☎ *524-9344)* is run by the owner, who attends to the tables, and his wife, who prepares the delicious meals. The wonderful flavours make you forget the small portions.

A lovely modern decor and very high ceiling give the local French restaurant **L'Entre-Miche** *($$; 2275 Sainte-Catherine Est,* ☎ *521-0816)* a certain elegance. The service is friendly, attentive and professional.

Le Petit Extra *($$; 1690 rue Ontario Est,* ☎ *527-5552)* is a large European style bistro and a distinguished spot for a good meal in a lively setting. There is a different *table d'hôte* each day. The clientele includes many regulars.

Maisonneuve

Le Goût de la Thaïlande *($; wine; 6361 rue Sherbrooke Est,* ☎ *272-7031)*, see description p 187.

The **Jardin du Baron Fou** *($$$; 5020 rue Notre-Dame Est,* ☎ *257-0666)* is frequented by people out to enjoy themselves heartily without drinking. On Friday, Saturday and Sunday, some 150 artists and extras liven up the evening. Staging, costumes and sets—everything comes together to make the evening fun and relaxing. The simple menu lacks polish, but its the show people come here for.

Little Burgundy and Saint-Henri

The **Green Spot** *($; 3041 rue Notre-Dame Ouest,* ☎ *932-2340)* is another temple to the French fry that has established a solid reputation among hot-dog and *poutine* connoisseurs. Everything reeks of grease and the decor is non-existent, but this just adds to the charm... For fast food fans only.

In the same category as above, try **New System** *($; 3419 rue Notre-Dame Ouest,* ☎ *932-1484)*, for barbecued chicken.

Pointe-Saint-Charles and Verdun

Right in the heart of industrial Pointe-Saint-Charles, is **Magnan** *($; 2602 rue Saint-Patrick, Pointe-Saint-Charles,* ☎ *935-9647)*, one of the best known taverns in Montréal. The house specialty is steak, ranging from 6 oz to 22 oz (170 g to 625 g) - hey why not get your yearly ration of red meat in one shot? The high quality beef and lobster festival attracts large crowds. Arrive by 11:30 a.m. to get a table for lunch.

The West Island

■ **Lachine**

Located near of Lachine's marina, **Il Fornetto** *($; 1900 boulevard Saint-Joseph, Lachine,* ☎ *637-5253)* is ideal for those who like taking after-dinner strolls - especially if that stroll is along the water and you've just eaten one of the generous portions served here. With its noisy crowd and friendly service the place is reminiscent of a trattoria. The pizzas cooked in the wood-burning stove are worth a try.

For real Italian food, head to **La Fontanina** *($$; 3194 boulevard Saint-Joseph,* ☎ *637-2475)* restaurant located in a charming renovated old house.

Chinese-food lovers should remember **Le Caveau Szechwan** *($$; 1798 boulevard Saint-Joseph,* ☎ *639-1800)* in Lachine.

■ **LaSalle**

Ristorante Andrea *($; 7 8ᵉ Avenue, LaSalle,* ☎ *366-7000)* is just a few minutes from the Lachine rapids, and is an enchanting spot that is not to be missed. It is frequented by a noisy, lively crowd, who come to celebrate special occasions. Simple family-style meals are served.

■ **Pointe-Claire**

Calories *($; 6729 autoroute Transcanadienne,* ☎ *630-6729)* : for the finest in cheesecake (see also p 183)

Chi-Chi's *($; 985 Saint-Jean,* ☎ *694-6346)* is usually packed with lively groups enjoying deliciously huge portions of Mexican food in a relaxed and friendly atmosphere.

Where to Get a Good Breakfast in Montréal

■ **Downtown**

If you are looking for a cute little restaurant for breakfast, try **La Tulipe Noire** (see p 181). It opens on weekday mornings at 7:30 a.m. and 8 a.m. on Saturdays. Brunch is served on Sundays.

The **Jardins du Ritz** (see p 174) is beautiful on sunny morning, and ideal for a relaxing breakfast. Sunday brunch *($38 per person)* is served as of 11:30 a.m.. The same menu is also served year round at the **Café de Paris**. Reservations are required.

An excellent breakfast is served in the refined setting of **Le Cercle** (see p 175) at the Hôtel Quatres-Saisons. Brunch is served on Sundays *($26.75 per person)*.

■ **Village Shaughnessy**

On Sundays the **Ambiance** tea room (see p 179) serves brunch as of 11:30 a.m.. Enjoying a good brunch and then exploring the several antique dealers in the area make a pleasant outing.

■ **Around the Hôtel-Dieu**

Beauty's is literally overrun on weekends by hungry crowds who come for the brunch which includes among other things a delicious bagel and lox (see p 183).

■ **Plateau Mont Royal**

Hearty breakfasts, including baked beans, eggs, bacon and sausages are served every morning at **Chez Claudette** (see p 187), and at a price to suit all appetites!

Delicious, nutritious breakfasts can be enjoyed at the **Aux Entretiens** (see p 187) restaurant in a relaxed atmosphere.

The terrace of the **Café Cherrier** (see p 188) is busy every morning with a clientele looking to enjoy a delicious breakfast in a pleasant environment.

■ **Quartier Latin**

The doors open early every morning at the friendly **Le Pélerin** (see p 186) café, where breakfasts, Viennese pastries of all sorts and delicious coffees are served (see p 186).

Just steps from UQAM, the **Second Cup** (see p 186) restaurant serves a variety of pastries and coffees.

■ **Outremont**

La Croissanterie (see p 191) has a charming terrace opening up onto a quiet street, and is an ideal spot to enjoy breakfast on a summer morning.

The Italian restaurant **Eduardo** (see p 190) prepares a delicious brunch.

ENTERTAINMENT

Montréal's reputation as a vibrant and unique city in North America is well established. Whether it be cultural activities, huge festivals, or simply the countless bars and discotheques of all kinds, Montréal is a fascinating city with something for everyone. Sports enthusiasts will also get their fill with professional hockey and baseball, as well as the international sporting events that take place here each year.

 Bars and Discotheques

From sundown until early morning, Montréal is alive with the sometimes boisterous, other times more romantic rhythm of its bars. Crowded with people of all ages, there are bars designed to suit everyone's tastes, from the sidewalk bars along Rue Saint-Denis to the underground bars of Boulevard Saint-Laurent; from the most fashionable bars on Rue Crescent to the gay bars in the "Village"; there are whole other worlds to discover.

Though it is located in the heart of the Gay Village, **Le Big Bang** *(cover charge $6 on Thursdays when drinks are served at reduced prices, Sat and Sun $3; 1400 rue Montcalm)* attracts a young, fashionable, straight clientele. An energetic crowd lets loose on the vast, multi-level dance floor. The club features techno-rave music and incredible lighting.

L'Air du Temps *(194 rue Saint-Paul Ouest)* ranks among the most famous jazz bars in Montréal. Set in the heart of Vieux-Montréal, it has a fantastic interior decorated with scores of antiques. As the place is often packed, it is necessary to arrive early to get a good seat. The cover charge varies according to the show. For more information, call ☎ 842-2003.

Dark, smoky, jam-packed, hot, hectic and noisy, Le Balattou *(4372 boulevard Saint-Laurent)* is without a doubt the most popular African nightclub in Montréal. On weekends, the cover charge is $7 (including one drink). Shows are presented only during the week, when the cost of admission varies.

A clientele composed mainly of junior executives crowds into the Belmont *(4483 boulevard Saint-Laurent)*. On weekends, the place is literally overrun with customers. Cover charge: $3 on Thursdays, $4 on Fridays and Saturdays.

La Bibliothèque *(1647 rue Saint-Denis)* is a quiet bar with a beautiful terrace overlooking the hustle and bustle of Rue Saint-Denis.

A bar with a modest decor, Les Beaux Esprits *(2073 rue Saint-Denis)* presents good jazz and blues shows.

Obliged to move from its location in front of the Université de Montréal, Café Campus *(57 Prince Arthur)* has settled into a large place on Rue Prince Arthur. Over the years, it had become a Montréal institution, but now that it has moved, it has to prove itself all over again (will its regular clientele follow it?). The decor is still quite plain. Good musicians are frequently invited to give shows here.

Le Central *(4479 rue Saint-Denis)* is an old unpretentious jazz bar, popular among students because the drinks are

so inexpensive and there is no cover charge. The Quai des Brumes on the first floor has a calmer, warmer atmosphere.

Bar La Cervoise *(4457 boulevard Saint-Laurent)* is a small laid-back *brasserie* with a young clientele. An interesting mix of music adds to the atmosphere. Pool tables are available for any and all interested.

Le Cheval Blanc *(809 rue Ontario Est)* is a Montréal tavern, which does not appear to have been renovated since the 1940's; hence its unique style! A few beers are brewed on the premises, and vary depending on the season.

Young professionals are the typical crowd at Crocodile *(5414 rue Gatineau; 4238 boulevard Saint-Laurent; 636 rue Cathcart)*. They come to dance to popular music, have a few drinks and to see and be seen. The restaurant offers a traditional menu in the early evening.

A noisy, enthusiastic crowd is drawn to Aux Deux Pierrots *(cover charge $5; 104 rue Saint-Paul Ouest)* to sing along with Quebecois variety singers. During summer, there is a pleasant outdoor terrace.

Di Salvio's *(3519 boulevard Saint-Laurent)* art deco interior and fifties-style furniture create a unique and original setting. Patrons lucky enough to get picked from the line-up (it can be difficult to get in) dance to underground music.

The discotheque Eugène Patin *(5777 boulevard Saint-Laurent, at the corner of Bernard)* is frequented by a clientele of junior executives, who meet to enjoy an original blend of popular music and oldies.

Les Foufounes Électriques *(87 rue Sainte-Catherine Est)*, the place with the bizarre name (The Electric Buns), is in fact a fantastic, one-of-a-kind bar-discotheque-meeting place. The best bar in Québec for dancing to non-traditional music, it attracts a motley crowd of young Montrealers, ranging from punks to medical students. The decor, consisting of graffiti and strange sculptures, is wacky, to say the least. Don't come here for a quiet night.

The **Fûtenbulle** *(273 avenue Bernard Ouest)* is open to everyone. Besides the simple menu, customers can choose from probably the largest selection of beers in Montréal.

During summer, **Le Grand Café** *(1720 rue Saint-Denis)* is at the heart of the action on Rue Saint-Denis. Jazz and blues bands provide the entertainment.

The **Île Noire** *(342 rue Ontario Est)* is a beautiful bar, in the purest Scottish tradition. The abundance of precious wood used for the decor gives the place a cosy charm and sophisticated atmosphere. The learned staff guide guests through the impressive list of whiskeys. The bar also has a good selection of imported draft beer. Unfortunately, the prices are high.

The biggest discotheque in Montréal, the **Métropolis** *($5 cover charge during the week, $8 on Sat.; 59 rue Sainte-Catherine)* occupies what was once an immense theatre.

The **Loft's** *(1405 boulevard Saint-Laurent, ☎ 281-8058)* austere techno interior, accented in mauve, and alternative music attract a varied clientele between the ages of 18 and 30. Interesting exhibits are occasionally presented. Pool tables provide some

diversion, and the roof-top terrace is pleasant.

A young clientele packs the **Passeport** *(4156 rue Saint-Denis)* every night of the week.

Le Pub... de Londres à Berlin *(4557 rue Saint-Denis)* has a somewhat austere decor with the added bonus of free popcorn and a wide selection of draft beers.

The **Saint-Sulpice** *(1682 rue Saint-Denis)* occupies all three floors of an old house and is tastefully decorated. Its front and back terraces are perfect places to make the most of summer evenings.

Noisy students crowd the **Bar Salon Saint-Laurent** *(3874 boulevard Saint-Laurent)*, to discuss the latest news or dance to South-American and Caribbean rhythms.

The **Set** *(5301 boulevard Saint-Laurent)* is a small cosy bar, decorated with antiques. The pleasant choice of music is always at just the right volume so as not to interfere with conversation. This is a popular spot on weekends.

Le Sherlock *(1010 rue Sainte-Catherine Ouest)* has a very lovely decor, including busts of Sherlock Holmes, reminiscent of an English pub. It also has the advantage of being very big and very popular! Everything, however, is quite expensive, and the restaurant is not recommended. About 15 pools tables are also at the disposal of customers.

The **Sir Winston Churchill Pub** *(1459 rue Crescent)*, an English-style bistro, attracts crowds of singles, who come here to cruise and meet people. It has pool tables and a small dance floor.

The entrance to **Swimming** *(3643 boulevard Saint-Laurent)* leads through the dilapidated vestibule of a building dating back to the beginning of the century, making the view from the third floor of this gigantic pool room even more striking. The large rectangular bar and endless rows of pool tables and players are surrounded by glazed concrete columns, deliberately emphasized and topped by strange polyhedrons. The patterned sheet metal ceiling is a reminder of both the industrial city of the early 20th century, and the building's original purpose.

Thursday's *(1449 rue Crescent)* bar is very popular, especially among the city's anglophone population. It is a favourite meeting place for business people and professionals.

The **Vieux Dublin Pub** *(1219 A rue University)* is an Irish pub with live Celtic music and an impressive selection of draft beer.

Located inside a large Bavarian-style building, the **Vieux Munich** *(1170 rue Saint-Denis)* is frequented by folks of all ages, who come to drink beer and enjoy the excellent Bavarian music.

The **Whisky Café** *(3 rue Bernard Ouest)* has been so conscientiously decorated that even the men's bathrooms are on their way to becoming a tourist attraction. The warm colours used in a modern setting, the tall columns covered with woodwork and the 1950's-style chairs all create a sense of comfort and elegance. The well-off, well-bred clientele consists of a gilded youth between the ages of 20 and 35.

The **Zoo** *(3556 boulevard Saint-Laurent)* is a hot dance bar where beautiful people come to check each other out. The modern decor, female mannequins dressed in zebra-stripes and leopard-spots hanging from the ceilings, and triangular bar all make it a popular spot with young professionals. Alternative, dance and rap music add to the melée!

■ Gay Bars and Discotheques

The **Cabaret l'Entre-Peau** *(1115 rue Sainte-Catherine Est)* puts on transvestite shows. The place attracts a lively, mixed clientele.

Intellectuals get together at the quiet **La California** *(1412 rue Sainte-Élizabeth)*. In the summer, patrons enjoy a superb terrace laid out in an inner court, forming a lovely urban garden.

The **Club Date** *(1218 rue Sainte-Catherine Est)* piano-bar is located in the village. Singers are often presented. The clientele is mainly older men.

Located in an old post office and still carrying its old name, **Station C** *(1450 rue Sainte-Catherine Est)* is a veritable gay complex, not lacking in charm. There are two nightclubs inside, **K.O.X**, which attracts a mixed crowd and **Katacombes**, for men only.

Max *(1166 rue Sainte-Catherine Est)* is a comfortable discotheque with a varied crowd of all ages.

A trendy bar in the village, **Sky** *(1474 rue Sainte-Catherine Est)* attracts a young gay crowd. Techno-pop music.

La Track *(1584 rue Sainte-Catherine Est)* is a lively men's gay bar, most of whose patrons dress in leather and come to cruise.

Cultural Activities

Montréal has a distinct cultural scene. All year round, there are shows and exhibitions, which enable Montrealers to discover different aspects of the arts. Accordingly, shows and films from all over the world, exhibitions of art of all different styles, and festivals for all tastes and ages are presented here. The free weekly newspapers *Voir*, *The Mirror* and *Hour* summarize the main events taking place in Montréal.

■ Theatres

Prices vary greatly from one theatre to the next. Most of the time, however, there are student rates.

Club Soda
5240, avenue du Parc
☎ 270-7848
Great shows are presented here, particularly during the Just for Laughs Festival and the Jazz Festival. During these festivals, the shows are free after 11 pm.

Place des Arts
260, boulevard de Maisonneuve Ouest
☎ 285-4200, ☎ 842-2112 (for reservations)
The complex contains five theatres: Salle Wilfrid-Pelletier, Théâtre Maisonneuve, Théâtre Jean-Duceppe, Théâtre du Café de la Place and the Cinquième Salle, opened in 1992.

Théâtre du Nouveau Monde
84, rue Sainte-Catherine Ouest
☎ 861-0563

Théâtre du Rideau Vert
4664, rue Saint-Denis
☎ 844-1793

Théâtre Saint-Denis
1594, rue Saint-Denis
☎ 849-4211

Théâtre d'Aujourd'hui
3900, rue Saint-Denis
☎ 282-3900

Théâtre Espace GO
5066, rue Clark
☎ 271-0813

Théâtre de Quat'Sous
100, rue des Pins Est
☎ 845-7277

Théâtre de Verdure
Parc Lafontaine
☎ 872-2644
Set up in the heart of Parc Lafontaine, the Théâtre de Verdure puts on free open-air shows all summer long.

Spectrum
318, rue Sainte-Catherine Ouest
☎ 861-5851
Shows usually begin around 11 p.m.. Count on at least $10 to get in. As with Club Soda, shows after 11 p.m. are usually free during the Festival de Jazz.

■ Ticket Sales

There are two major ticket agencies in Montréal, which sell tickets for shows, concerts and other events over the telephone. Service charges, which vary according to the show, are added to the price of the ticket. Credit cards are accepted.

Admission
☎ (514) 790-1245
☎ 1-800-361-4595

Ticketmaster
☎ (514) 790-2222

Billetterie Articulée (an *Admission* ticket outlet)
☎ (514) 844-2172

■ **Information on the Arts**

Montréal Aujourd'hui
☎ 790-1234
The telephone service **Montréal Aujourd'hui** provides free information on the major cultural events taking place that day. The service is free.

Info-Arts (Bell)
☎ 790-ARTS
This service's operators provide information on current cultural and artistic events in the city.

■ **Museums**

Permanent exhibits at most museums are free on Wednesday evenings between 6 p.m. and 9 p.m. Special rates are available for temporary exhibits during the same period. Call ahead to check.

■ **Movie Theatres**

Montréal has many movie theatres; here is a list of the major downtown theatres. Special rates are offered on Tuesdays and for matinees. The regular price of a ticket is $8 (except at repertory theatres).

The following show films in French:

Berri
1280, rue Berri
☎ 849-3456

Complexe Desjardins
Rue Sainte-Catherine Ouest, between Jeanne-Mance and Saint-Urbain
☎ 849-3456

Le Parisien
480, rue Sainte-Catherine Ouest
☎ 866-3856

The following show films in English:

Égyptien
Cours Mont-Royal, 1455, rue Peel
☎ 849-3456

Loews
954, rue Sainte-Catherine Ouest
☎ 861-7437

Palace
698, rue Sainte-Catherine Ouest
☎ 866-6991

Impérial
1430, rue de Bleury
☎ 288-1702
This is the oldest movie theatre in Montréal.

The following are repertory theatres:

La Cinémathèque Québécoise
335, boulevard de Maisonneuve Est
☎ 842-9763
shows films in French

Le Nouvel Élysée
35, rue Milton
☎ 288-1857
shows films in French

Le Cinéma Parallèle
3682, boulevard Saint-Laurent
☎ 843-6001
shows films in French

Cinéma de Paris
896, rue Sainte-Catherine Ouest
☎ 875-7284
shows films in English

Le Rialto
5723, avenue du Parc
☎ 272-3899
shows films in English, or with subtitles
A one-of-a kind theatre with out-of-the-ordinary films, and plays.

Le Cinéma Imax
at the Vieux-Port de Montréal, on Rue de la Commune corner Boulevard Saint-Laurent
☎ 496-4629; for reservations
☎ 496-1799
Films are presented on a giant screen (see p 64).

Complex dedicated to Quebecois and Canadian cinema :

**Office National du Film
(National Film Board)**
1564, rue Saint-Denis
☎ 496-6301
A *cinérobothèque* allows several people to watch NFB films at once. A robot, the only one like it in the world, loads each machine.

■ **Cultural Centres**

Cultural centres have been established to help young artists of all disciplines become professionals. In order to make these exhibits and shows accessible to all, admission is free. Schedules of the specific exhibits at these *Maisons de la Culture* are published in the "Show" section of *The Gazette* every Friday.

Ahuntsic/Cartierville
12137, rue Bois-de-Boulogne
☎ 872-8749

Chapelle Historique du Bon Pasteur
100, rue Sherbrooke Est
☎ 872-5338

Côte-des-Neiges
5290, chemin de la Côte-des-Neiges
☎ 872-6889

La Petite Patrie
6707, avenue de Lorimier
☎ 872-1730

Maisonneuve
4120, rue Ontario Est
☎ 872-2200

Marie-Uguay
6052, rue Monk
☎ 872-2044

Mercier
8105, rue Hochelaga
☎ 872-8755

Notre-Dame-de-Grâce
3755, rue Botrel
☎ 872-2157

Parc Frontenac
2550, rue Ontario Est
☎ 872-7882

Plateau Mont-Royal
465, avenue du Mont-Royal Est
☎ 872-2266

Pointe-aux-Trembles
12045, rue Notre-Dame Est
☎ 872-2240

Rivière-des-Prairies
8075, rue Hochelaga
☎ 872-9814

Villeray/Saint-Michel/Parc-Extension
7920, rue Hochelaga
☎ 872-1730

Festivals

During summer, festival fever takes hold of Montréal. From May to September, the city hosts a whole series of festivals, each with a different theme. One thing is for certain—there is something for everyone. As the summer season draws to a close, these events become less frequent.

During the **Concours International d'Art Pyrotechnique** (International Fireworks Competition) (☎ 514-872-6222), during the months of June and July, the world's top pyrotechnists present high-quality pyro-musical shows every Saturday in June and every Sunday in July. Montrealers crowd to the La Ronde amusement park (tickets cost $21.15; call ☎ 514-790-1245), on the Pont Jacques-Cartier or alongside the river (both at no cost) to admire the spectacular blossoms of flame that colour the sky above the city for over half an hour.

During the **Festival International de Jazz de Montréal** (☎ 514-871-1881), hundreds of shows set to the rhythm of jazz and its variations are presented on stages erected around Place des Arts. At the beginning of July, this part of the city and a fair number of theatres are buzzing with activity. The event offers people an opportunity to take to the streets and be carried away by the festive atmosphere of the fantastic, free outdoor shows, which attract Montrealers and visitors in large numbers.

Humour and creativity are highlighted during the **Festival Juste pour Rire** (Just for Laughs Festival) (☎ 514-845-3155 or 790-HAHA), held at the end of July. Theatres host comedians from a variety of countries for the occasion. Théâtre Saint-Denis presents shows consisting of short performances by a number of different comedians. Given the growing numbers of spectators, all outdoor activities will now take place at the Vieux-Port. Outdoor shows will take place on Quai Jacques-Cartier and the two small islands adjacent. An admission fee of $2 for adults and $1 for children will be charged to help finance the festival.

The **FrancoFolies** (☎ 514-871-1881) are organized to promote French-language music and song. At the beginning of August, artists from all Francophone countries (Europe, Africa, French Antilles, Québec and French Canada) give shows, providing spectators with a unique glimpse of the world's French musical talent.

The **Fêtes Gourmandes** (☎ 861-8241), organized in mid-August on Île Notre-Dame, is the perfect opportunity to sample gastronomic goodies from Québec, Canada and several other countries. Over a kilometre of international tables are set up, allowing visitors to taste and discover the exotic flavours of the world.

At the end of August beginning of September, the **Festival International des Films du Monde** (World Film Festival) (☎ 514-848-3883) is held in various Montréal movie theatres. During this competition, films from different countries are presented to Montréal audiences. At the end of the competition, prizes are awarded to the most praiseworthy films. The most prestigious category is the Grand Prix des Amériques. During the festival, films are shown from morning to night, to the delight of movie-goers across the city.

During the **Cent Jours d'Art Contemporain de Montréal** (Hundred Days of Contemporary Art), from September 1st to November 27th, about thirty artists from Québec, Canada and abroad present their works of sculpture, painting or video. This contemporary visual art extravaganza takes place at 3576 Avenue du Parc, ☎ 288-0811.

Winter's cold does not preclude the festival spirit, it merely provides an opportunity to organize another festival in Montréal, this time to celebrate the pleasures and activities of this frosty season. The **Fête des Neiges** takes place on Île Notre-Dame, from the end of January to mid February. Skating rinks and giant toboggans are set up for the enjoyment of Montréal families. The ice-sculpture competition also attracts a number of curious onlookers.

Sporting Events

The Forum
2313, rue Sainte-Catherine Ouest
☎ 932-2582
Starting in the fall, the Montréal Canadiens' hockey games are held at the **Forum**. The team plays 42 games during the regular season. Then come the play-offs, when the Stanley Cup Champions are decided.

The Stade Olympique
4141, avenue Pierre-de-Courbertin
☎ 846-3976
Spring signals the beginning of baseball season. At the **Stade Olympique** *(4141 avenue Pierre-de-Courbertin,* ☎ *846-3976)*, the Expos play against the various teams of the National Baseball League.

■ Big Events

The **Tour de l'Île** takes place in early June. The event can accommodate a maximum of 45,000 cyclists, who ride together for some 65 km around the island of Montréal. Registration begins in April, and costs $19 for adults and $8 for children under 11 and senior citizens. Registration forms are available at Canadian Tire stores (in Québec) and from *Tour de l'Île de Montréal* 3575 Boulevard Saint-Laurent, office 310, H2X 2T7, ☎ 514-847-8356).

Mid-June is marked by an international event that captivates a large number of fans from all over North America—the **Grand Prix Molson du Canada** *(to reserve seats, call* ☎ *514-392-0000)*, which takes place at the Circuit Gilles Villeneuve on l'Île Notre-Dame. This is without question one of the most popular events of the summer. During these three days, it is possible to attend a variety of car races, including the roaring, spectacular Formula One competition.

From August 13th to 21st, 1994, tennis enthusiasts flock to the **Internationaux Matinée de Tennis** *(*☎ *273-1515)*. The top women players compete this year and other even-numbered years (it is a men's competition in odd-numbered years). Tickets can be purchased by phone at ☎ 790-1245.

September 18th, around 8,000 runners participate in the **Marathon de Montréal** *(*☎ *284-5272)*. Four races are scheduled, one for wheelchairs (10 km), one for young people aged 6 to 17 (3 km), a relay (42,2 km) and the classic marathon (42,2 km).

SHOPPING

Whether it be original Québec creations or imported articles, Montréal's shops sell all sorts of merchandise, each item more interesting than the last. To assist visitors in their shopping, we have prepared a list of shops with exceptionally high-quality, original or inexpensive products.

"En vente" and *"en solde"* both mean on sale, therefore the price is reduced.

The Underground City

The 1962 construction of Place Ville-Marie, with its underground shopping mall, marked the origins of what is known today as the underground city. The development of this "city under the city" was accelerated by the construction of the Métro, which opened in 1966. Soon, most downtown businesses and office buildings, as well as a few hotels, were strategically linked to the underground pedestrian network and, by extension, to the Métro.

Today, the underground city, now the largest in the world, has five distinct sections. The first lies at the very heart of the Métro system, around the Berri-UQAM station, and is connected to the buildings of the Université du Québec à Montréal (UQAM), the Galeries Dupuis and the bus station. The second stretches between the Place-des-Arts and Place-d'Armes stations, and is linked to Place des Arts, the Musée d'Art Contemporain, Complexe Desjardins, Complexe Guy Favreau and

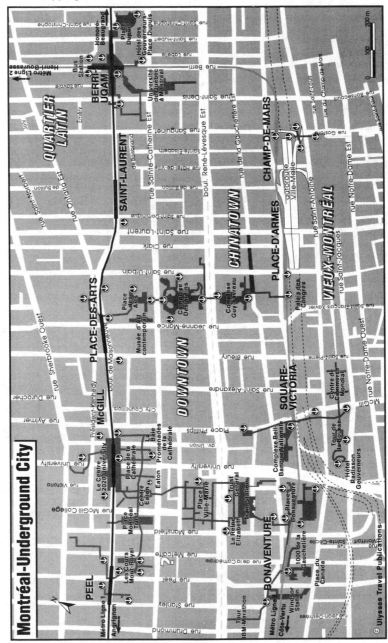

Montréal-Underground City

the Palais des Congrès, forming an exceptional cultural ensemble. The third, at the Square-Victoria station, serves the business centre. The fourth, which is the busiest and most important one, is identified with the McGill, Peel and Bonaventure stations. It encompasses the La Baie and Eaton department stores; the Promenades de la Cathédrale, Place Montréal Trust and Cours Mont-Royal shopping centres, as well as Place Bonaventure, 1000 de la Gauchetière, the train station and Place Ville-Marie. The fifth and final area is located in the commercial section around the Atwater station; it is linked to Westmount Square, Collège Dawson and Place Alexis Nihon (see detailed map of underground city).

Haute Couture

The fashion industry is flourishing in Montréal. The city is a multiethnic crossroads where Quebecois and Canadian designers show their latest creations alongside those from the United States, Italy, France and elsewhere. Streets like Saint-Denis, Laurier, Saint-Laurent and Sherbrooke stand out for the numerous boutiques that line their sidewalks. A visit to the shops is sure to turn up something that is just your size.

■ Shopping Centres, Department Stores and Fashion

Several downtown shopping centres offer a good selection of clothing by well-known fashion designers, including Jean-Claude Chacok, Cacharel, Guy Laroche, Lily Simon, Adrienne Vittadini, Mondi, Ralph Lauren and many others.

Holt Renfrew
1300, rue Sherbrooke Ouest, ☎ 842-5111

Ogilvy
1307, rue Sainte-Catherine Ouest, ☎ 842-7711

Place Montréal Trust
1600, avenue McGill College, ☎ 842-8000

Place Ville-Marie
5, Place Ville-Marie, ☎ 861-9393

Westmount Square
4, Westmount Square, ☎ 932-0211

Certain department stores carry *haute couture* lines in a broad range of prices. These stores also carry Canadian designs, such as those by Simon Chang, Michel Robichaud and Alfred Sung, as well as fashions by foreign designers like Mondi, Jones New York and Adrienne Vittadini. Leather goods can also be had for respectable prices.

Eaton
677, rue Sainte-Catherine Ouest, ☎ 284-8411

La Baie
Square Phillips (on rue Sainte-Catherine Ouest), ☎ 281-4422

■ A Few Small Clothing Boutiques

L'Aventure
277, avenue Laurier Ouest, ☎ 948-3805 (women)
5107, avenue du Parc, ☎ 274-4184 (men)

Collection 24 (women)
90, avenue Laurier Ouest, ☎ 273-4682
1334, Fleury Est, ☎ 387-6712

Henriette L. (women)
1012, avenue Laurier Ouest,
☎ 277-3426

Il n'y a que deux (men and women)
1405, rue Crescent, ☎ 843-5665

Old River (men)
1115, rue Sainte-Catherine Ouest,
☎ 843-5520

■ Québec Designs

Artefact
4117, rue Saint-Denis, ☎ 842-2780

Revenge
3852, rue Saint-Denis, ☎ 843-4379

Splash
1397, rue Sainte-Catherine Ouest,
☎ 845-0545

■ Hats

Chapofolie
4129, rue Saint-Denis, ☎ 982-0036

Henri Henri
189, rue Sainte-Catherine Est,
☎ 288-0109

Sieur Duluth
4107, rue Saint-Denis, ☎ 843-8933

■ Lingerie

Deuxième Peau
4457, rue Saint-Denis, ☎ 842-0811

Jacob Lingerie
4067, rue Saint-Denis, ☎ 844-0190

La Senza
Place Montréal Trust, ☎ 288-8775

La Vie en Rose
Place Montréal Trust, ☎ 844-2704

Lyla
1087, avenue Laurier Ouest,
☎ 271-0763

Madame Courval
4861, rue Sherbrooke Ouest,
☎ 484-5656

Moments Intimes
Centre Eaton, ☎ 847-0856
1, Place Ville-Marie, ☎ 874-9480

Un Homme la Nuit
Place Ville-Marie

■ Fur

Desjardins Fourrure
325, boulevard René-Lévesque Est,
☎ 288-4151

Fourrure Oslo
2863 A, boulevard Rosemont,
☎ 499-1777

McComber
440, boulevard de Maisonneuve Ouest,
☎ 845-1167

■ Boots

Top Western (for cowboy boots)
4314, rue Saint-Denis, ☎ 843-6069
1384, rue Sainte-Catherine Ouest,
☎ 875-4972

■ Jeans

Dalton
4339, rue Saint-Denis, ☎ 845-8819
3794, boulevard Saint-Laurent,
☎ 843-3320

Pantorama
Place Montréal Trust (corner of rue Sainte-Catherine Ouest and rue McGill College)
This boutique sells all sorts of denim clothing, and often has specials.

Paris-Texas
4201 B, rue Saint-Denis, ☎ 281-6686
This boutique has a wide variety of brands of jeans, as well as a funky selection of suede and leather coats.

Superior Pants
69, rue Sainte-Catherine Est, ☎ 842-6969
This boutique specializes in Levi's; they also do alterations.

■ **Sportswear**

Azimut
1781, rue Saint-Denis, ☎ 844-1717
1324, rue Sherbrooke Ouest, ☎ 849-2193

La Cordée
2159, rue Sainte-Catherine Est, ☎ 524-1106

Kanuk
752, rue Rachel, ☎ 527-4494

Tilley Endurables (easy-wash travel wear)
158, avenue Laurier Ouest, ☎ 272-7791

Le Yéti
5127, boulevard Saint-Laurent, ☎ 271-0773

■ **Children's Clothing**

Am Stram Gram
1279, avenue Bernard Ouest, ☎ 272-0751

Boutique Enfants Deslongchamps
1007, avenue Laurier Ouest, ☎ 274-2442

Boutique Fiou
3933, rue Saint-Denis, ☎ 844-0444

Maison Lalongé
7088, Plaza Saint-Hubert, ☎ 273-3329

Noisette et chocolat
316, avenue Duluth Est, ☎ 844-0394

Pom'Canelle
4860, rue Sherbrooke Ouest, ☎ 483-1787

Bookstores

There are francophone as well as anglophone bookstores in Montréal. American, Canadian and Quebecois books are sold at reasonable prices. Visitors interested in literature from Québec will find a large selection in bookstores in Montréal, now is the time to stock those library shelves! Books imported from Europe are generally a bit more expensive, due to shipping costs.

■ **General**

Champigny (francophone)
4380, rue Saint-Denis, ☎ 844-2587
5054, avenue du Parc, ☎ 495-9297

Coles (francophone and anglophone)
1171, rue Sainte-Catherine Ouest, ☎ 849-8825

Librairie Gallimard (francophone)
3700, boulevard Saint-Laurent, ☎ 499-2012

Librairie Paragraphe and Café (anglophone)
2065, rue Mansfield, ☎ 845-5811

Librairie Renaud-Bray (francophone)
5219, chemin de la Côte-des-Neiges, ☎ 342-1515
4233, rue Saint-Denis, ☎ 499-3656
5117, avenue du Parc, ☎ 276-7651

WH Smith (francophone and anglophone)
Place Ville-Marie, ☎ 861-1736
Place de la Cathédrale, ☎ 289-8737

■ **Specialized**

Double Hook Bookshop (Canadian books)
1235 A, avenue Greene, ☎ 932-5093

Librairie Artexte (contemporary art)
185, rue Sainte-Catherine Ouest, ☎ 847-6903

Librairie Allemande (German books)
418, rue Sherbrooke Est, ☎ 845-7489

Librairie l'Androgyne (gay and feminist literature)
3636, boulevard Saint-Laurent, ☎ 842-4765

Librairie C.E.C. Michel Fortin (education, languages)
3714, rue Saint-Denis, ☎ 849-5719

Librairie du Centre Canadien d'Architecture
1920, rue Baile, ☎ 939-7028

Librairie Ésotérique (esotericism and New Age)
1707, rue Saint-Denis, ☎ 844-1719

Librairie Las Americas (Spanish books)
10, rue Saint-Norbert, ☎ 844-5994

Librairie Italiana (Italian books)
6792, boulevard Saint-Laurent, ☎ 277-2955

Librairie du Musée des Beaux-Arts (art)
1368, rue Sherbrooke Ouest, ☎ 285-1600, poste 350

Librairie Olivieri (foreign literature, art)
5200, rue Gatineau, ☎ 739-3639

Éditions Paulines (religion)
4362, rue Saint-Denis, ☎ 849-3585

Librairie Renaud-Bray (children)
5219, chemin de la Côte-des-Neiges, ☎ 342-1515

Librairie Stratégie (business)
4174, rue Saint-Denis, ☎ 843-9875

Librairie Ulysse (travel)
4176, rue Saint-Denis, ☎ 843-9447
560, avenue du Président-Kennedy, ☎ 843-7222
Ogilvy, 1307, rue Ste-Catherine Ouest, ☎ 842-7711 ext.362

■ **Magazines**

Le Lux
5220, boulevard Saint-Laurent, ☎ 271-9272

Maison de la Presse Internationale
1393, rue Sainte-Catherine Ouest, ☎ 844-4508
1128, rue Sainte-Catherine Ouest, ☎ 874-1676
4201, rue Saint-Denis, ☎ 289-9323

Stationery Stores

Carton
4068, rue Saint-Denis, ☎ 844-9663

Essence du Papier
4160, rue Saint-Denis, ☎ 288-9691
393, rue Saint-Jacques Ouest, ☎ 842-2272
Ogilvy, 1307, rue Sainte-Catherine Ouest, ☎ 844-8244

Papillote
1126, avenue Bernard, ☎ 271-6356

Raymond DesCartes
5171, boulevard Saint-Laurent, ☎ 270-7442

Compact Discs and Cassettes

Archambault Musique
500, rue Sainte-Catherine Est, ☎ 849-6201

HMV
1035, rue Sainte-Catherine Ouest, ☎ 844-8468

Rayon Laser (sales and rental, alternative music)
19, rue Prince-Arthur Ouest, ☎ 848-6300

Sam the Record Man
399, rue Sainte-Catherine Ouest, corner Rue Saint-Alexandre

Tres-Arts
1633, rue Saint-Denis, ☎ 849-9417

Electronics

Montréal is an interesting place to purchase electronic equipment, like telephone answering machines, fax machines and cordless telephones. These units can be used in the United States and Europe, however in the latter case, the electric wires and cards must be adapted to your country's telephone system.

Téléboutique Bell
Place Alexis-Nihon, 1500, avenue Atwater, ☎ 287-5045
Galeries Dupuis, 1475, rue Saint-Hubert, ☎ 287-5045

Radio Shack
Place Montréal Trust, 1500, avenue McGill College, ☎ 499-9922

On Boulevard Saint-Laurent, between Boulevard de Maisonneuve and Rue Sherbrooke, several stores sell electronic equipment of all kinds. The merchandise is sold as is; bargain and expect to pay from 10% to 20% less than the sticker price.

Computer Stores

Dumoulin Informatique
8251, rue Saint-Hubert, ☎ 385-1777

Micro Boutique
6615, avenue du Parc, ☎ 270-4477

Softmagic Computer Software inc.
9740, Henri-Bourassa Ouest, ☎ 335-0195

Solide Logique
5177, boulevard Décarie, ☎ 481-7777

■ Computer Books and Software

Camelot Info
1191, Square Phillips, ☎ 861-5019

Crazy Irving
1219, Square Phillips, ☎ 398-0737

Crafts

Craft boutiques, known as *boutique d'artisanat* in French, offer an impressive selection of pieces illustrating the work and specific themes dear to artisans from here and abroad.

■ Local Crafts

Local crafts include Canadian, Native and Inuit, as well as Québec works. Each year during the month of December, the *Salon des Métiers d'Art du Québec* (Québec Art and Crafts show) is held at Place Bonaventure *(901 rue de la Gauchetière Ouest)*. The show lasts about ten days and provides Québec artists the opportunity to display and sell their work.

Le Rouet
136, rue Saint-Paul Est, ☎ 875-2333
4201, rue Saint-Denis, ☎ 842-4306
1500, avenue McGill College, ☎ 843-5235
700, rue Sainte-Catherine Ouest, ☎ 861-8401

Galerie d'Art Inuit Baffin
4, rue Saint-Paul Est, ☎ 393-1999
Specialzes in Inuit crafts.

Guilde Canadienne des Métiers d'Arts
2025, rue Peel, ☎ 849-6091
A small boutique sells pieces of Canadian and Quebecois art, and two small galleries exhibit Inuit and Native art and crafts.

Le Chariot
446, Place Jacques-Cartier, ☎ 875-6134
Offers a good selection of Inuit and Native art and crafts.

Manu Reva (pottery)
20, rue Fairmount Ouest, ☎ 948-1717

■ International Crafts

Artefact
102, avenue Laurier Ouest, ☎ 278-6575

Galerie Ima
3839, rue Saint-Denis, ☎ 499-2904
Works from Iran are for sale.

Giraffe
3997, rue Saint-Denis, ☎ 499-8436
A good selection of African art is sold.

Art Galleries

■ Traditional

Centre d'Art Morency
2180, rue de la Montagne, ☎ 845-6442

Galerie Dominion
1438, rue Sherbrooke Ouest, ☎ 845-7471

Galerie Clarence Gagnon
1108, avenue Laurier Ouest, ☎ 270-2962

Galerie Claude Lafitte
1480, rue Sherbrooke Ouest, ☎ 939-9898

Galerie Jean-Pierre Valentin
1434, rue Sherbrooke Ouest, ☎ 849-3637

Waddington & Gore
2155, rue Mackay, ☎ 847-1112

■ Contemporary and *Avant-Garde* Art

Galerie Clark
1591, rue Clark, ☎ 288-4972

Galerie Michel-Ange
430, rue Bonsecours, ☎ 875-8281

Galerie Oboro
4001, rue Berri, ☎ 844-3250

Galerie Prince
55, rue Prince, ☎ 878-2787

Galerie Samuel Lallouz
372, rue Sainte-Catherine Ouest,
☎ 398-9806

Galerie Simon Blais
4521, rue Clark, ☎ 849-1165

Galerie Skol
279, rue Sherbrooke Ouest,
☎ 842-4021

Galerie Trois Points
307, rue Sainte-Catherine Ouest,
☎ 845-5555

The cultural centres (*maisons de la culture*) of the Université du Québec à Montréal (UQAM) present exhibits of local artists' works.

■ Glasswork

Elena Lee
1428, rue Sherbrooke Ouest,
☎ 844-6009

Antique Dealers

Antique dealers stock an assortment of eccentric items to suit every taste. Visitors looking for quality antiques irregardless of price should check out the respectable stores in Westmount along Rue Sherbrooke. Those searching for lost treasures in all price ranges should check out the antique and used furniture dealers along Rue Notre-Dame close to Rue Guy (see 141-142).

The following sell beautiful pieces of furniture :

Antiquité Phyllis Friedman
5012, rue Sherbrooke Ouest,
☎ 483-6185

Henrietta Anthony
4192, rue Sainte-Catherine Ouest,
☎ 935-9116

Petit Musée
1494, rue Sherbrooke Ouest,
☎ 937-6161

■ Light Fixtures

L'Allumeur (antique lamps and fixtures, 1850 to 1950)
1126, boulevard de Maisonneuve Est,
☎ 522-0961

Food

From French pastries to Belgian chocolates, to Chinese, Italian and German specialties, Montréal is well-served when it comes to international gastronomic delights.

■ Specialty Grocers

Anjou-Québec (butcher)
1025, avenue Laurier Ouest,
☎ 272-4065

Atlantic Meat & Delicatessen (German specialties)
5024, chemin de la Côte-des-Neiges,
☎ 731-4764

Chinatown is full of shops selling all the necessary ingredients for Chinese cuisine.

Gérard Van Houtte
1042, avenue Laurier Ouest,
☎ 274-5601
On Thursdays, Fridays and Saturdays, this shop offers a special selection of cheeses.

Eaton (basement)
677, rue Sainte Catherine Ouest,
☎ 284-8411

Faubourg Sainte-Catherine
1616, rue Sainte-Catherine Ouest,
☎ 939-3663

Le Fromentier (bakery)
5090, rue Fabre, ☎ 527-3327

La Foumagerie (cheese)
4906, rue Sherbrooke Ouest,
☎ 482-4100

Marché Andes
4387, boulevard Saint-Laurent

Milano (Italian foods)
6884, boulevard Saint-Laurent,
☎ 273-8558

Optimum (natural foods)
630, rue Sherbrooke Ouest, ☎ 845-1015

Tau (natural food)
4238, rue Saint-Denis, ☎ 843-4420

La Vieille Europe
3855, boulevard Saint-Laurent,
☎ 842-5773

■ A Few Public Markets

Public markets where Quebecois farmers come to sell their harvests still exist in Montréal. Some of them also sell imported goods.

Marché Atwater
138, avenue Atwater

Marché Jean-Talon
7075, rue Casgrain

■ Pastry Shops

Le Nôtre
1050, avenue Laurier Ouest,
☎ 270-2702
1600, avenue McGill College,
☎ 844-2244
1277, avenue Greene, ☎ 939-6000

Pâtisserie Belge
3483, avenue du Parc, ☎ 845-1245
1075 A, avenue Laurier, ☎ 279-5274

Pâtisserie de Nancy
5655, avenue Monkland, ☎ 482-3030

Duc de Lorraine
5002, chemin de la Côte-des-Neiges,
☎ 731-4128

Pâtisserie de Gascogne
6095, boulevard Gouin Ouest,
☎ 331-0550

Pâtisserie Bruxelloise
860, avenue du Mont-Royal Est,
☎ 523-2751

Pâtisserie La Brioche Lyonnaise
1593, rue Saint-Denis, ☎ 842-7017

■ **Chocolate Shops**

Andrée
925, boulevard de Maisonneuve,
☎ 282-7517
5328, avenue du Parc, ☎ 279-5923

Au Festin de Babette
4118, rue Saint-Denis, ☎ 849-0214

Pâtisserie Bruxelloise
860, avenue du Mont-Royal Est,
☎ 523-2751

Daskalidès
5111, avenue du Parc, ☎ 272-3447

Chocolats Belges Léonidas
605, boulevard de Maisonneuve Ouest,
☎ 849-2620

Godiva
Ogilvy, 1307, rue Sainte-Catherine
Ouest, ☎ 849-4789

■ **Cookie Shops**

Monsieur Félix et Mr. Norton
732, rue Sainte-Catherine Ouest,
☎ 861-4961
1661, rue Saint-Denis, ☎ 844-9332

Home

These stores offer a wide selection of decorations and articles for the home.

■ **For the Home**

Cache-Cache - La Cache
2185, rue Crescent, ☎ 842-0276
3941, rue Saint-Denis, ☎ 842-7693
1051, avenue Laurier Ouest,
☎ 273-9700

Omorpho
3497, boulevard Saint-Laurent,
☎ 848-0812
5065, rue Saint-Denis, ☎ 849-6575

■ **For the Kitchen**

Arthur Quentin
3960, rue Saint-Denis, ☎ 843-7513

Caplan Duval
5800, boulevard Cavendish,
☎ 483-4040

Maison d'Émilie
1073, avenue Laurier Ouest,
☎ 277-5151

Ma Maison
4279, rue Saint-Denis, ☎ 499-3026

■ **Bedding**

Bleu Nuit
3913, rue Saint-Denis, ☎ 843-5702

Décor Marie Paule
4918, rue Sherbrooke Ouest,
☎ 486-7305
1307, rue Sainte-Catherine Ouest,
☎-844-2393
1090, avenue Laurier Ouest,
☎ 273-8889

Linen Chest
625, rue Sainte-Catherine Ouest,
☎ 282-9525

■ Posters

À L'Affiche (movie posters)
4415, rue Saint-Denis, ☎ 845-5723

Atelier 68
5190, boulevard Saint-Laurent,
☎ 276-2872

Carterie Saint-Denis
1579, rue Saint-Denis, ☎ 281-2083

For Special Occasions...

■ Gift Shops

Boutique du Musée d'Art Contemporain
185, rue Sainte-Catherine Ouest,
☎ 847-6226

Boutique du Musée des Beaux-Arts de Montréal
1379, rue Sherbrooke Ouest,
☎ 285-2600

Cartier (fine china)
1498, rue Sherbrooke Ouest,
☎ 939-0000

Fushia (decorative houseware)
361, avenue Victoria, ☎ 488-9690

Les Millésimes (everything for the wine cellar, imported wines)
3901, rue Saint-Denis, ☎ 284-2613

Pier 1 Imports (clothing, dishes, decorative houseware)
1319, rue Sainte-Catherine Ouest,
☎ 985-2401

Tintin Montréal (different articles, all decorated with Tintin, the cartoon character created by Hergé)
4419, rue Saint-Denis, ☎ 843-9852

Vignette de la Vie (decorative houseware)
5157, boulevard Saint-Laurent,
☎ 277-9580

Zone (decorative houseware)
4246, rue Saint-Denis, ☎ 845-3530

■ Intimates

Capoterie (condoms of all types)
2061, rue Saint-Denis, ☎ 845-0027
2015, rue Crescent, ☎ 847-9297

Priape (gay boutique : clothing, magazines, accessories)
1311, rue Sainte-Catherine Est,
☎ 521-8451

■ Jewelry and Accessories

Agatha
1054, avenue Laurier Ouest,
☎ 272-9313

Birks
1240, Square Phillips, ☎ 397-2511

Kyose
Cours Mont-Royal, rue Sainte-Catherine Ouest, ☎ 843-3129
380, rue Saint-Antoine Ouest,
☎ 847-7572

Moug
1429, rue Crescent, ☎ 844-6844

Oz Bijoux
3955, rue Saint-Denis, ☎ 845-9568

Suk Kwan Design
5141, boulevard Saint-Laurent,
☎ 278-4079

■ Games and Toys

Boutique Gabriel Filion
1127, avenue Laurier Ouest,
☎ 274-0697

Le Coin du Cheminot (miniature trains
of all sorts)
5344, rue Bélanger Est, ☎ 728-8443

Franc Jeu
4152, rue Saint-Denis, ☎ 849-9253

Pikolo
4261, rue Saint-Denis, ☎ 844-0595

Toys R US
3600, chemin Côte-Vertu, ☎ 333-8697

Valet de Cœur (children of all ages)
4408, rue Saint-Denis, ☎ 499-9970

Victoire Victorine (imported toys)
4859, rue Sherbrooke Ouest,
☎ 486-7418

■ Florists

Jean-Jacques Fauchois
4008, rue Saint-Denis, ☎ 844-6576

Fleuriste Folle Avoine
16, rue Maguire, ☎ 270-8609

Madame Lespérance
365, avenue Laurier Ouest,
☎ 277-2173

Marcel Proulx
3835, rue Saint-Denis, ☎ 849-1344

Marie Vermette
801, rue Laurier Ouest, ☎ 272-2225

Photography

■ Photo Equipment

NDG Photo
1108, boulevard de Maisonneuve
Ouest, ☎ 844-1766

L.L. Lozeau
6229, rue Saint-Hubert, ☎ 274-6577

L.R. Viala
1280, boulevard de Maisonneuve Est,
☎ 526-2535

La Place
2050, boulevard Saint-Laurent,
☎ 288-7755

■ Photo Developing

Astral Photo
Complexe Desjardins, ☎ 843-8219
Place Montréal Trust, ☎ 843-8836
Place Ville-Marie, ☎ 878-9821

Centre Japonais de Photo (one-hour
developing)
Centre Eaton, ☎ 842-5133
Promenades de la Cathédrale,
☎ 849-4877

Camtec photo
26, rue Notre-Dame Est, ☎ 875-5110

Selected Recommended Reading

Guidebooks

Québec	Ulysses Travel Publications (1994)
Hiking in Québec	Ulysses Travel Publications (1994)
Best B&B in Québec	Ulysses Travel Publications (1994)
The Guide to Ethnic Montréal	Véhicule Press (1992)
The Great Montréal Bike Path Guide	Éditions Tricycle (1994)

Classics

Mordecai Richler	*The Apprenticeship of Duddy Kravitz* (1959)
	St. Urbain's Horseman (1971)
Leonard Cohen	*Beautiful Losers* (1966)
	Selected Poems 1956-1968 (1968)
Irving Layton	*The Collected Poems of Irving Layton* (1971)
Hugh MacLennan	*Two Solitudes* (1945)
Mavis Gallant	*Home Truths; Selected Canadian Stories* (1981)
Morley Callaghan	*The Loved and the Lost* (1951)

Contemporary

Julie Bruck	*The Woman Downstairs*
Joe Fiorito	*Comfort Me With Apples*
Gail Scott	*Heroine, Main Brides*
Robert Majzel	*Hellman's Scrapbook*
P. Scott Lawrence	*Missing Fred Astaire*

Other fine local contemporary writing includes novels by **Carole Corbeil, Trevor Ferguson, David Homel** and poet/novelist **Mary di Michele**; short stories by **Neil Bissondath, Yann Martel, Robyn Sarah** and **Terry Rigelhof**; and poetry by **Charlotte Hussey** and **Erin Mouré**.

In French (translated)

Michel Tremblay	*La Grosse femme d'à côté est enceinte (The Fat Woman Next Door is Pregnant)* (1981)
	Les Belles Soeurs (1968)
Gabrielle Roy	*Bonheur d'Occasion (The Tin Flute)* (1945)
Yves Beauchemin	*Le Matou (The Alleycat)* (1981)

Collections

Montréal Mon Amour - A collection of Montreal short fiction by some of Canada's finest authors.

Parallel Voices - Voix Parallèles - A bilingual anthology with prominent English-speaking Canadian writers translated by nine French-speaking counterparts, and vice-versa.

For a literary taste of Montréal in English, look at Double Hook Canadian Books (1235A Greene, 932-5093), Paragraphe (2065 Mansfield, 845-5811), Danger! (3968 St-Laurent), or the multi-level Coles (1171 Ste-Catherine at Stanley, 849-8825).

FRENCH GLOSSARY

GREETINGS

Hi (casual)	Salut
How are you?	Comment ça va?
I'm fine	Ça va bien
Hello (during the day)	Bonjour
Good evening/night	Bonsoir
Goodbye, See you later	Bonjour, Au revoir, à la prochaine
Yes	Oui
No	Non
Maybe	Peut-être
Please	S'il vous plaît
Thank you	Merci
You're welcome	De rien, Bienvenue
Excuse me	Excusez-moi

I am a tourist.	Je suis touriste
I am American (male/female)	Je suis Américain(e)
I am Canadian (male/female)	Je suis Canadien(ne)
I am British	Je suis Britannique
I am German (male/female)	Je suis Allemand(e)
I am Italian (male/female)	Je suis Italien(ne)
I am Belgian	Je suis Belge
I am French (male/female)	Je suis Français(e)
I am Swiss	Je suis Suisse

I am sorry, I don't speak French	Je suis désolé(e), je ne parle pas français
Do you speak English?	Parlez-vous anglais ?
Slower, please.	Plus lentement, s'il vous plaît.
What is your name?	Quel est votre nom?
My name is...	Je m'appelle...
spouse (male/female)	époux(se)
brother, sister	frère, soeur
friend (male/female)	ami(e)
son, boy	garçon
daughter, girl	fille
father	père
mother	mère
single (male/female)	celibataire
married (male/female)	marié(e)
divorced (male/female)	divorcé(e)
widower/widow	veuf(ve)

DIRECTIONS

Is there a tourism office near here?	Est-ce qu'il y a un bureau de touris près d'ici?
There is no..., we have no...	Il n'y a pas de..., nous n'avons de...
Where is...?	Où est le/la ...?
straight ahead	tout droit
to the right	à droite
to the left	à gauche
beside	à côté de
near	près de
here	ici
there, over there	là, là-bas
into, inside	à l'intérieur
outside	à l'extérieur
far from	loin de
between	entre
in front of	devant
behind	derrière

FINDING YOUR WAY AROUND

airport	aéroport
on time	à l'heure
late	en retard
cancelled	annulé
plane	l'avion
car	la voiture
train	le train
boat	le bateau
bicycle	la bicyclette, le vélo
bus	l'autobus
train station	la gare
bus stop	un arrêt d'autobus
The bus stop, please	l'arrêt, s'il vous plaît
street	rue
avenue	avenue
road	route, chemin
highway	autoroute
rural route	rang
path, trail	sentier
corner	coin
neighbourhood	quartier
square	place
tourist bureau	bureau de tourisme

bridge	pont
building	immeuble
safe	sécuritaire
fast	rapide
baggage	bagages
schedule	horaire
one way ticket	aller simple
return ticket	aller retour
arrival	arrivée
return	retour
departure	départ
north	nord
south	sud
east	est
west	ouest

CARS

for rent	à louer
a stop	un arrêt
highway	autoroute
danger, be careful	attention
no passing	défense de doubler
no parking	stationnement interdit
no exit	impasse
stop! (an order)	arrêtez!
parking	stationnement
pedestrians	piétons
gas	essence
slow down	ralentir
traffic light	feu de circulation
service station	station-service
speed limit	limite de vitesse

MONEY

bank	banque
credit union	caisse populaire
exchange	change
money	argent
I don't have any money	je n'ai pas d'argent
credit card	carte de crédit
traveller's cheques	chèques de voyage
The bill please	l'addition, s'il vous plaît
receipt	reçu

ACCOMMODATION

inn	auberge
youth hostel	auberge de jeunesse
bed and breakfast	gîte du passant
hot water	eau chaude
air conditioning	climatisation
accommodation	logement, hébergement
elevator	ascenseur
bathroom	toilettes, salle de bain
bed	lit
breakfast	déjeuner
manager, owner	gérant, propriétaire
bedroom	chambre
pool	piscine
floor (first, second...)	étage
main floor	rez-de-chaussée
high season	haute saison
off season	basse saison
fan	ventilateur

SHOPPING

open	ouvert(e)
closed	fermé(e)
How much is this?	C'est combien?
I would like...	Je voudrais...
I need...	J'ai besoin de...
a store	un magasin
a department store	un magasin à rayons
the market	le marché
salesperson (male/female)	vendeur(se)
the customer (male/female)	le / la client(e)
to buy	acheter
to sell	vendre
T-shirt	un t-shirt
skirt	une jupe
shirt	une chemise
jeans	un jeans
pants	des pantalons
jacket	un blouson
blouse	une blouse
shoes	des souliers
sandals	des sandales
hat	un chapeau
eyeglasses	des lunettes
handbag	un sac

gifts	cadeaux
local crafts	artisanat local
sun protection products	crèmes solaires
cosmetics and perfumes	cosmétiques et parfums
camera	appareil photo
photographic film	pellicule
records, cassettes	disques, cassettes
newspapers	journaux
magazines	revues, magazines
batteries	piles

watches	montres
jewellery	bijouterie
gold	or
silver	argent
precious stones	pierres précieuses
fabric	tissu
wool	laine
cotton	coton
leather	cuir

MISCELLANEOUS

new	nouveau
old	vieux
expensive	cher, dispendieux
inexpensive	pas cher
pretty	joli
beautiful	beau
ugly	laid(e)
big, tall (person)	grand(e)
small, short (person)	petit(e)
short (length)	court(e)
low	bas(se)
wide	large
narrow	étroit(e)
dark	foncé
light (colour)	clair
fat (person)	gros(se)
slim, skinny (person)	mince
a little	peu
a lot	beaucoup
something	quelque chose
nothing	rien
good	bon
bad	mauvais
more	plus
less	moins

do not touch	ne pas toucher

quickly	vite
slowly	lentement
big	grand
small	petit
hot	chaud
cold	froid

I am ill	je suis malade
pharmacy, drugstore	pharmacie
I am hungry	j'ai faim
I am thirsty	j'ai soif
What is this?	Qu'est-ce que c'est?
Where?	Où?

fixed price menu	table d'hôte
order courses separately	à la carte

WEATHER

rain	pluie
clouds	nuages
sun	soleil
It is hot out	Il fait chaud
It is cold out	Il fait froid

TIME

When?	Quand?
What time is it?	Quelle heure est-il?
minute	minute
hour	heure
day	jour
week	semaine
month	mois
year	année
yesterday	hier
today	aujourd'hui
tommorrow	demain
morning	le matin
afternoon	l'après-midi
evening	le soir
night	la nuit
now	maintenant
never	jamais

Sunday	dimanche

Monday	lundi
Tuesday	mardi
Wednesday	mercredi
Thursday	jeudi
Friday	vendredi
Saturday	samedi
January	janvier
February	février
March	mars
April	avril
May	mai
June	juin
July	juillet
August	août
September	septembre
October	octobre
November	novembre
December	décembre

COMMUNICATION

post office	bureau de poste
air mail	par avion
stamps	timbres
envelope	enveloppe
telephone book	bottin téléphonique
long distance call	appel outre-mer, une longue distance
collect call	appel collecte
fax	télécopieur, fax
telegram	télégramme
rate	tarif
dial the regional code	composer le code régional
wait for the tone	attendre la tonalité

ACTIVITIES

recreational swimming	la baignade
beach	plage
scuba diving	la plongée sous-marine
snorkelling	la plongée-tuba
fishing	la pêche
recreational sailing	navigation de plaisance
windsurfing	la planche à voile
bicycling	faire du vélo
mountain bike	vélo tout-terrain (VTT)
horseback riding	équitation
hiking	la randonnée pédestre
to walk around	se promener

museum or gallery	musée
cultural centre	centre culturel
cinema	cinéma

TOURING

river	fleuve, rivière
waterfalls	chutes
viewpoint	belvedère
hill	colline
garden	jardin
wildlife reserve	réserve faunique
reserve where hunting is allowed	ZEC (Zone d'Exploitation Contrôlée)
peninsula	péninsule, presqu'île
south/north shore	côte sud/nord
town or city hall	hôtel de ville
court house	palais de justice
church	église
house	maison
manor	manoir
bridge	pont
basin	bassin
dam	barrage
workshop	atelier
historic site	lieu historique
train station	gare
stables	écuries
convent	couvent
door, archway, gate	porte
customs house	douane
locks	écluses
market	marché
canal	canal
channel	chenal
seaway	voie maritime
museum	musée
cemetery	cimitière
mill	moulin
windmill	moulin à vent
general hospital	Hôtel Dieu
high school	école secondaire
college attended after high school	CEGEP
lighthouse	phare
barn	grange
waterfall(s)	chute(s)
sandbank	batture
neighbourhood, region	faubourg

NUMBERS

1	*un*
2	*deux*
3	*trois*
4	*quatre*
5	*cinq*
6	*six*
7	*sept*
8	*huit*
9	*neuf*
10	*dix*
11	*onze*
12	*douze*
13	*treize*
14	*quatorze*
15	*quinze*
16	*seize*
17	*dix-sept*
18	*dix-huit*
19	*dix-neuf*
20	*vingt*
21	*vingt-et-un*
22	*vingt-deux*
23	*vingt-trois*
24	*vingt-quatre*
25	*vingt-cinq*
26	*vingt-six*
27	*vingt-sept*
28	*vingt-huit*
29	*vingt-neuf*
30	*trente*
31	*trente-et-un*
32	*trente-deux*
40	*quarante*
50	*cinquante*
60	*soixante*
70	*soixante-dix*
80	*quatre-vingt*
90	*quatre-vingt-dix*
100	*cent*
200	*deux cents*
500	*cinq cents*
1 000	*mille*
10 000	*dix mille*
1 000 000	*un million*

THEMATIC INDEX

Restaurants and Cafés in Alphabetical Order

Restaurants by Type of Cuisine

Acadian

African

Arabic

British Columbian

Belgian

Brazilian

Cafés and Tea Rooms

Caribbean

Chicken and Ribs

Accommodation in Alphabetical Order

INDEX

Travel Notes _____

Travel Notes _____

Travel Notes _____

■ ULYSSES TRAVEL GUIDES

☐ Best Bed & Breakfasts
   in Québec $9.95
☐ Dominican Republic
   2nd Edition $22.95
☐ Guadeloupe $22.95
☐ Martinique $22.95
☐ Montréal $22.95
☐ Ontario $14.95
☐ Panamá $22.95
☐ Québec $24.95

■ ULYSSES GREEN ESCAPES

☐ Hiking North-East USA $19.95
☐ Hiking Québec $19.95

■ ULYSSES TRAVEL JOURNAL

☐ Ulysses Travel Journal $9.95

QUANTITY	TITLES	PRICE	TOTAL

Name :_____

Address :_____

City :_____

Postal Code :_____

Payment : ☐Money Order ☐Visa ☐MC ☐Cheque

Card Number :_____

Expiry Date :_____

Signature :_____

Sub-total	
Postage & Handling	3.00 $
Sub-total	
G.S.T. in Canada 7 %	
TOTAL	

ULYSSES
TRAVEL PUBLICATIONS

4176, Saint-Denis
Montréal, Québec
H2W 2M5
Tel : (514) 843-9882
Fax: (514) 843-9448